D0299859

Managing information services

Sue Roberts and Jennifer Rowley

Edge Hill University
WITHDRAWN

facet publishing

© Sue Roberts and Jennifer Rowley 2004

Sue Roberts and Jennifer Rowley have asserted their right under the Copyright, Designs and Patents Act, 1988 to be identified as authors of this work.

Published by
Facet Publishing
7 Ridgmount Street
London WC1E 7AE

Facet Publishing is wholly owned by CILIP: the Chartered Institute of Library and Information Professionals.

Except as otherwise permitted under the Copyright, Designs and Patents Act, 1988 this publication may only be reproduced, stored or transmitted in any form or by any means, with the prior permission of the publisher, or, in the case of reprographic reproduction, in accordance with the terms of a licence issued by The Copyright Licensing Agency. Enquiries concerning reproduction outside those terms should be sent to Facet Publishing, 7 Ridgmount Street, London WC1E 7AE.

First published 2004

British Library Cataloguing in Publication Data
A catalogue record for this book is available from the British Library.

ISBN 1-85604-515-3

Every effort has been made to contact the holders of copyright material reproduced in this text, and thanks are due to them for permission to reproduce the material indicated. If there are any queries please contact the Publishers.

Typeset in 10/14 pt Bergamo and Chantilly by Facet Publishing.
Printed and made in Great Britain by MPG Books Ltd, Bodmin, Cornwall.

Contents

ＸEdge Hill College
Learning Resource Centre

Author   RoBERTS. S

Class No.   025.1

Book No.   661273

Introduction

This book is an introductory textbook on information services management. It draws together in an accessible form the principles of management as they need to be understood by library and information professionals. The text is not a substitute for reading on general management, but supplements it by reviewing well established management concepts and practices from the perspective of the management of public libraries, academic libraries and other information services. Examples from this context are used throughout.

Written by a team that comprises a management academic and a practising information services manager, the text introduces and applies established management concepts and models to information service management practice. The book's underpinning philosophy is that theory and practice should be tightly intertwined. Theoretical models and concepts have their foundations in practice. The applications of theories and concepts can assist in sense making, communication, sharing and analysis. They can act as frameworks for the articulation and sharing of best practice and promote shared learning. Such application of theory in its turn advances and develops theory to allow it to accommodate a wider variety of contexts, and to evolve in line with practice.

Since most library and information services are part of a wider organization, their management practice will be influenced by that organizational setting, whether the setting is a university, a local authority or a business organization. Responding effectively within this organizational context is a key theme that runs through this text. Library management is concerned with managing people, services, information, collections and resources, and finance, but managers also need to work beyond the confines of the library. They need to understand and influence their environment, to respond to the power and politics of a situation, to contribute to strategic direction in arenas related to knowledge management, learning and information, and to promote their own careers. In a changing environment, they need to be clear about the contribution that information services can make.

Library and information services in the 21st century face a number of challenges. Managing digital resources and achieving a balance between the access and archive functions is a key issue for all information service managers. A library and information service is no longer delivered only through the library building and issue desk, and users and staff may be remote. In extreme examples the library is entirely virtual but the more common dilemma facing most library managers is the hybrid library, with its blended multi-channel information service delivery. In addition to this erosion of the importance of physical presence, functional boundaries between information professionals and other groups are being eroded. In universities, teamworking with academics in the design and delivery of learning experiences promotes library professionals' understanding of pedagogy and academics' understanding of information retrieval and the use of digital information resources. Economic and political agendas associated with digital citizenship, social inclusion and learning in the information society provide strong drivers for change. Information service managers need a positive and flexible engagement with change. They need to inspire and challenge their staff and others in their organizations to think creatively about the importance of information management. This is the background against which this text is written.

The scene is set through the first two chapters, on information organizations and management and leadership. Chapter 1 is an introduction to both the range and role of information organizations. More importantly for those whose experience of these organizations is limited it explores the complexity, diversity and the networked and global nature of such organizations, and how their roles are changing in increasingly digital environments. Chapter 2 explores the nature of management, managing and leadership, through an exploration of management roles, and how individuals can develop into ever more effective leaders and managers.

The next two chapters are about people, or staff in information services. Staff motivation, competences, attitudes and the way in which they are managed have a big impact on the quality of the information service delivered to users. Chapter 3 examines people in organizations, covering both the factors that affect, for example, motivation, job satisfaction and teamworking, and also the management of such issues. Sections covering mentoring and coaching, managing conflict and managing stress introduce perspectives on how people can be supported, challenged and developed to be successful for themselves and for the information service. Chapter 4 looks at the contractual aspects of staff management. Working within parameters and guidelines established by the wider organization, the information service manager will need to engage in human resource planning, job design, recruitment and selection of staff, appraisal, and training and development.

The next two chapters are united by their focus on customers. The customer orientation, with its focus on customer relationships, that drives much current marketing practice, is echoed in the conceptual frameworks associated with service quality and quality management. Chapter 5 encourages consideration of the nature of the offering or product being delivered to information service customers or users, and the importance of understanding and interpreting the concept of customer value. Later sections introduce some practical approaches to marketing communications. Chapter 6 focuses on quality management. After an exploration of the nature of service and information service quality and approaches to its measurement, the chapter introduces total quality management approaches to the accreditation of quality, benchmarking, and performance management.

Finally, the concluding two chapters deal with strategy and direction, and the allocation of resources to support progress towards strategic objectives. Chapter 7 examines the key financial challenges for information services managers, covering topics such as sources of funding, budget setting and planning, and costing and pricing. Entrepreneurial approaches to resource capture and utilization, and the 'bidding' culture are the topics of specific sections. Chapter 8 puts strategic planning processes under the microscope. It explores the nature of strategy and planning, and looks at the stages in the strategic planning process, introducing some useful tools.

The sequence of chapters has been carefully designed. After the first chapter, which provides context for management in information organizations, the following three chapters focus on aspects of organizational behaviour and people in organizations; this order communicates the importance that managers must place on working with people. The next two chapters have a stronger external focus, considering marketing, and quality management. The final two chapters address processes associated with the integration of internal and external perspectives.

Bland generalizations and dry theory would not communicate the reality. We have therefore used examples and cameos to tell the story. Because we are based in the United Kingdom (UK), we have greater awareness of the developments in the UK, and many of our illustrations are UK based. We apologize to our international readers for this. We cannot claim to be able to competently monitor or cover the specifics of relevant policy agendas in all parts of the world, and we are aware that governments and other organizations worldwide are more or less committed to the role of information organizations, and more or less able or willing to invest resources to support developments. Nevertheless governments and other organizations in all communities are struggling with the same social, technological and economic drivers for change. Accordingly, whilst the specifics of the UK-based examples may not be generally applicable, they are illustrative since the drivers, issues and approaches are widely shared, and these set the longer-term agendas for management practice.

The book features:

- *Learning objectives* – Study objectives are identified at the beginning of each chapter.
- *Summaries* – Summaries review the content of each chapter and draw together the key themes that have been developed.
- *Reflections* – Reflection points are distributed throughout each chapter. These questions are intended to encourage the reader to pause and think about the text. They can also be used as group discussion points.
- *Review questions* – Review questions appear at the end of each chapter. These are examination-type assessment questions designed to encourage readers to review, interpret and apply the material in the chapter. They provide an opportunity to test retention. The questions also flag the key issues that are addressed in each chapter and in that sense provide an additional summary of key themes. Although all questions can be answered from the material in this book, better answers will also draw illustration from professional practice and experience, and concepts from wider reading.
- *Challenges* – Each chapter has a list of Challenge questions. These should not be confused with the Review questions. Although the basic concepts for thinking about the questions are embedded in the text of the respective chapter, these Challenge questions are designed to provoke further investigation, discussion and debate. There are no easy answers to these questions; they are precisely the imponderable questions that information service managers and researchers know to be at the heart of practice and theory, but for which if there is an answer it will be contingent on the context, and likely to change tomorrow. These dilemmas are what makes management interesting!
- *Case studies* – Each chapter includes a case study to further illustrate the application and relevance of the concepts in the chapter. Each case study is accompanied by case study questions that can be used as the basis for individual reflection or group discussion.
- *References and additional reading* – Sources cited in the text and other useful sources, including as appropriate both print documents and websites, are listed at the end of each chapter.

We have tried to pack as much as we can into the pages of this book, and have continually been frustrated by what it has been necessary to omit. We hope that the book nevertheless serves as a sound starting point for the adventure of management in information organizations. Management involves people and politics, and is never straightforward or predictable. It can be challenging, surprising, frustrating, disappointing, satisfying, inspiring and exhausting, and often several of these simultaneously. Enjoy!

Audience

This book is designed to introduce students of library and information management to the practice, experience and theoretical principles of information services management. In particular it should prepare them for their first posts as library and information service managers and alert them to the challenges and rewards of management. Indeed, the book can be used as an on-the-job training guide for staff new to management, helping them with those difficult first steps. Practising information service managers might also enjoy revisiting some of the topics covered in the book.

Acknowledgements

We are grateful to various organizations for permission to reproduce extracts from their documents or websites. Acknowledgement is included adjacent to the individual items. We would also like to express our thanks to the very professional team at Facet Publishing for supporting the idea and realization of this book from its conception. We have both been blessed with patient families who know that writing is just one of those things that we have to do. Our appreciation goes to Steve, Peter, Shula and Zeta, for giving us space and showing just the right amount of interest!

1 Information organizations

LEARNING OBJECTIVES

After reading this chapter you should be able to:

- describe the environmental factors that act as drivers for change and evolution on information services
- discuss the range of different types of information organizations and differentiate between their roles
- identify information service activities and processes
- discuss different approaches to organizational structures within information organizations, and their implications for job roles
- understand the roles of partnerships in the delivery of information service.

Introduction

This chapter is designed to communicate a realistic and challenging image of the role and activities in information organizations, and the policy and other agendas that are increasingly laying expectations on such organizations in terms of the *impact* that they can have on the processes associated with their respective communities. With the advance of information societies, governments are increasingly recognizing that libraries and other information organizations have a significant contribution to make, and targeted funding is often available to support the change and development that policy agendas arising from social, economic and technological change dictate. This lays the gauntlet at the feet of library managers. As discussed later in this chapter there are many different types of information organization, including public libraries, academic libraries, school libraries, college libraries, health information services and a wide variety of different kinds of workplace library and information services. Each of these information organizations has different communities, and within those communities specific user groups. Their activities are unique to those user groups, but as discussed in the section that follows they share some common objectives and common processes. They also frequently work in partnership both with other information organizations, or other organizations, such as schools, voluntary groups, advice centres and other health service information agencies.

In seeking to offer a flavour of information organizations, their role and activities, this chapter cannot be comprehensive. Such an enterprise would occupy several books on its own. The purpose here is to provide a context for the subsequent chapters in this book by starting the discussion of factors such as activities and staff roles (continued in Chapters 3 and 4), funding (continued in Chapter 7), communities and users (continued in Chapter 5) and policies and strategy (continued in Chapters 6 and 8).

Information organizations and their environment

Why should I become an information professional?

You will be at the heart of a profession that is vital in the 21st century. You can aim to head up information departments, manage projects, rise through local government, become a consultant, become the director of an information services at a law firm. You will have the opportunity to make a difference in the community, in law, in education. You will have a profession that is recognized and needed all over the world.

Doctors and nurses need to know the latest medical findings. Children and teachers need support for the National Curriculum, lawyers have to be informed about case law, business has to have the gen on International Trade Agreements, the Public want to know what's the best read, Parliament needs facts to debate properly, Government has to know what's going on.

(www.cilip.org.uk/jobs_careers.html)

The above quote from the CILIP (Chartered Institute of Library and Information Professionals) website captures the essence and diversity of the role of an information professional, and thereby the information services or organizations in which they work. Information organizations and the information professional and other staff who work in them are focused on making sure that information users get the right information or document as quickly and conveniently as possible. In the knowledge-based society and economy of the 21st century, users' expectations and engagement with knowledge and information have grown in sophistication, and technology is ever changing. Information professionals need to lead the way. They need to be curious, innovative, adaptable, gregarious; they need to be good communicators, effective team members, conscious trainers, careful and supportive service deliverers, meticulous with detail, and yet forward thinkers, seeing wider horizons. Without a good smattering of such traits and characteristics the information professional will not be able to add value and make an impact to their user community, and the information service will fail. These descriptors characterize the information service manager for the 21st century and, at least as significantly, they characterize their staff. Managing outgoing, well-informed, communicative, energetic and innovative staff is both a delight and a challenge. The manager needs to facilitate the use of talents and not squander them. But the challenge does not end there. The information profession has legacies that are likely to mean that some staff will not always come up to these exacting standards. Factors such as relatively poor pay in some sections of the profession, coupled with the 'shhh!' image, have not always attracted staff who are naturally innovative, confident presenters, and gregarious. The second challenge for the information service manager is to work with these people and support them so that they continue to make a valuable contribution into the 21st century (see Chapter 2, Management and Leadership).

As suggested by the quote, there is a wide range of different types of information organization, but before discussing these in more detail, a couple of definitions provide a useful focus. What is meant by the term 'organization'? The definition provided by Buchanan and Huczynski (2004, 5) offers a useful starting point:

> An organisation is a social arrangement for achieving controlled performance in pursuit of collective goals.

Key elements of this definition are:

- social arrangements in which groups of people participate
- collective goals and shared objectives

- controlled performance, through standards, and the measurement of performance against those standards.

We define an information organization thus:

> An information organisation is a social arrangement for achieving controlled performance in pursuit of collective goals that relate to information provision, sharing, and management.

Each information organization has been established to meet the information requirements of a different community. Information is critical to the achievement of the social, educational, professional and business goals of these various user communities. Information services variously help to:

- bridge the digital divide, empowering those with poorer access to digital resources than others
- enable the independent learning of students, workers, the retired and, indeed, anybody
- support evidence-based decisions, through the sharing of research and practice-based data in support of scientific, professional and technological developments
- counter information overload in a data-rich but knowledge-poor society, evaluating and filtering data and information
- retrieve information from wherever it may be found, including documents, databases and experts
- manage knowledge and intellectual capital in support of the learning of individuals, teams, organizations and communities.

The Wider Information and Library Issues Project (WILIP), a consultation on the issues facing libraries as they move towards the future, generated a vision shared by all types of libraries in the UK. Key elements of this vision were:

1   Information-literate users have seamless and unfettered access to information resources at the time and place of their choosing and in the form that they want, no matter where the resources are located.
2   Access is facilitated by more and more information being available electronically, including a wider range of older resources made accessible through digitization.
3   The library becomes the focus for access to the wider range of services.

4 The library role becomes more closely geared to customers' needs, supporting self-navigation by users, helping them develop information literacy skills or providing intermediation, according to their requirements.

(www.mla.gov.uk/action/wilip/wilip.asp)

This vision suggests that information organizations will impact on society in the areas of:

- learning
- developing sustainable communities
- health
- the economy, and
- modernizing government.

Progress in delivering the vision is dependent upon:

- improving funding and the sustainability of initiatives
- developing the workforce
- creating a policy framework linking information strategies in each sector so that the full power of the library and information world can be harnessed
- advocacy to convince industrialists and the policy makers in the various sectors of government that they should give higher priority to information as the catalyst for achieving their objectives
- improving access for users.

Reflection: *Discuss the implications of this vision articulated above for a library known to you.*

In summary, increasing digitization of information resources or content delivered to a networked society is already impacting on people's opportunities to access the world's information resources. A transformation is under way on the way in which individuals, groups, communities and societies live learn, work, trade and communicate. These developments are changing the role of library and information services, and revitalizing their contributions in promoting democracy, inclusiveness, public information, lifelong learning, economic growth and business success. Policy making by government and professional bodies is pivotal in defining and promoting the contribution of library and information services.

---

*Reflection: Why have governments identified libraries as key agents in moving forward
the information and knowledge society agenda?*

Information organizations and their services

Most developed countries have a rich variety of information organizations. These
include public libraries, school library services, college libraries, higher education
libraries, national libraries, health sector libraries, prison libraries, cultural and
heritage libraries, government libraries, corporate libraries, libraries for research
institutions, and voluntary sector libraries. Boundaries are difficult to draw and
some would also include content providers (such as print publishers, digital and
other media publishers) and distributors (such as booksellers, and book suppliers)
and other information and advice providers within the general category of
information organization.

This section briefly outlines the role of and services offered by each of the main
types of information organization or library. Although details focus on the UK
context, the types of information service exist in most countries, and they
experience similar environmental, technological and policy agendas.

Public libraries

Public libraries are established in many parts of the world, in order to provide the
general public with access to books, periodicals and other publications for their
education and cultural and recreational needs. The extent of collections and
services varies between countries depending on resources available. The UK has
a long tradition of free public libraries, supported by the Public Libraries Act of
1850, and they are managed by local authorities, which under the terms of the
Public Libraries and Museums Act of 1964, are expected 'to provide a
comprehensive and efficient library service for all persons wishing to make use
thereof'. The Department for Culture, Media and Sport (DCMS) holds policy
responsibility for libraries and museums, as well as for the built heritage, the arts,
sport, education, broadcasting, the media, tourism and the National Lottery.
Until 1998, 'local authority' referred to councils of counties, metropolitan
districts and London boroughs. but since the reorganization of local government
in 1998, some public libraries have been the responsibility of new unitary
authorities that manage all local government services in a particular area. Under
the emerging English regional agenda new regional authorities are setting the
strategic direction for and have control of cultural services, including public

libraries, museums and archives. The Scottish Parliament, the Welsh Assembly and the devolved bodies in Northern Ireland already have similar responsibilities for libraries, museums and archives.

Public libraries are being expected to respond to social, economic and technological changes in society that include:

- changes in working patterns
- increased leisure time
- the spread of leisure over seven days a week and almost 24 hours a day
- the rapidly increasing significance of the internet and the world wide web, and public demand for access to these resources
- increased government interest in the role of libraries in supporting initiatives such as lifelong learning, access for all to information, and the creation of a National Grid for Learning.

These agendas have led to increased expectations on public libraries from their users, especially from children, young people, their parents and teachers. A recent US-based study showed that the internet has revolutionized the way in which libraries provide community education (Durrance and Pettigrew, 2002). New funding for public libraries for network developments, staff training and new digital content has been made available in the UK through the People's Network project (www.peoplesnetwork.gov.uk). In addition, since 2000, public libraries have been required to meet benchmarks set by the DCMS. In 2003, the DCMS published its *Framework for the Future*, which outlines the UK government's ten-year vision for public libraries, in terms of how they can best service their communities in the 21st century (see Figure 1.1).

What exactly are the services that public libraries offer to their community? Most public libraries operate through a headquarters or central library,

1. **Capacity to deliver transformation through innovative and effective management**

2. **Books, reading and learning**
   Knowledge, skills and information are at the heart of economic and social life. Libraries can provide access to virtually all books ever published and much more. In an informal, supportive and stimulating environment, libraries can encourage reading and provide access to learning for everyone.

3. **Digital citizenship**
   Libraries are providing access to vastly more information than ever before through the internet. They enable all citizens to have access to information and services and are central to the delivery of electronic government.

4. **Community and civic values**
   Libraries are safe, welcoming, neutral spaces open to all the community. They are particularly well placed to engage hard to reach groups, working with education, social, health and leisure services.

Figure 1.1 Central themes of *Framework for the Future* (DCMS, 2003)

a series of branches, a mobile library service, and services for specific groups of users. Central libraries are typically located in urban areas such as town or city centres and have a more extensive specialist stock and range of services; administrative, processing and management functions are often located at the central library. Central libraries may have special business, reference and information, and local studies collections. Branch libraries serve their local communities, through information services, loans of books, CDs, videos, DVDs and other resources, host art exhibitions and events, run sessions for children, hold special resources and provide services for ethnic communities, and support local clubs and societies in various other ways. Mobile services take a limited range of information service and resources to locations remote from branches, and home library services may deliver a service to those with limited personal mobility. Figure 1.2 is an extract from the website of one public library, showcasing their services. Many public libraries in the developed world have websites; these are a useful source of information on the nature of service delivery in different parts of the world.

Figure 1.2 A public library website homepage
(www.kent.gov.uk/e&l/artslib/libraries/home.html)

Reflection: Which public library services do you use and why? Do you expect your use of
public libraries to change in the future?

Library and information services for schools

Library provision in schools is widely recognized to have an important role in supporting learning through promoting literacy, encouraging students to enjoy reading, and supporting the development of information literacy skills such as elementary information retrieval, comprehension, information organization and presentation.

At primary level (up to age 11), the school library is often poorly resourced or non-existent, with a limited collection of resources. It is too often located in a corridor or other 'corner', and sometimes may be barely organized and poorly controlled. Too often the quality and extent of the resource is dependent on donations and voluntary staffing, with possibly one member of teaching staff having a general overview of the collection.

Secondary school libraries (age range typically 11–16) are generally better resourced and organized, although even in this sector practice varies, and a recent survey (cited in Villa, 2002) showed that 40% of schools covered by the survey had no full- or part-time librarian or teacher involved with the library. Sound provision at this level involves a dedicated space, with desks and chairs for study space and preferably some computers for independent study use. Stock comprises books, and some multimedia resources, with some newspapers and newsletters. This is catalogued and classified, and reasonably appropriately shelved. Better libraries have a small computer-based library management system; training literature and sessions may be available to students, working independently or working with teachers in class time. A professional librarian on a full- or part-time basis is necessary to maintain this level of service, and to work effectively with teachers to ensure that the library supports learning. Student volunteers may assist and learn at the same time.

In English schools the government's literacy programmes have increased demand for special fiction collections, 'guided reading', genre collections, books on fairy and folk tales, author studies and poetry. School libraries are also faced with a challenge in terms of their engagement with the provision of access to web-based resources to support student learning. The ultimate challenge is to change, with limited budgets and staff resource.

Library and information services for further education and related colleges

The further education college sector, which is responsible for the delivery of post-16 education not offered in higher education institutions, supports a wide range of academic and vocational training. Colleges in the further education sector include generalist colleges covering a wide range of academic, vocational and community learning programmes; specialist colleges such as schools of art and design, colleges of technology, and colleges of agriculture and horticulture; and, sixth-form colleges specializing in academic courses for 16–19 year olds. Students may be full or part time, on short or longer courses, focused on developing vocational skills and qualifications or engaged in lifelong learning or programmes that support social inclusion. Further education colleges have a significant contribution to make in the economic, social and cultural development of the skills base of a community or region. In the UK, the Learning and Skills Development Agency (www.lsda.org.uk) has overall responsibility for the development of policy and practice in post-16 education and training. The Learning and Skills Council in England and equivalent further education funding councils in Scotland, Wales and Northern Ireland provide funding for the sector.

Libraries in further education colleges support the activities of the college. The diversity of the sector in terms of size of college, range of programmes offered and profiles of communities served is matched by the diversity of library and information provision. The best libraries have a basic but current and relevant collections of books, professional magazines and a few academic journals, housed in dedicated and purpose-built accommodation that includes study space. A computerized library management system supports the control of the resource, offering students and staff an online public access catalogue and a library web page that directs to selected web and other electronic resources. The resource centre is staffed by a small team of professional and non-professional staff, who work with academic staff and learning support staff to help staff and students in the use of both print and online resources. A collection of workstations providing web access may also be part of the library service, and in some instances such a service may take responsibility for the loan of portable PCs and other educational media and equipment. There has been a considerable drive for improvement in recent years as a result of initiatives that promote the use of information and communications technology in learning, such as the National Grid for Learning and the National Learning Network. The JISC Regional Support Centres have been a significant source of support for colleges in the development of digital learning environments.

Library and information services in higher education

The higher education sector, including universities and colleges, supports learning at undergraduate (degree), and postgraduate (Masters and Doctoral) levels. Most higher education institutions also have a significant research and knowledge development role, and there is increasing emphasis on 'third-mission' activities designed to promote knowledge exchange, transfer and creation with business and other organizations. Student communities are diverse; many students study part time, and some study on distance learning programmes. Many universities have franchise and other arrangements with colleges, other universities and private sector organizations for the delivery of their programmes. In addition, higher education institutions attract significant international cohorts of students, particularly from Europe (often as exchange students), and Asia (particularly, in recent years, China).

Programmes offered cover all subject disciplines, including, for instance, medical sciences, health sciences, the physical sciences, the social sciences, arts and humanities, teacher education, business and management studies, engineering, computing and information systems.

Thus, library and information provision in universities needs to be designed to support teaching, learning, research and other activities across a wide range of discipline areas, and for a diverse range of users. These users include not only students with a variety of different levels and modes of engagement with the university, but also staff and research students in research and third-mission activities.

In recent years there has been a significant debate about the shift in the role of university libraries. The traditional focus of the *archival* function of such libraries, in which their role in collection building and the maintenance of as comprehensive a book and journal collection as resources would allow, has received less emphasis, as their *access* role has come to the fore. The access role recognizes that any individual information service cannot 'own' all of the information resources to which its users might need access. This debate is continued in Chapter 7, Finance and Resources. This shift in emphasis in role has been accompanied by structural changes often characterized by the *convergence* of library and information services with information systems departments, to form an integrated information service organization. Even where such convergence is not symbolized by structural changes, these two departments work closely together.

The Joint Information Systems Committee (JISC), a collaborative venture initially by the three UK higher education funding councils, has been an agent through which research, development and change in relation to information systems, networking and digital libraries have been promoted collaboratively throughout UK higher education over the last 20 years. Early focus was on the development of networking capacity through the Joint Academic Network (JANET) and SuperJanet, the negotiation of software deals for the sector, and the development of specialist data centres. More recently greater focus has been on the role of digital resources in learning, the development of digital content (focused on the Resource Discovery Network (RDN), and the Information Environment) and support for learners and other users.

Controls on university libraries derive from the funding regime of their parent university. Virtually all universities in the UK are public sector universities; in other parts of the world, including the USA and some countries in Europe, there is a stronger tradition of private universities. In these institutions funding, standards and quality management for information services will be determined through the political processes that determine the allocation of resources for competing priorities in the university. In the UK public-sector-based universities, funding is administered and allocated by the Higher Education Funding Council for England (HEFCE), the Higher Education Funding Council for Wales, the Department of Education for Northern Ireland and the Scottish Higher Education Funding Council (SHEFC). Within their budgets, universities have considerable freedom in terms of budgetary arrangements and mechanisms for the allocation of resources between departments, and practices vary (see Chapter 7, Finance and Resources). Clearly the level of resource allocation impacts on the quality of the information service. The primary responsibility for maintaining the standards and reputation of higher education, including their library and information services, rests with the higher education institutions. Periodic quality assessment (see Chapter 6) through the Quality Assessment Agency (QAA), an agency of the funding councils, embraces learning resources, of which information services are one element. In addition universities are required to develop a rolling strategic plan that includes reference to information and learning resources strategies.

Distance learning has become an increasingly popular means of delivering learning to remote audiences and many universities in the USA, Australia and the UK have distance learning programmes. Digital resources and digital learning platforms have made it much easier to deliver access to information resources to support distance learning, and to integrate such access into the distance learning experience. The Open University is the UK's leading institution working with open and distance learning. Open Libr@ry, the university's electronic library, is a significant enterprise offering links to information services, staff, online resources, electronic journals and guides to the use of resources at a distance. Open University students, like other distance learning students, often look to the resources of local libraries, whether university, college or public, to support their studies.

Reflection: *What special difficulties might academic library and information services*
face in supporting: (a) part-time students and (b) remote, distance learning
students?

National libraries

Many countries have national libraries. Some of the major national libraries are the Library of Congress, National Library of Australia, National Library of Canada and the Bibliothèque Nationale de France. National libraries have a significant role in building and maintaining a record of documents published in their country and beyond, and making this often significant collection available to users, many of whom will interact with the library and its services remotely, and sometimes through other university or public libraries.

The UK has three national libraries: the British Library, the National Library of Scotland and the National Library of Wales. These libraries, together with three other libraries – the Library of Trinity College, Dublin, the Bodleian Library, the University of Oxford, and Cambridge University Library – constitute the group of legal deposit libraries. Under the Copyright Act of 1911 and it successors, a copy of all UK publications must be deposited in the British Library, and the other five legal deposit libraries are entitled to receive copies of publications on request. In addition to the national collections deriving from their legal deposit status, the National Library of Wales and the National Library of Scotland have significant collections of works about Wales and other Celtic countries, and Scotland, acting as the archive for the record of the history and culture of their respective countries. Their collections include books, pamphlets, magazines, newspapers, microforms, ephemera, manuscripts, pictures, photographs, maps, sound recordings and moving images, as well as significant and growing archives of electronic resources.

The British Library offers a wide range of different services to different market segments, as shown in Figure 5.7, on page 153.

Reflection: *Examine Figure 5.7 on page 153 and make a list of the services offered by*
the British Library.

Workplace information services

Workplace libraries, often described as 'special' libraries or information services, are instituted and designed to meet the specialized needs of specific user communities. Many such information services exist in business organizations such as management consultancies, pharmaceutical research organizations, market research agencies and legal advice centres. A number also fall within the public or voluntary sector. This group includes:

- government libraries, such as those of government departments and ministries, in areas such as defence, international affairs, trade and industry, and the environment
- medical and healthcare library and information services, as discussed further below
- research council libraries, such as the libraries of the Economic and Social Research Council and of the Engineering and Physical Science Research Council
- professional body libraries, including those of professional associations, learned societies, trade unions and employers' bodies. Particularly significant are the libraries of the Royal Society of Chemistry, the Institution of Mechanical Engineers, the Institution of Electrical Engineers and the British Computer Society.

Reflection: *Why would a management consultancy need an information service? What subjects might such a service cover and what kinds of information resources might be used in the delivery of such a service?*

These information services are united in their need to define and continuously evolve the scope of the information offered to users, and to demonstrate impact through working in partnership with others in their organization. Staff delivering such services often apply subject expertise (in, say, healthcare, science or defence) together with their expertise as an information professional. Currency and intelligence are pivotal, some of which will be derived from personal contacts rather than documentary information sources. Staff may be involved in the interpretation of information and the preparation of reports. Functions such as translation and the management of intellectual property rights may also be closely aligned with the provision of information services.

Libraries in this sector have been particularly affected by digitization. Many are significant users of subject-based databases and collections of electronic journals, although they often do not have the benefits of consortia purchasing open to some of the other sectors. In this sector, the access role is even more to the fore than in university libraries, and many have been operating remote electronic information services for a considerable number of years; particularly in business organizations, these remote services may be delivered to a global audience, with all of the interesting cultural and linguistic challenges that this poses.

As business and other organizations have become increasingly aware of the significance of information and knowledge as assets and the basis of competitive advantage, several have sought to embrace the philosophies, culture and technologies of knowledge management. Increased investment in information systems, and the embedding of information systems – initially in business processes (such as sales ordering, inventory control, product design and production control), but more recently in organizational processes (such as those associated with communication, innovation, knowledge creation and knowledge dissemination) – has led organizations to focus more directly on their knowledge management philosophy, processes and technology, and to appoint individuals with overarching and strategic responsibility for knowledge in organizations, sometimes called Chief Knowledge Officers (Abell and Oxbrow, 2001). Related to interest in knowledge management is the growing interest within organizations in information literacy as a key skill for staff (Winterman, Skelton and Abell, 2003).

While workplace libraries share some of the same environmental influences and challenges, the other chief characteristic of this sector is its variability. Such information services are generally much smaller than university or public libraries, and some are 'one-person' services. Staffing roles and structures are equally variable and are likely to be influenced by the cultural and structural approach adopted by the parent organization. The primary group of users is other members of staff of the same organization, or organizational members. Some services also offer some access to broader publics.

Medical and healthcare libraries

Medical and healthcare libraries are a significant group of library and information services, which traditionally would have been grouped with 'special' libraries because the primary role of most of them was to support medical practitioners or researchers. However, within the UK, since the publication in 1988 of the National Health Service (NHS) information strategy *Information for Health*, their roles are changing. Healthcare libraries have a pivotal role in the establishment of 'evidence-based' practice, and patient empowerment (Booth and Brice, 2004).

Medical and healthcare libraries can be categorized into several groups:

- government libraries, such as the libraries of the Department of Health
- national libraries, such as the British Library's Health Care Information Service
- professional association and research library and information services, such as the libraries of the Royal Society of Medicine, the British Medical Association, the Royal College of Nursing and the Wellcome Institute
- NHS libraries, located in NHS regions, to provide information to doctors and other health service professionals and the community.

The keystones of the vision for NHS libraries in the UK are NHS Direct, and the National electronic Library for Health (NeLH).

NHS Direct (www.nhsdirect.uk) seeks to provide information and possibly advice on healthcare issues to the general public; its role is to support the development of a better-informed public who are, in turn, in a stronger position to take responsibility for their own health and make informed decisions about when to refer to a healthcare professional. Figure 1.3 shows some of the

Figure 1.3 NHS Direct Online (www.nhsdirect.nhs.uk)

information and advice to which it provides access.

The National electronic Library for Health (www.nelh.nhs.uk) is working with NHS libraries to develop a digital library and information portal for NHS staff and patients and the public. Access is offered to a considerable range of sources including clinical databases, full-text journals, bibliographic databases (e.g. MEDLINE), reviewed internet resources and current awareness services. The resource is designed for the healthcare professional, but patients and the public can access selected resources, on registration.

Reflection: *Why are there so many different medical and healthcare libraries? How do their roles differ?*

The rest!

Information is an extremely pervasive commodity and there is a wide range of other services that provide some kind of information service, possibly coupled with advice or commercial promotion of other products and services. These include both physical centres with face-to-face contact and online information intermediaries, for example:

- consumer and community advice centres – often established by charitable organizations to offer advice to the public on their rights and options in commercial and other contractual relationships
- tourist information centres – providing information to visitors to a town or region, with a focus on travel, accommodation and attractions
- legal advice services – providing advice and information to the general public on legal matters, and access to further legal services
- financial advice services and cybermediaries – providing advice and information on financial matters, often with a view to encouraging engagement with financial services, insurance or banking
- careers information services – offered by both public and private sector organizations seeking to offer employment advice and promote employment
- government education and information services – for example, in the UK, the National Grid for Learning (NGfL) (www.ngfl.gov.uk) and Ufi/Learndirect (www.ufi.co.uk), which are both designed to offer learning opportunities, and Culture Online (www.cultureonline.gov.uk) which provides access to cultural treasures and cultural organizations online, and UK Online (www.ukonline.gov.uk), a portal which supports citizen interaction with government.

Processes in information organizations

The great diversity of the purposes, services, communities, subjects and resources of information organizations leads to diversity in processes and job roles. Nevertheless, the shared role of offering information services to a community makes it possible to identify a common core of processes that are at the heart of the job roles, and therefore experiences and competencies of information staff, whatever their professional status. This section is intended to provide a brief glimpse of 'what information organizations do' in order to deliver their services. An appreciation of job roles is an important precursor to any discussion of organizational structure, since structures are often based on the job tasks to be completed.

This section explores the theme of processes at two levels: operational and strategic. At the operational level, the focus is on the processes that make appropriate and relevant resources available to users. At the strategic level, the focus is on overall direction for the information service and, more widely, for information policy and strategy within organizations and society. Library managers are responsible for strategy and planning, and typically manage others who are responsible for the day-to-day execution of operational processes. Both of these themes surface repeatedly throughout later chapters in this book. Chapter 8, Strategy and Planning, explicitly focuses on the processes associated with strategic management.

Operational processes

Operational processes form the basis of many of the job roles in an information organization, and the information manager is charged with the effective execution and co-ordination of these processes. Different aspects of management processes (as discussed in later chapters of this book) will impact variously on these operational processes. These processes focus on the identification, selection and making accessible of documents and other information resources. Most of the stages are executed with the assistance of a computer-based library management system, which records transactions in relation to individual items or documents at each stage of this cycle. Summarized in Figure 1.4, these processes include:

1   *Establishing and reviewing scope of service* – As discussed further in Chapter 8, Strategy and Planning, a mission and corporate objectives need to be established for an organization. This is a strategic process, but it forms the

foundation for the establishment of the scope of the service, with regard to the resources to be included in terms of subject (e.g. physics, social care, gardening), level (e.g. general public, children's, research) and form (e.g. books, journals, electronic journals, web resources, music, artworks). Traditionally such scope definition would be described as the collection development criteria.

2 *Evaluation and selection of information resources* – This process involves the identification of potentially relevant resources, through web scanning, book selection tools made available by book suppliers, monitoring announcements of new journals, and scanning a variety of other sources of announcements. In open archive and institutional electronic repository contexts, this stage may also involve working with other partners inside or beyond the organization in designing documents for inclusion in an archive or learning platform. Documents and other information resources will be selected for inclusion on the basis of selection criteria established in the previous process.

3 *Acquisition, ordering and contracting of information resources* – In the print world, this process focuses on the acquisition of print copies of books, journals, reports and other items. These processes are facilitated by book suppliers and periodical subscription agents, who typically have information systems that link to the library's management system, making it easier to conduct the processes of evaluation and selection, acquisition ordering and contracting, and creating records and access links. For print documents, such as books, this stage involves the regular placing of orders to stock the collection. For electronic documents, this stage focuses on the establishment of any bulk licence arrangements or contracts which grant information service users the right to access the document. For documents internal to the organization, such as reports or course materials, this stage should be interpreted as the stage at which the documents are quality assured.

4 *Creating records and access links* – Once an item has been selected for inclusion, a record of that decision needs to be made for both administrative and access purposes. Again, for print documents, libraries need a unique record of all of the items that are added to the collection, and they need to be able to match the record to the item for administrative, inventory and insurance purposes. They need similar administrative records relating to any electronic resources for which they have a contractual arrangement. In addition, a record of all resources, including print, electronic contracted resources (such as image collections or electronic journals) and web resources to which links might be provided, needs to be created for user access. The processes described as

cataloguing and classification generate records of documents or items, together with subject access keys such as keywords, subject descriptors and classification codes.

5 *Making information resources available* – Items are made available by adding records to databases and/or links to library web pages or portals. This stage could be summarized as creating and maintaining the information service portal so that it provides appropriate links to online catalogues, electronic newspapers, full-text databases, bibliographic databases, internet resources and digitized objects. In applications where the library is involved in the creation of open archives or institutional electronic repositories this stage might extend to the electronic publication of, for example, course materials, multimedia documents, preprints and research data.

6 *Managing and supporting access* – At this stage the focus shifts from processing information resources to user-based activities. This stage involves the management of user registration and authentication (authorization to access, for example, electronic resources), circulation control (for print materials) and user training and development. Feedback from these processes is one source of input into the review of the service, as discussed in Chapter 6, Quality Management.

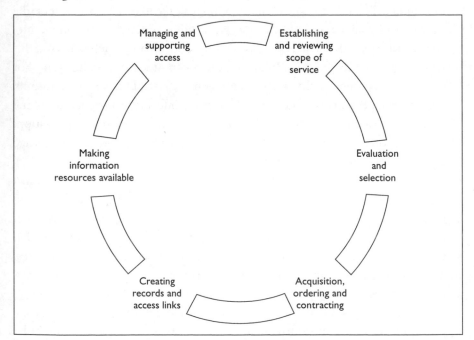

Figure 1.4 Operational library management processes

The balance between these stages depends on the nature of the organization and its services. Each of these stages relates to both printed and digital resources, although the component processes are different for these two categories of resources. Since most information services are 'blended', working with both print and digital resources, they need to engage with both sets of processes.

Reflection: How should job roles be mapped on to the various activities described in the above processes?

Strategic processes

Strategic processes are designed to ensure that the information service has a clear direction and purpose, formulates objectives that make explicit the elements of adhering to a strategic direction, and has strategies for ensuring that objectives are achieved. Strategy involves attention to people issues, such as culture and leadership style, as well as quality management processes, finance and the allocation of resources, and marketing. These are variously discussed in later chapters in this book. For now it is sufficient to identify these processes as part of the work of the information service and to move on to observe that none of these processes are completed in isolation. Strategic direction must be defined in relation to the contribution that the information service seeks to make, and is expected by various other stakeholders to make, to its community, university, college, school or research or professional group.

Early sections of this chapter offer many examples of government direction affecting public and health service libraries directly, and education libraries indirectly. This means that it is not sufficient for senior information service managers to be content with managing the direction of their own service; they also need to participate in wider information strategy and policy issues. Within organizations such as universities, local authorities and businesses, information service managers need to participate and sometimes lead in establishing objectives in areas such as communications strategy, information systems strategy, knowledge and information sharing and associated issues such as intellectual property, transparency, privacy, trust and data protection. In the wider societal context senior information managers, working with professional bodies and in partnership with other professional and community groups, need to be central to the development of information policy relating to issues such as learning, citizen empowerment, e-government, intellectual property, access and accessibility, and data protection legislation.

Organizational structures

Organizational structures provide an important framework for influencing how information organizations do what they do. Organizational structure refers to the formal system of task and reporting relationships that controls, co-ordinates and motivates employees so that they work together to achieve organizational goals. It is integrally related to 'how the organization gets the job done'. It therefore sets the scene for issues discussed in Chapter 3, People and Organizations, such as job roles, culture, learning, communication, motivation, stress and job satisfaction. Organizational structures in information organizations tend to mirror the approach taken by their parent organization, but there is also considerable bench-marking across the various sectors discussed above.

Organizational structures can be designed in two different ways – top down or bottom up. The top-down approach to organizational structure design starts from an assessment of the strategic direction and objectives of the organization, and identifies what needs to be done to meet those objectives. On the basis of these activities, first departments and then teams and individual staff are identified to take responsibility for these activities, and specific job roles defined. The bottom-up approach identifies tasks and groups these into job roles; job roles are then grouped together into departments. Most existing organizational structures are the result of evolution over time, and probably reflect a recognition both that all information services need to undertake the roles in Figure 1.4, in relation to operational processes, but also that change in the nature of these roles, and specific strategic initiatives, sometimes imposed or at least urged by funding bodies, leaves most organizational structures reflecting elements of both of these approaches.

Organizational structures can also be classified on the basis of whether they are hierarchical or matrix in nature. Hierarchical structures (in our view!) are easier to understand, and communication channels and lines of responsibility are more clearly defined. Figure 1.5 shows an example of a typical organization structure for an academic library. This figure illustrates a number of features of a hierarchical organization structure:

- There is a hierarchy of managers, with each manager having a number of subordinates and one more senior, line manager.
- The average number of subordinates that a manager has responsibility for is described as the span of control. The wider the span of control of a hierarchical organizational structure the fewer the levels in the hierarchy. A hierarchy with few layers is described as a flat hierarchy. Hierarchies in both public and private

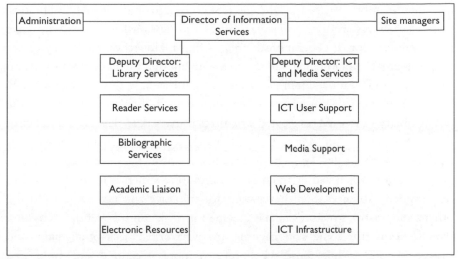

Figure 1.5 Organization structure for an academic information service

sectors have become flatter in recent years, through 'delayering' restructuring that has eliminated 'middle' layers of management.

- Flat hierarchies with few layers reduce the communication down the 'line-of-command', and therefore increase the accuracy of messages between the top and bottom of the hierarchy.
- Flat hierarchies have many people at each level, which means that opportunities for promotion are limited, and staff must find job satisfaction and motivation through other roots than promotion; also flat hierarchies increase the importance of communication between colleagues on the same level in the hierarchy, or team communication.

Matrix organizational structures are structures in which managers may be accountable or answerable to more than one line manager, or take on more than one role. In such a structure individuals are also likely to be members of more than one team. For example, a Director of Information Resources (a converged service embracing library resources, information systems and educational media) in a university might also have responsibility for the strategic management of one of the sites of the university. The Director may be accountable to the Vice Chancellor for both roles, but will manage two different teams. Lower down the hierarchy, an academic librarian may have responsibility for the library website, in which role they may be managed by the University Web Resources Manager, and also have a role as subject librarian for the Psychology Department, in which role they may be managed by the User Services Librarian. In public libraries, matrix structures are used to create teams of professional librarians who have responsibility for a geographical area. One member of staff may share responsibility for four branches in the area with another member of staff and also have responsibility for children's services across the area. In this second role, they will be a member of the team that co-ordinates children's services across the public library service. Matrix-based structures allow staff to develop a number of different areas of competence, and particularly to couple general management experience with the development of areas of specialism. They can also be flexible, because multi-skilled staff should make it easier to re-structure to cover new roles or temporary absences. Staff have scope for initiative and innovation. On the other hand, matrix structures can be a recipe for weak control over staff activities, which means that some staff become an overworked 'jack-of-all-trades and master-of-none', while those who prefer a more structured and monitored management regime may be at a loss to make an appropriate contribution.

Although structures in many information organizations are fairly hierarchical, new projects and special initiatives often generate project teams or special roles, which allow individuals to experience different roles within a hierarchy and to work with different managers and teams. In addition, the level of formality of the operation of a hierarchical structure is at the discretion of the manager and will depend on management and leadership style (as discussed in Chapter 2, Management and Leadership).

Reflection: *Examine Figure 1.5 on page 23 and propose an alternative organizational structure for this library and information service.*

Partnerships

> Partnership is one of the most complex and difficult ways in which to work. When it works even reasonably well, however, it can bring some of the best results for the end-user.
>   (Dakers, 2003, 47)

One of the most exciting aspects of the information profession has always been the extent to which libraries and other information organizations work together to support each other in meeting the needs of users. Early examples of partnership working were the union catalogues of regional and other library co-operation schemes – and those enormous card catalogues were truly resource intensive, and a credit to a considerable level of attention to detail – and related interlibrary loan schemes. Collaboration across the library and information profession has always had national and international aspects; perhaps the most significant legacy of earlier years in this area are the standards that underlie cataloguing and classification practices today, such as the Dewey Decimal Classification Scheme, the Anglo-American Cataloguing Rules, and Machine-Readable Cataloguing (MARC). The information profession's enthusiasm for standards and standardization that supported networking and exchange predated and underpinned the current fashion for web-enabled networking and interoperability.

This brief section is designed to emphasize the importance of networking and working together to build and share information and knowledge bases. Information services staff and managers participate in numerous consortia and partnerships, in the pursuit of offering the best possible service to their users. These partnerships are both internal and external to the organization. They may be long-lived or short term. Partnerships can be grouped into three types. Information service managers or their staff may be leaders or contributors in these partnerships:

- *Project-based partnerships*. Project teams may be drawn together by the parent organization or the information service to work on a specific time-limited project, such as a website for a hospital trust, an e-government initiative or the selection and installation of a new managed learning environment. Project-based consortia may come together in response to specific and possibly funded initiatives at regional, national or European level.
- *Operational alliances*. Internally this may mean two departments working together or being merged. External operational alliances include partnerships in the supply chain (working with publishers and book suppliers), and outsourcing and subcontracting of specific processes or aspects of service delivery.
- *Strategic partnerships* are concerned with the long-term strategic position of the information service or its parent organization. For example, an information service manager might be engaged in the aspects of the relationships arising from a merger between two higher education institutions, or a franchise arrangement between a university and a further education college. Regional networks of library and information services and national networks of research libraries also have a strategic role.

As Dakers (2003) suggests, partnership working is not easy. Working in partnership requires individuals and organizations to direct considerable effort toward agreeing a shared agenda from which both parties are convinced that they will benefit and to which both parties are committed to contribute, not just at the beginning, but over the lifetime of the relationship. Successful partnership working requires:

- clear identification of objectives and strong commitment to the fulfilment of those objectives
- clear statements of the responsibilities of the respective partners
- schedules and staff resources that allow for individuals from different organizations to learn how to work effectively together
- effective communication between organizations and within organizations – those with lead responsibility for the collaborative venture also need to manage communication within their own organizations
- persistence in managing the partnerships against a backdrop of changing organizational agendas and funding and resource situations.

And specifically in the context of seamless information service delivery, in partnership it is also important to address:

- compatibility of communication network infrastructures and standards
- electronic resources access and authentication mechanisms, which need careful negotiation when some users may be full-time 'government-funded' students, while others may be on 'fee-paying' short or distance learning courses
- user cultures, between different user groups. For example, in the health service, doctors seek personalized support and quiet space, while nurses are more likely to work in teams and seek space and resource access that supports group working.

Summary and conclusions

Governments are becoming increasingly committed to the roles of information organizations in areas such as learning, digital citizenship, cultural and community values, and economic opportunity. There are many different types of information organizations or library and information services, each of which is designed to deliver an information service to a different community. This chapter has outlined the context for and nature of public libraries, library and information services for schools, colleges and universities, national libraries, workplace information services, and medical and healthcare libraries. All information services share a common core of processes, at strategic and operational levels. Strategic processes are important in defining the direction of the service, whereas operational processes are important in processing and providing access to an appropriate collection or information resource. Organizational structures define jobs and the way in which the work of the organization is completed and progress is made towards the fulfilment of strategy objectives. Organizational structure has significant consequences for the experience of the organization as discussed in Chapter 3, People in Organizations, and Chapter 2, Management and Leadership. An additional layer of complexity in working relationships arises from working in partnership with other teams in the partner organization and in external organizations, at project, operational and strategic levels.

REVIEW QUESTIONS

1 What are the key drivers for change for information organizations in the early years of the 21st century?
2 Discuss the role of UK government initiatives in changing the nature and role of library and information services.
3 Identify the main types of information organization or information service. Discuss the differences between these services in terms of the services that they offer and the user groups that they serve.
4 Explain the difference between an operational and a strategic process, as these might apply in information organizations. How are operational processes essential to service delivery?
5 What do you understand by the term 'organizational structure'? Evaluate the difference between a hierarchical organizational structure and a matrix-based structure.
6 Describe some of the different kinds of partnerships in which information services, their staff and managers may participate.

CASE STUDY

Investigating information organizations

Visit one of the following websites (or other equivalent website) to locate a list of library and information services in a specific sector. Select three services in one sector from one of these lists, and visit the websites of these services. The following websites provide lists of information organizations:

- public libraries on the web: http://dspace.dial.pipex.com/town/square/ac940/ weblibs.html
- higher education library websites: www.ex.ac.uk/library/uklibs.html and www.scit.wlv.ac.uk/ukinfo/uk.map.html.

Compare and contrast the information services in terms of:

- the profile of the communities that they serve
- the information resources available
- the nature of the library and information services on offer
- any evidence of working in partnership.

CHALLENGES

1 Will government support, through initiatives like the UK People's Network, succeed in revolutionizing the role and public perception of public libraries?
2 Do multiple government initiatives in areas such as lifelong learning improve access for a wide range of different communities or confuse users and citizens? Does this initiative culture produce sustainable change and development?
3 In an environment in which parent organizations may be in competition with each other, such as universities in a region, does it make sense for them to share their resources? If so, what should be the basis for any collaborative contract?
4 How can information services achieve the maximum benefit from working in partnership, without spending too many staff resources maintaining complex sets of external relationships?

References and additional reading

Note: These lists at the end of each chapter include documents cited in the text, but are also amplified with a range of current readings that tell further stories about the nature of information services. These readings are representative rather than comprehensive.

Abell, A. and Oxbrow, N. (2001) *Competing with Knowledge: the information profession in the knowledge management age*, London, TFPL and Library Association Publishing.
Anderson, G. (2003) No More Ivory Towers, *Library + Information Update,* **2** (10), 37.
Blanshard, C. (1994) *Managing Library Services for Children and Young People: a practical handbook*, London, Library Association Publishing.

Booth, A. and Brice, A. (2004) *Evidence-based Practice for Information Professionals: a handbook*, London, Facet Publishing.

British Standards Institution (2003) *Managing Culture and Knowledge: guide to good practice*, London, BSI.

Buchanan, D. and Huczynski, A. (2004) *Organisational Behaviour: an introductory text*, 5th edn, Harlow, FT Prentice Hall.

Carpenter, H. (2004) Welcome to Your Library, *Library + Information Update*, **3** (5), 40–1.

Chiorazzi, M. and Russell, G. (eds) (2002) *Law Library Collection Development in the Digital Age*, New York, Haworth Information Press.

Cox, L. (2003) Define Your Principles, Raise Your Status, *Library + Information Update*, **2** (9), 50–1.

Dakers, H. (2003) The BL Reaches Out, *Library + Information Update*, **2** (10), 46–7.

Department for Culture, Media and Sport (2003) *Framework for the Future*, London, DCMS.

Durrance, J. C. and Pettigrew, K. E. (2002) *Online Community Information: creating a nexus at your library*, Chicago/London, American Library Association.

Eskins, R. and Willson, J. (2003) Rebuilding with Information Architecture, *Library + Information Update*, **2** (10), 44–5.

Hannah, K. (2003) Developing Accessible Library Services, *Library + Information Update*, **2** (11), 50–2.

Hopson, I. (2003) Develop the Job, *Library + Information Update*, **2** (11), 48–9.

Howell, M. (2004) Doing Business in the City, *Library + Information Update*, **3** (4), 26–8.

Kakabadse, N. K., Kakabadse, A. and Kouzmin, A. (2003) Reviewing the Knowledge Management Literature: towards a taxonomy, *Journal of Knowledge Management*, **7** (4), 75–91.

Levett, S. (2004) Profile, *Library + Information Update,* 3 (4), 16–17.

McKearney, M. (2003) Let's Focus on Reading, *Library + Information Update*, **2** (9), 48–9.

Marfleet, J. (2003) C. R. M. with J. P. Morgan, *Library + Information Update*, **2** (9), 52–3.

Markless, S. and Streatfield, D. (2004) *Evaluating the Impact of Your Library: a practical model*, London, Facet Publishing.

Prosser, C. (2003) Getting Down to Business, *Library + Information Update*, **2** (11), 42–3.

Rowley, J. (2001) Knowledge Management in Pursuit of Learning: the learning with knowledge cycle, *Journal of Information Science*, **27** (4), 227–37.

Stott, V. (2003) A Museum Library in Transition, *Library + Information Update*, **2** (11), 36–7.

Thompson, P. (2003) A Fanfare for Music, *Library + Information Update*, **2** (10), 30–1.

Villa, P. (2002) *An Investment in Knowledge: library and information services in the United Kingdom 2002*, London, CILIP, British Council.

Winterman, V., Skelton, V. and Abell, A. (2003) A New Kind of Worker, *Library + Information Update*, **2** (10), 38–9.

2 Management and leadership

One does not 'manage' people.
The task is to lead people.

(Drucker, 1999, 21)

LEARNING OBJECTIVES

After reading this chapter you should be able to:

- discuss definitions of management
- understand the broad trends in management thought and theory
- demonstrate an overview of generic management competencies and how they apply to the information service context
- explore the issues relating to women and management
- discuss approaches to change management
- explore the differences between management and leadership
- appreciate the leadership challenges for the 21st century
- be aware of how individuals can develop into ever more effective leaders and managers.

Introduction

What do we mean by management in the early 21st century? How does this apply to the information services context and how can individuals make both the successful transition to management and continue to develop to become more effective managers? This chapter will aim to provide models, frameworks and suggestions to some of these challenging questions. As later emphasized in Chapter 3, People in Organizations, the organizational context is a critical shaping factor and an in–depth understanding of its culture is imperative to inform the manager's role, style and ultimate performance and success. Management and practitioner thinking with regard to competencies and skills are constantly evolving, and different trends are explored here, particularly in relation to emotional intelligence, empowerment and participation. Rapid and revolutionary change is now viewed as the norm within information services; models of changes management, barriers and enhancers, are closely considered with concepts of leadership – a term that has undergone several metamorphoses over the past few decades and that is the subject of considerable concern across the information profession. This chapter will provide a firm basis for progression to the more specific chapters in this book, raising questions and issues to provoke critical enquiry, and pointing to focused and detailed exploration in later sections. Both this chapter and many of the subsequent chapters concentrate on the human issues of management within information services; this emphasis is deliberate and unrelenting. Interestingly, the appreciation and interest in human skills, interaction and motivation (across management generally and within information services) has grown and not diminished as new technology advances, with manager–employee relations crucial for organizational success. The role of the manager, as Drucker emphasizes, is still to be 'the dynamic, life-giving element in every business' (1955, 3).

Management definitions and roles

There are many definitions of management and it remains a broad and generalist concept:

> a process which enables organizations to set and achieve their objectives by planning, organizing and controlling their resources, including gaining the commitment of its people.
>
> (Cole, 1996, 5)

Or, more basically, 'leading a team to achieve planned objectives' and 'directing resources towards a goal'. Changing theories and thoughts on modern management, particularly in relation to aspects of 'control', are calling into question such definitions and will be explored throughout this chapter. Writers certainly agree, however, that management is carried out within the organizational context and that it encompasses a range of processes and functions that vary according to role.

Mintzberg's (1973) organized set of behaviours usefully map out three functional groups and the skills required:

Interpersonal roles	Figurehead	*LEADER*
	Leader	
	Liaison	
Informational roles	Monitor	*ADMINISTRATOR*
	Disseminator	
	Spokesman	
Decisional roles	Entrepreneur	*FIXER*
	Disturbance handler	
	Resource allocator	
	Negotiator	

Handy (1993) has subsequently added three umbrella role types (highlighted in italics) that relate the three groups more closely to practical management experience. These are useful when considering the skills and abilities required of managers at different levels within information services and we will return to these at a later point. Interestingly, some of these roles can also apply to non-management posts (for example the entrepreneur or negotiator) and some writers would argue that management should not be rigidly viewed as the preserve of formal managers who manage resources and services. Another model for exploring a manager's role is a five-point task list, again related to specific functions and acts, illustrated in Table 2.1.

Table 2.1 The manager's role

Broad task	Specific functions
Planning	Mission, strategic planning
	Objective setting
Organizing	Organizing time, work, decision making
Leading	Direction, motivation
Controlling	Discipline, performance review
	Monitoring
Achieving	Results

Management thinking has also recently turned from a focus on management efficiency, i.e. evaluating the inputs (how individuals plan, monitor, control), to one of management effectiveness, i.e. evaluating outputs (the impact of how individuals manage on productivity, customer satisfaction, new-service development, staff motivation and morale).

Management theories and frameworks are the foundations for this text with the study and practice of management very much dependent on management concepts. Yet, as Billsberry (1996) provocatively demands, 'How can theory help managers become more effective?' and 'Why don't we just tell managers what to do?' Theory can be used to generalize, generate questions and invite criticism, enabling us to think about:

- appropriateness to our specific circumstances
- how theories might be applied (or not)
- how different theories may work in different situations
- how we can adapt and modify them.

A brief and broad overview of the Schools of Management Thought and how they have developed provides an interesting window on how management practices and approaches have shifted significantly over time, and how they continue to change. Early 20th-century theorists such as Fayol and Taylor – 'classical' or 'scientific' managers – were concerned primarily with the structuring of work and organizations and were generally prescriptive in their approach. The Human Relations and Social Psychological Schools, in contrast, were social scientists who researched and analysed the human element of management and organizational culture, including McGregor and Mayo (whose work encompassed motivation theories). Another group – contingency theorists – grounded their work in the idea of the organization as social systems with the view that there were multiple variables at play in any situation. More recent theorists (Mintzberg, Peters, Drucker) take a holistic and strategic perspective, encompassing all factors in their comprehensive views of organizations. Clearly, there has been a shift to more people-centred and holistic approaches in modern management, and these are reflected in approaches to management competencies, change and leadership.

Management of information services

The key management issues for information services are increasingly complex, set within the context of a hybrid environment with rapid advances in technology, globalization, the rise of the stakeholder and the search for continued quality enhancement and excellence. In many respects, the management challenges for information services are no different from those for any other profession (James, 1994). The specific context of the types of services and organizations (depicted in Chapter 1, Information Organizations) alludes to increasing need for change and effective management and leadership in both the public and private sectors. Figure 2.1 illustrates key management issues for information service managers; some of these challenges are explored in this chapter while others, such as devising strategy and planning, merit dedicated chapters.

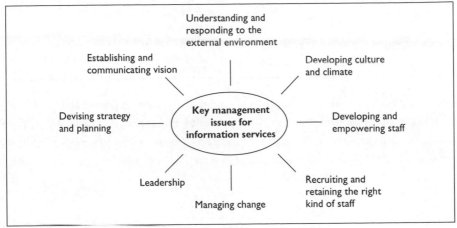

Figure 2.1 Key management issues for information services

The importance of effective management for information services is provocatively highlighted by Line (2002) in his checklist of the characteristics of 'bad bosses' with common faults such as: ignorance; interference; isolation; incoherence; intellectualism; inconsistency; inhumanity. Interestingly the majority of these faults are related to behaviour (and indeed to interpersonal behaviour) rather than knowledge and professional skills. This focus on behaviour is reflected throughout this chapter.

Reflection: Consider a 'bad boss' you have experienced. What were their characteristics and what was the impact on their staff?

Generic levels of management can be usefully mapped against information services management roles (see Table 2.2). At each level the information service manager must grapple with: people, work and structures, systems and procedures. Their approach will be defined by the goals of the organization, its culture, the resources available and factors such as technology. What becomes very clear is the variety of roles a modern information manager can and must take, with variety and fragmentation characteristic of their daily life (Handy, 1993). To illustrate this, Handy uses a powerful image of 'Manager as General Practitioner', seeing

Table 2.2 Generic levels of management and information services roles

Level of management	Example
Direct responsibility for other people	Team leader for electronic resources Small branch library supervisor Lending services supervisor
Responsibility for other managers	Operations manager Academic services manager Cross-site or regional manager
Responsibility for multiple functions	Chief librarian for local authority Head of an academic converged information service

them as the first recipient of problems who must first diagnose the problem, looking at the symptoms but also the root cause. The manager would also call on specialist help or a second opinion if required. Yet, how do information professionals make the move into a first management post and what can be done to help them?

Transition to management

Jordan and Lloyd (2002) have explored the inherent problems associated with the transition from information worker to manager (in whatever role and context), finding that people aren't aware of what management involves and believe that the skills are in built rather than being a set of competencies and abilities that can be acquired and developed. The transition to management often involves a move into a first-line supervisory post with responsibility for a small team, or a few individuals, their objectives and performance. The key elements of such a role can be described as:

- planning and allocating work
- goal setting for the unit/team
- monitoring and checking the work
- supporting and developing the staff
- motivating staff
- evaluating and providing feedback
- communicating with staff, senior managers and other colleagues.

Studies of staff views towards their supervisors within an information service context reveal that staff appreciate managers who are approachable, accessible and enthusiastic, who provide guidelines on the standards of work required, who cover problems and how to deal with them, and who are consultative. An aware-ness of the basic expectations of the supervisor is the first step in considering the competencies required.

With the transition into management and the (hopefully) resultant promotion to subsequent levels of management, there is an inherent conflict for many informa-tion professionals. As individuals move up the management ladder and develop and use their more generic manage-ment skills, their specialist skills (whether they be in academic liaison, enquiry work, web development, col-lections, etc.) will be needed much less, if indeed at all. This is illustrated in Figure 2.2.

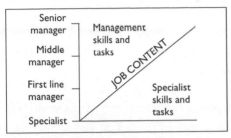

Figure 2.2 Transition to management levels

Reflection: *What guidance and support could be provided to assist an individual's transition into management?*

Management competencies

From the common tasks undertaken by managers highlighted above, it is then possible to describe and analyse a management competencies taxonomy. The popular concept of competency often lacks clarity of meaning. Introduced by Boyatzis, job competency is defined as 'an underlying characteristic of a person which results in effective and superior performance' in a specific role (1982, 21). As such, competency can be achieved by a range of factors – skill, knowledge, motivation, trait – and as such is interlinked with an individual's behaviour and personality as well as the development of skills and understanding. Management roles will therefore require certain competencies and within different roles, orga-nizations and levels of management such competencies will be balanced differ-ently and developed to greater or lesser extents. Effective manager frameworks have been developed and adopted by various organizations to provide direction and to draw competencies together; Figure 2.3 provides an example of a generic management competencies framework. Underpinning each section would be further detail as to skills, behaviours and knowledge required.

An interesting question to consider is: are there significant differences in the management competencies required for information professionals as compared with any other management role? A review of the literature and practice would

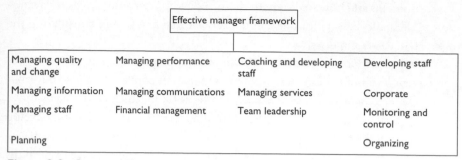

Figure 2.3   Generic effective manager framework

suggest that for information service managers there is an increased focus on service orientation, effective communication with stakeholders, partnership and teamworking, which taken together could privilege a certain type of manager and leader (see later sections on management style and leadership).

A key lesson for all information professionals is that there exists no finite point at which an individual can declare 'I am now an excellent manager' – there is always more to learn and more ways to develop competency. This section explores the core competencies that would be required of a manager at any level. Some of the more specific elements such as financial management and marketing are covered in other chapters, although it is important to recognize that all competencies are interlocking.

The following breakdown of management competencies, associated issues and areas for personal development has been synthesized from a range of authors on general management and information service management. Underpinning all competencies will be the specific management knowledge the manager will need to develop about their organization and role plus their attitude in dealing with people and priorities.

Organizing, planning and controlling

These management competencies are traditionally seen as the core of effective management. They have been touched upon briefly in this chapter and will be explored in further detail in Chapter 7, Finance and Resources, Chapter 8, Strategy and Planning, and Chapter 4, Human Resource Management. Interestingly, there has been a noticeable shift away from these 'harder' competencies to the 'softer' elements explored below. In order to function in areas such as HRM, financial planning and strategic management, a manager must be analytical, organized and evaluative, and be able to communicate effectively their plans and approaches. For example, in setting objectives they must be able to determine goals, break these down into activities, allocate the work, and measure performance. An understanding of the specific organizational context, particularly with regard to financial regulations and HR policies and procedures, is also fundamental to this aspect of a manager's role.

Problem solving and decision making

As Handy (1993) highlights, the first role of a manager is to analyse a problem before they even begin to consider how to solve it. Creative problem solving is often seen as a stumbling block within library and information services management. The rational left brain has been given priority over the creative right brain yet research shows that right-brain thinking can have longer-term results. There are numerous models and approaches to creative problem solving that the manager can usefully employ. These include:

- *lateral thinking* – thinking 'outside the box'
- *brainstorming* to generate as many ideas as possible without being judgemental
- *wish listing* to break the cycle of low expectations and negativity.

Personal effectiveness

Time management

Jordan and Lloyd (2002) and Lawes (1993) usefully identify time wasters or time robbers in relation to information services work, advocating self-analysis before taking action to eliminate as many time robbers as possible. These will be different for each distinct service sector but commonly include meetings (scheduled and unscheduled), e-mail, attempting too much and estimating time unrealistically, interruptions, inability to say no, personal standards (is it 'good enough'?). Strategies for time management include objective and priority setting and review, breaking tasks into manageable chunks, considering best use of time, setting and keeping to deadlines, using others (see 'Delegation' below).

Interpersonal communication skills

Excellent interpersonal skills are essential not only when managing staff but when fostering productive relationships at all levels – with users and both within and

outside an organization. Jordan and Lloyd (2002) identify four key areas and rec-
ommend that with interpersonal skills training the individual manager should
seek to develop and improve them:

- *Communication* – verbal and non-verbal, including presentation skills and the
  ability to persuade, influence and negotiate.
- *Self-management and awareness* – knowing yourself and how your behaviour
  affects others, how you can change your behaviour.
- *Team/group working* – in both formal and informal groups. Of growing
  importance in information services work (see Chapter 3, People in
  Organizations, for more on teams).
- *Assertiveness* – essential for dealing with others including managers, staff, users,
  particularly relevant in dealing with conflict (see Chapter 3, People in
  Organizations).

Reflection, own development, time for relaxation

Any manager must ensure time for their own learning and development,
reflection on successes and issues, and 'self-care' and 'self-pacing' in order to be
able to manage the pace of their work and alleviate stress.

Facilitation and counselling

Many authors and practitioners highlight facilitation and counselling skills as essential for an effective information manager. Such competencies can be particularly
invaluable when dealing, for example, with line-managed staff with problems such
as variable performance, lateness, absenteeism, in situations where conflict resolution is required, or simply when staff need support and counselling as a result of
events at work or in their personal lives. Facilitation and counselling are very different activities but require a range of similar skills. Facilitation aims to literally
'make things easy', with facilitators employing a range of skills and methods to bring
out the best in people as they work to achieve results; typical facilitation events
include meetings, brainstorming future scenarios for the service, alleviating conflict
within a team, and discussion around a theme. Counselling, in contrast, is a one-
to-one activity focusing on an individual and enabling them to take responsibility
for their actions and possible solutions. Three core conditions must be present for
effective counselling to occur:

1 Unconditional positive regard – accept people for who they are, see everyone as worthy
2 Empathy
3 Genuineness – to establish trust.

Both questioning and active listening skills are central to facilitation and counselling, and should be the priority for any manager. Facilitation skills encompass group management and communication techniques, including:

- setting the scene and building rapport
- stimulating interest within the group for the topic
- valorizing every participant – 'unconditional positive regard' as with counselling
- seeking consensus – when everyone agrees to agree
- providing focus particularly with regard to essential items and areas for discussion
- recognizing common themes and trends and highlighting these
- moving the group towards action.

With both counselling and facilitation (and generally in relation to any staff relationship), feedback is also a crucial stage and requires specific skills. Guidelines for providing feedback insist that it should be timely, specific, constructive, evidence based, action focused and, above all, a two-way dialogue between the manager and member of staff.

Delegation

Delegation is the process by which management makes it possible for other staff to share in the work. There are several advantages of delegation:

- Tasks are carried out at the right level with more effective use of resources (also a strategy in time management!)
- It can provide others with opportunities to develop, bring reward and recognition (linked to job enrichment)
- Decision making is better, responses are quicker
- There is professional development for the staff involved.

It is important that the member of staff to whom delegation is being made is given responsibility for the job, e.g. project management for a new library website, is given the authority and is accountable for their actions and outcomes. However, the manager remains ultimately accountable for the area of work. There are problems inherent in delegation, ranging from managers who won't delegate or delegate ineffectively, staff who don't want the increased responsibility, and lack of trust. Bryson (1999) suggests that staff have to be allowed to make mistakes and should be provided with support.

It is evident with this competencies overview that the 'softer' skills – a focus on the emotions rather than on the intellect and the technical – are very much to the fore in information services management. Line (2002) argues that the 'paper' aspects of management – preparing plans or budgets for example – can be learnt fairly easily but that the people aspects are by far the most important and by far the harder to learn. Figure 2.4 summarizes the key behaviours of effective people, taken from Covey's *The Seven Habits of Highly Effective People* (1989). Such behaviours underpin all the general management competencies and reinforce the need for personal development and awareness.

---

1. Be proactive – take responsibility as well as initiative.
2. Begin with the end in mind – where do you want to go?
3. Put first things first – identify priorities in light of your goals.
4. Think win–win.
5. Seek first to understand, then be understood – develop listening skills.
6. Synergize – think creatively.
7. Reflect and renew – allocate time for personal reflection and replenishment.

Figure 2.4 Key behaviours of effective people

Styles of management

Styles of management are in many respects viewed as more significant than management competencies, particularly in relation to staff motivation. Management style refers to the general approach taken by organizations or individuals towards managing employee relations. Styles of management are vital factors in staff motivation and thus managers need to be very conscious of the impact of their own style. McGregor's X and Y theory (in Handy, 1993) sets out two extreme propositions about human motivation, suggesting that people either subscribe to:

- *Theory X* – individuals are *not* self-motivated and thus staff must be directed, persuaded, rewarded and forced to submit to the needs of the organization

Or

- *Theory Y* – individuals *are* self-motivated and staff want to influence their own decisions, need to use their skills, can direct themselves and seek responsibility, wanting to be involved with contributing to the organization's goals and needs.

To generalize, as a consequence Manager X will have an authoritarian, hierarchical style depending on close supervision while Manager Y will be more participative, open in communication style, with staff establishing their own goals and using more initiative. This is an extreme juxtaposition but usefully illustrates the connection between management styles and beliefs, as clearly managers with different beliefs will have very different styles. Blake and Mouton's concept of *grid organization development* (in Jordan and Lloyd, 2002) provides a further model to consider different management styles in a less black-and-white fashion, with a self-scoring questionnaire to plot an individual's management style. The management or leadership grid is then used to plot a manager's approach to interpersonal relationships and has five styles:

1,1   *Impoverished management* – low concern for production with low concern for people. Minimum effort by manager, avoided conflict, abdicated management responsibility.

9,1   *Authority-compliance management* – high concern for production with low concern for people. Close supervision and control of staff, concentration on maximizing output, ignoring employee attitudes, feelings and needs.

1,9   *Country club management* – high concern for people with low concern for output. Concentrate on employee needs potentially at expense of output.

9,9   *Team management* – high levels of concern for both employees and output. Belief that organizational and employee needs are compatible. Managers develop teamwork and involvement of staff.

5,5   *Middle-of-the-road management* – moderate levels of concern for people and output, dependent on compromise.

The most satisfactory position would be a high concern for output married with a high concern for people, although within any given organizational context managers will, and should, adapt their style and behaviour differently at different times.

Reflection: *What are the advantages of completing a management-style assessment?*

A great deal has been written in the late 20th and early 21st centuries on the benefits of participative management, linked to high staff morale and motivation, as reflected in the Human Relations School of Management, and in Blake and Mouton's preferred management approach. Theorists argue that participative management both meets people's needs more effectively at work but is also more closely aligned to the future shape of organizations required for flexibility, responsiveness and survival in a climate of rapid and continuous change. Features of participative management within an information services context include:

- increased delegation – of particular task or projects, e.g. delegation to a small group to design a user survey
- decision-making pushed down the structure – e.g. enquiry staff to discuss and decide on improvements to the enquiry service
- involvement of staff in objective setting and evaluating their achievements – via performance review
- open communication – more informal, face-to-face as well as virtual, group and team meetings, lateral communication
- emphasis on initiative and creative problem solving across the organization – e.g. introduce 'idea of the month' scheme, reward and recognize creativity
- team emphasis with each member valued for their contribution and specialism – use of cross-service project or themed groups.

Participative management is not always easy if staff are accustomed to a more authoritarian style and therefore possibly suspicious of new approaches. Managers can encourage and support their staff by delegation, coaching, feedback and constant and open communication. It is also important to note that management style is not simply affected by the individual manager but by the dominant culture of the organization which may not provide appropriate conditions for participation. Participation is often used synonymously with *empowerment*, defined as 'an approach to managing people which permits team members to exercise greater decision-making on day-to-day matters in their work' (Cole, 1996,190). Clearly, empowerment, participation and delegation are closely inter-related and are fundamental to staff motivation, day-to-day operations, service developments and individual development, and the ability of the organization to change and respond to new imperatives.

Reflection: *Consider a manager that you have worked with. How would you describe their management style? How is this transmitted via their behaviour?*

Women and management

Does the glass ceiling still exist?

Unfortunately, there remains a need to consider women and management as a separate issue within this chapter as, although the situation has improved somewhat within information services and general management, there is still progress to be made in the appointment of women to middle and senior management positions. The metaphor of the glass ceiling was coined in the 1980s to describe the 'transparent barrier that kept women from rising above a certain level in corporations' (Simon, 1995). As Alimo-Metcalfe (1995) powerfully states, 'About the single most uncontroversial, incontrovertible statement to make about women in management is that there are very few of them.' In relation to library and information management this is further highlighted by the 'sexual segregation' of the workforce (McDermott, 1998), as most workers are women yet the higher salaries and status levels are often still occupied by men. This is supported by research undertaken by Nankivell (1992) and the American Library Association (Lynch, 1999) whose statistics also demonstrate that men's salaries tend to be higher than women's even for the same position. More recent research is sparse and there have certainly been more women promoted to prominent positions, but clearly it remains a significant concern.

Barriers to women's progress

Whilst undoubtedly many obstacles have been removed in the UK and elsewhere by legislation such as the Sex Discrimination Act (1975), Equal Pay Act (1970), and the Flexible Working Time Directive (2003), writers such as Burrington (1993) and Simon (1996), commenting on the UK and Australian perspectives respectively, identify other, more deeply entrenched and 'social' barriers:

- double burden of career and family (still seen as the female domain) – 'one cannot deny the enormous pressure that working women face on a daily basis as they attempt to balance their home and career' (Simon, 1996)
- typical myths and prejudices that assume women aren't ruthless enough or assertive enough and dislike power
- organizational culture that is dominantly male
- structure of work that doesn't allow for the flexibility that many women need and desire
- lack of mentors and role models.

What else can be done?

Mentoring is recognized as the most important factor in the career success of women and therefore should be encouraged and developed. In addition, women must fight socialization and begin to change cultures from within. Organizations themselves can also continue to develop more flexible working practices and family-friendly policies.

Interestingly, research shows that while both sexes have male and female values to differing degrees, female values and characteristics are now more highly rated with the shift to people-centred and participative styles of management. Table 2.3 illustrates the different values.

Table 2.3 Marshall's male and female values (in Cole, 1996, 106)

Male values	Female values
Self-assertion	Interdependence
Separation	Cooperation
Control	Receptivity
Competition	Merging
Focused perception	Acceptance
Rationality	Awareness of patterns, wholes and contexts
Clarity	Emotional tone
Discrimination	Being
Activity	Intuition

Consequently, writers are now arguing that we may be seeing the 'feminization' of management as flatter structures with a focus on teamworking and participation require collaborative approaches that are more closely associated with female values (note that not all women will necessarily have 'female' values). This context may provide a more receptive environment for the female manager and will hopefully lead to further changes within the library and information service workforce.

Management of change

One cannot manage change. One can only be ahead of it.

(Drucker, 1999, 73)

To 'manage change' is wishful thinking, implying as it does that one not only knows where to go and how to get there but can persuade everyone else to travel there. To 'cultivate change' is something different, suggesting an attitude of growth, of channelling rather than controlling, of learning not instruction.

(Handy, 1993, 292)

The ability to cope with radical and constant change is a prerequisite for the modern information service manager. They are working in a context influenced by multiple variables, most notably the balance between the virtual and the physical, the demands and expectations of users and stakeholders, changes to culture, climate and structure to meet objectives, rapid advances in information, technology and systems and their interface with human interactions and roles. Figure 2.5 demonstrates the complexity of this environment, highlighting the key organizational features. This section will explore concepts of change, the development of flexible responses and the cultivation of conducive conditions, in particular the human dimension. Specific models for achieving change are explored in detail in Chapter 8, Strategy and Planning.

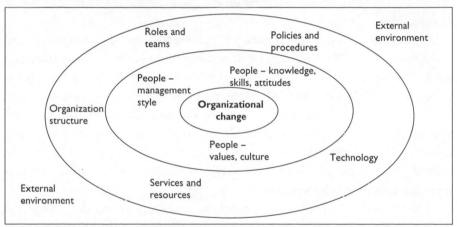

Figure 2.5 Organizational change features

Concepts of change and its 'management'

The ability to adapt, to redesign structures and services and to continuously realign them to stakeholder needs, is critical to organizational performance. Corrall (2000) stresses that the process of planning and implementing change deserves 'special attention' as it remains a difficult and pertinent issue for information services. Leadership is often discussed in relation to change and is a key aspect of change success; it will be explored here as a separate issue as it is felt to be of wider significance than a change agent but the two are unarguably intrinsically linked. Echoing Drucker and Handy, there are two common types of change:

- *conservative*: response to external environment that is reactive – attempt to 'manage' imposed change

- *entrepreneurial*: proactive decision to change from within – attempt to 'stimulate' change or remain ahead of it.

There has also been an evident shift in the management literature from 'mechanistic' and planned models of change (the idea of being able to control change) to a 'radical/dynamic' view where change has to be viewed as essentially chaotic, transformational and never-ending. Another view is that the exclusive concern in the late 20th century has been with making things happen and happen very quickly, often resulting in innovation fatigue. Some writers argue for 'painless change', which is small and ongoing, rather than radical revolution. This concept of change would appear to be organic and integrative, and would also seem to prioritize a concern for people and their capacity to cope with constant and radical change.

Approaches to change are very much dependent on organizational culture and management style. Moss Kanter (1984) suggests two interesting and contrasting models for ways in which organizations deal with change: the *integrative* organization that deals holistically with problems and is willing to try out new ideas, seeing change as an opportunity, and the *segmentalist* organization that sees itself as a collection of segments and consequently deals with change in a compartmentalized way rather than as a whole. The integrative organization can be aligned with the entrepreneurial, proactive approach to change while the segmentalist appears much more conservative.

Lewin's models (1951) have very much influenced approaches to change and its 'management' but are now seen as rather mechanistic. His three-step model provides a framework to consider a step-by-step approach, moving from one fixed state to another that is logical and systematic, from

Unfreeze – current situation
Move – to a desired new state
Refreeze – stabilize the changes.

As Corrall (2000) highlights, this fails to recognize the cyclical nature of change – where 'repeat freeze' is the norm – and 'the importance of treating it as an iterative and interactive process' (209). There are many expert views on approaches to change initiatives but there are common elements to most models that the information service manager must consider:

- a *pressure* for change – to ensure it is given high priority and has a rationale

- a clear shared *vision* – to ensure ownership and to sustain momentum
- actionable *first steps* – to ensure direction and early wins
- *capacity* for change – in terms of leadership, people and learning.

(after Corrall, 2000)

The key element, yet again, is people, with the need for a strategic approach to human resource development, often neglected by management, to ensure that staff have both the capacity for flexible responses to the unknown (an attitude conducive for change) and the appropriate education, training and development.

Reflection: Why do you think there has been a shift from 'mechanistic' to 'dynamic' approaches to change? How does this relate to the information services context?

People and change

While people are central to the change process, their responses to change can be extremely problematic, resulting in low morale and motivation, and problems of retention. Workplace stress is also often associated with poor change management; the psychological consequences of rapid change have been explored by theorists such as Toffler (1970) who coined the term 'future shock' to express the stress and lack of control experienced by people confronted by the pace of change. Resistance to change should be anticipated as people will see both the positives: creation of the new, innovation, improvements, and the negatives: discontinuity, loss of the familiar, fear of the unknown. A participative management style, as discussed previously, can facilitate staff engagement and ownership of change but there are other, inter-related models, that are also worth exploring.

Lewin's *force field analysis theory* (1951) is a widely used and effective tool for thinking through change strategies, particularly in relation to people and resistance. The theory suggests that all behaviour is the result of a balance between two sets of opposing forces (driving and restraining) with driving forces attempting to bring about change and restraining forces maintaining the status quo. The challenge for the manager is to not simply increase the driving forces but to remove or reduce the restraining forces; in summary, begin with the staff views and concerns and consider 'how can we deal with them?' Again, this is a people-centric model. For example, mergers between libraries could be resisted because staff fear loss of status or redundancies and are suspicious of the other teams. Instead of continuing to exert pressure by insisting the change needs to happen for financial reasons, managers should explore with staff their fears and concerns, communicating openly and honestly to alleviate fears, to establish clearly what will happen and to negotiate and agree actions.

Kubler-Ross's *coping cycle* (1969), illustrated in Figure 2.6, is a further useful diagnostic tool as it provides a framework to enable an understanding of how individuals deal with traumatic personal loss by moving through a variety of stages. It has been applied to individuals coping with radical organizational change, and can help managers to consider the impact of change on their staff. A note of caution is that the individualistic nature of anyone's response would not necessarily comply with the cycle.

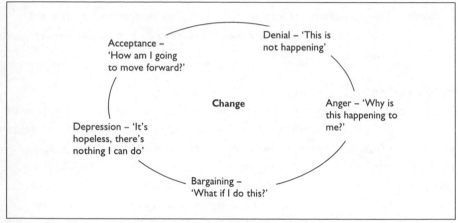

Figure 2.6 The coping cycle (after Kubler-Ross)

An *action research* and participative approach to change can provide a team approach that will engender consultation, collaboration and hopefully ownership of the change. This is reflected in a simple model as shown in Figure 2.7.

Figure 2.7 Action research model

With any model, there remain multiple impact factors that can critically affect the change process; these include:

- *organizational culture* – awareness, flexibility, responsiveness, willingness to embrace change
- *management style and leadership* – effective two-way communication, participative, empowering, motivating, facilitative
- *HRM policies and practices* to provide a supportive framework for change – staff development approaches, flexible approaches to staffing
- *change agents and champions* – to drive change forward, influence, make a case for change. These can be at different levels of the organization.

One of the key contextual factors is readiness for change. Eccles (in Huczynski and Buchanan, 2004, 620) identifies several questions to test out readiness for change: Is there pressure for change? Is there a clear and shared vision of the goal and direction? Do we have effective liaison and trust between those concerned? Is there the will and power to act? Do we have enough capable people with sufficient resources? Do we have suitable rewards and defined accountability of action? Have we actionable first steps? Does the organization have the capacity to learn and adapt? The information service manager must ask, discuss and attempt to answer such questions before moving forward with any change implementation strategy.

On assessing the effectiveness of change management, writers such as Hooper and Potter (2001) stress that if behaviour is to change long term, there must be changes in values and beliefs and people must understand the reason for change. The key to influencing individuals, and therefore moving forward with change successfully, is for managers to operate at the level of identity, belief and values rather than simply trying to change behaviour. For example, an attempt to make a service more customer focused by introducing a customer charter without ensuring that staff really do believe that the customer comes first will lead to problems as people's behaviour cannot truly change unless their beliefs and values do.

Technology and change

Change theorists within an information service context often focus on technology, because of the significant impact it has had on working practices, services and roles. Technology can be seen as both an enabler and a driver of change and is often promoted as a solution to resourcing problems, e.g. the implementation of new systems to save staff time and to streamline activities. Corrall (2000) argues convincingly that technology should, however, be seen as a 'value-adding' process rather than a cost-cutting one, enabling the enhancement of services and resources through innovation, for example the development of the e-book to meet remote user needs, and cross-database searching to simplify research needs. Technology is certainly no longer seen as a panacea to all problems but can nevertheless provide creative possibilities with new opportunities driving change or providing solutions to challenging problems (see the Case Cameo below).

Common themes underpinning current thinking with regard to change and its facilitation highlight a shift from change as radical and quick to change as painless and slower, with a 'people-oriented' focus (advocated by authors such as Yukl, 2002) that recognizes the individual's capacity to deal with change must be part of the equation and strategy. Change is viewed as a learning process that must be bottom-up and open-ended, and there should be a continuous and organic cycle of change and reflection rather than a one off, momentous event. Above all, organizations must create an in-built flexibility and ability to change, undoubtedly dependent on their culture.

CASE CAMEO

Change and the electronic library

The massive rate of change in academic libraries in the 1990s in higher education in the UK, USA and Australia has been effectively captured by many authors' and government reports, including Hanson and Day (1998), HEFCE (1993) and John Fielden Consultancy (1993). As Riggs (in Hanson and Day, 1998, 129) noted, 'The libraries of colleges and universities are changing faster than their respective parent institutions. Essentially everything in and around the library is changing: services, technologies, organisational constructs, ownership and access policies, values and most of the rest.' This type of change was influenced by multiple factors including government agendas for greater participation in HE, the rise of student-centred learning, skills agendas and technological advances (most obviously the rise of the internet) and changes within the workplace including the influence of the customer, teamworking and a quality enhancement focus. IMPEL (Impact on People of Electronic Libraries) and IMPEL 2 projects researched the impact of such change on library and information services in the UK, particularly on organizations, cultures and people, finding evidence of the impact of electronic libraries (and particularly the tensions between access and holdings) on professional roles, structures and working methods. Four key points that reinforce the change concepts and models outlined above are:

- the importance of the role of training and development to enable staff to manage change
- the significance of an organizational development approach that considers readiness for change
- cultural issues and difficulties
- technology acting as a catalyst for change and also as an enabler.

Reflection: What are the challenges associated with managing and change issues in the electronic or hybrid library?

Leadership

> Surely a group of intelligent, well-meaning individuals can tackle any problem without the need for a leader?
>
> (Handy, 1993, 96)

Change and leadership

As many management authors highlight, there is an intrinsic link between change and leadership. The success of the former is dependent on the latter with the leader ensuring 'emotional alignment' between individuals and organizational goals (Hooper and Potter, 2001) and with leadership seen as a critical determinant of organizational success, whatever the type of organization. This is strongly supported within information services – 'There is no doubt that all activity towards change and transformation of services always refers to the importance of good and strong leadership' (Gent and Kempster, 2002, 53) – with the additional recognition that the 'task of leading such services has changed beyond recognition' (Corrall, introduction to Parsons, 2004). But what constitutes *good and strong leadership*? How does this impact on services, staff, stakeholders and cultures? What are the main theories and thoughts on leadership? And how can leadership potential be developed?

The study of leadership is a relatively recent discipline and is fascinating to explore as concepts have developed significantly. Writers have discussed and argued extensively the distinction between leadership and management. Most agree that there is a distinction, summarized by:

Manager – internally focused, will complete the task, an operator, problem solver
Leader – externally focused, has vision, a strategist, catalyst, looking to the future

Management – concerned with what people with responsibility for others actually *do*
Leadership – ability of people to *influence* others towards achievement of goals.

Such distinctions are felt by some to be unhelpful, as they portray leadership as
positive and management as negative. In addition, some authors view the two
concepts and roles as mutually exclusive – one person cannot be both as they have
incompatible values. Other writers believe that the words manager and managing
should be discarded as leadership is all important in our current context.
However, Yukl (2002) argues convincingly that while they are distinct processes,
and that people can lead without being a manager and can manage without being
a leader, they are interlinked as leadership is an essential management role that
pervades other roles. Writers such as Rost (In Huczynski and Buchanan, 2004)
also stress the value of effective management and feel strongly that it should not
be denigrated as a function. Consequently it can be argued that the two are mutually supportive in that people need to feel well led *and* well managed.

Reflection: Consider a leader whom you admire. What are their characteristics?

Trends in leadership theories

Leadership has been defined in many ways and the theoretical approaches are
numerous. The main trends can be summarized as:

- trait spotting
- style counselling
- context fitting
- twenty-first-century leadership
- emotional intelligence

Trait spotting

Based on the assumption that the personality traits of a good leader could be identified, this is often referred to as the 'great man theory', which supposes that leaders are born not made. Such traits include drive, self-confidence and the ability to
influence others. Until the 1980s there was also the assumption that leadership
was masculine.

Style counselling

This is based on the view that individuals can be developed as leaders and enabled to adopt appropriate behaviour. Two dimensions of leadership behaviour identified by research are: employee centred (focused on relationships and employee needs) and job centred (focused on the task). Likert's (1961) work reinforced the benefits of the former, as out of his four systems of leadership (see Table 2.4) the considerate, performance-oriented approach (3 and 4) is viewed as the most successful.

Table 2.4 Likert's four systems of leadership

System	Examples of behaviour
1. Exploitative autocratic	No trust in staff, no delegation, threatens, little teamwork and poor communication
2. Benevolent authoritative	Imposes decisions, paternalistic towards employees, motivates by reward
3. Participative	Incomplete trust, uses ideas of employees, still controls decision making but does listen
4. Democratic	Complete trust, shares ideas and opinions, employees make own decisions

Reflection: *Considering Likert's systems of leadership, what are the similarities between System 3 and 4 behaviours and a participative approach to management? What lessons can we learn from this?*

Context fitting

This is based on the view that leadership is context specific, and consequently a leader's style is based upon the situation they find themselves in. Choice is dependent on numerous variables within the individual leader (values, personality, beliefs, confidence), their employees (expectations, knowledge, values) and within the particular situation (culture, teamworking, nature of problem). As a result of consideration of all these factors, a leader would adapt their approach and style. Some authors argue strongly that there is no one right way to lead (contrasting with trait and style-counselling theories) and that leaders can and must vary their style to fit the context – sometimes having to *tell, sell, be participative* or *delegate*. A major factor in style is the employees' readiness to change or perform a task. If this is low then a leader must be more directive.

Twenty-first-century leadership

The leader of the twenty-first century is viewed as someone who has the right traits and style and can adapt to context; in brief, someone who conforms to all the theories highlighted above. There remain tensions in concepts of leadership with the 'new leader' still seen as a visionary, charismatic individual, seemingly at odds with the concept of the 'superleader' who aims to develop leadership at all levels of the organization. Authors are certainly more critical of the 'larger-than-life' leader who leads from the front, seeing effective leadership as a process created by an individual (the 'learning leader') rather than dependent on their personal qualities (Hooper and Potter, 2001). This is illustrated by the following:

Heroic individuals   *vs*   **Shared leadership**
Heroic leader who can   Leadership across teams,
transform the organization   shared by different
and motivate staff   members of staff.

Emotional intelligence (EI)

Management and leadership approaches do now take into account the emotional aspects of working. This is particularly reflected in the concept of emotional intelligence, led by Goleman (1995), which is seen by many as the key to effective leadership. EI can be defined as the capacity for recognizing our own feelings and those of others, for motivating ourselves, and for managing emotions well in ourselves and in our relationships. Goleman has established four quadrants individuals must reflect upon and develop:

Internal/Personal   *External/Inter-personal*
Self-awareness   Social awareness
Self-management   Relationship management.

Coaching   – develops people for the future, impacts on organizational culture
Democratic – collaborative, team approach, aims to build consensus
Affiliative – creates harmony, builds relationships
Visionary – motivates people towards a vision, change catalyst
Pace setting – gets moving quickly, drive to achieve
Directive – demands compliance, direction to achieve

Figure 2.8 Goleman's six EI leadership styles

He has also defined six leadership styles, stressing that we need to know when to use each one (reinforcing the view that different styles and approaches are needed for different occasions). These are reflected in Figure 2.8.

There is an evident concern within library and information services literature about leadership for the future. Corrall (2003) identifies that 'There is a serious shortage of candidates for senior positions', while the Public Library workforce study (Usherwood et al., 2001) paints a worrying picture of a sector in a state of crisis. Despite the view that leadership is key to the future of services and professional practice, there is little written on models of future leadership outside a few interesting US writers (for example, Urgo, 2000). It should also be stressed that leadership is a concern right across organizations, required in all levels and functions. Eastell (2003) also highlights this non-hierarchical approach: 'It's much less about finding the next head of library service and far more about finding ways of offering library staff at all levels the opportunity to demonstrate and develop their leadership skills.' Demands on leaders within the information services context are greater than ever before with the pace of change previously illustrated, the demands of stakeholders and rising expectations of staff. The challenge is to identify, support and reward leaders, enabling them to improve their leadership abilities. Several authors have also pointed to the role of information services leadership beyond the actual service, as 'community leaders' taking on roles across their organizations, particularly in relation to stakeholders.

What do effective leaders do?

It is helpful to consider how effective leaders behave and what they do in practice. As Hooper and Potter (2001) highlight, leaders are important role models and as such what they do must be a true reflection of their communicated values and beliefs. Most importantly, they must demonstrate integrity and inspire trust. Effective leaders are involved in:

- *Creation, sharing and communication of vision* – vision is explored in more detail in Chapter 8, Strategy and Planning, but must be incorporated briefly here to signal the critical role of the leader in developing a shared vision of the future of the service and organization, involving their staff and maintaining constant and consistent dialogue and communication of that vision.
- *Shaping of cultures* – the importance of organizational context and culture to enable successful change and innovation to occur has already been well established, and the concept of organizational culture is further developed in Chapter 3, People in Organizations. Leaders can and should shape organizational culture in powerful ways, including:
  — *primary mechanisms*: what they *do* (role modelling), how they allocate rewards and recognition, what they see as important and attend to as priorities; how they communicate which should be inspiring, clear, consistent

— *secondary mechanisms*: design of systems and procedures, organizational structure, stories, myths.

Within the information services context, effective leaders must also engender creativity, energy and communication across the organization at every level of staff, moving away from rigid structures and traditional hierarchies.

Manager and leadership development

A great deal is expected of managers and leaders within information services; consequently, management and leadership development are imperative. Strategies and approaches to generic staff training and development are explored in Chapter 4, Human Resource Management, but it is importantl to consider here the needs of managers and leaders. Management development methods include:

- formal education (MBA, DMS, IPM)
- training, e.g. emotional intelligence programmes
- experiential learning (often seen as the most effective) – incorporating secondments, job rotation, coaching
- leadership programmes – e.g. the Educause Leadership Programme (for IT leadership in US higher education) aims to develop leadership potential via topics such as 'Setting strategic expectations and service strategies' and 'Creativity and innovation'.

However, while specific skills have been highlighted throughout this chapter, management and leadership development should not simply be viewed as purely competency based. It must aim to challenge all staff to self-develop through increased self-knowledge, personal reflection and personal challenges. As such, it cannot be learnt by adhering to one particular model and the focus should be upon 'manager development', which nurtures personal qualities and behaviours, rather than 'management development', which looks specifically at skills. The development of effective leadership is thus a complex process, summarized by Adair (2003, 17) as encompassing a blend of:

- leadership quality – what you are
- leadership situational – what you know
- leadership functional – what you do
- leadership values – what you believe.

Summary and conclusions

Concepts of management and leadership have evolved throughout the 20th century and will continue to do so. The different theories and frameworks provide the information service manager with tools to consider their own skills, style, approach and techniques. Management must be considered as multifaceted, contextual and increasingly challenging given the nature of change and environmental issues. Undoubtedly the transition to management must be approached carefully, with the required skills and abilities identified and developed; but personal and professional development does not end there as management competencies and personal attributes will require constant development over an individual's career. Consideration of management styles is important for individuals and organizations, with management literature advocating a participative approach. Debates in relation to women in management are still necessary and barriers to their progression must be considered. The challenge for the information profession is to develop responsive and flexible managers who are both task and people oriented, within a climate that is inclusive and supportive. As highlighted in this chapter, the management of change is viewed as fundamental to any organization, and is crucial within the information services context; effective approaches are now seen as dynamic, continuous and people centred. Leadership must also be developed at all levels and, while viewed differently by various theorists, it can be an intrinsic part of management and also distinctive. What is evident is that information services need effective management *and* inspirational leadership. Being a manager and leader in today's environment undoubtedly requires more subtle skills and a different emphasis than in the past, with the ' "uncomfortable" requirement to be an empowerer, a coach, a facilitator and an educator' (Hooper and Potter, 2001, 69). For both managers and leaders their values and behaviours are in many ways more important than their competencies. This is particularly pertinent in their relationships with their staff as 'Managers need to genuinely listen to people, seek to understand them and mentor them. They need to demonstrate respect, and communicate people's worth and potential so clearly that they come to see it themselves – which is the true essence of leadership' (Gent and Kempster, 2002, 57).

REVIEW QUESTIONS

1 What are the key activities undertaken by a manager?
2 Describe the management challenges for information service managers.

3   What is a competency and can you describe information services management competencies?

4   Explain the differences between counselling and facilitation. When would you use each approach?

5   What are the features of a participative management style? Why is it viewed as desirable?

6   What are the barriers to women's progression to management?

7   Why is Lewin's three-step change management model now outdated?

8   What are the stages of Kubler-Ross's coping cycle and how could it be used with staff?

9   What are the main arguments in the differences between management and leadership?

10   Describe three key trends in leadership theories.

11   What is the difference between manager and management development?

CASE STUDY

Management competencies for higher education information services: the HIMSS project (Hybrid Information Management: skills for senior staff)

A project undertaken in UK higher education institutions, led by Birmingham University, explored recruitment, training and succession-planning issues for heads of information services. Challenges included obstacles to recruitment, skills gaps, training and development needs, the increased pace of change for managers and the increase in hybrid roles that encompassed diverse services, not simply libraries. The key management skills found to be lacking were:

- strategic management and leadership
- ability to manage change
- customer focus-orientation.

The list of generic management skills and personal qualities could relate to any type of information service and reinforce the management competencies discussed previously but also with a focus on change management and leadership skills. HIMSS have developed a Learning Framework Online aimed at helping the career development of staff aspiring to be heads of services (www.himss-lfo.bham.ac.uk) which allows staff to plot their experience, skills and achievements against those required to become head of a converged information service in higher education.

Considering the above overview, explore the Learning Framework Online and reflect on the following:

- How useful is this as a tool for individuals aspiring to become heads of service?
- How user friendly is the website?
- What did you find most relevant to your own career development?
- How could it be improved?

CHALLENGES

1 Do you agree with Drucker's view that people can't be managed and must only be led?
2 How can a participative approach be introduced into a service where the staff have been rendered passive during an authoritative style of management? What change management models could you employ?
3 Is all management the management of change? What are the consequences of the answer to this in relation to management and leadership styles?
4 How can a leader create a climate where change is embraced and not feared?
5 What are the possible consequences of a leader's personal values and beliefs being at odds with those of the organization?

References and additional reading

Adair, J. (2003) *The Inspirational Leader: how to motivate, encourage and achieve success*, London, Kogan Page.

Alimo-Metcalfe, B. (1995) An Investigation of Female and Male Constructs of Leadership and Empowerment, *Women in Management Review*, **10** (2), 3–8.

Billsberry, J. (ed.) (1996) *The Effective Manager: perspectives and illustrations*, London, Sage Publications in association with The Open University.

Boyatzis, R. E. (1982) *The Competent Manager*, New York, Wiley.

Bryson, J. (1990) *Effective Library and Information Centre Management*, Aldershot, Gower.

Bryson, J. (1999) *Effective Library and Information Centre Management*, 2nd edn, Aldershot, Gower.

Burrington, G. A. (1993) *Equally Good: women in British librarianship*, London, Association of Assistant Librarians.

Cole, G. A. (1996) *Management Theory and Practice*, 5th edn, London, Continuum.

Corrall, S. (2000) *Strategic Management of Information Services: a planning handbook*,

London, ASLIB/Information Management International.

Corrall, S. (2003) How Can Our Leaders Thrive? *Library and Information Appointments*, **6** (1), 1–2.

Corrall, S. and Brewerton, A. (1999) *The New Professional's Handbook: your guide to information services management,* London, Library Association Publishing.

Covey, S. R. (1989) *The Seven Habits of Highly Effective People*, New York, Simon and Schuster.

Drucker, P. (1955) *The Practice of Management*, Oxford, Butterworth-Heinemann.

Drucker, P. (1999) *Management Challenges for the 21st Century,* Oxford, Butterworth-Heinemann.

Eastell, C. (2003) The Key to Ciara and the Next Generation of Public Library Leaders, *Library + Information Update*, (April), 40–1.

Gent, R. and Kempster, G. (2002) Leadership and Management. In Melling, M. and Little, J. (eds), *Building a Successful Customer-service Culture: a guide for library and information managers*, London, Facet Publishing, 53–73.

Goleman, D. (1995) *Emotional Intelligence: why it can matter more than IQ*, London, Bloomsbury Publishing.

Handy, C. (1993) *Understanding Organizations,* 4th edn, London, Penguin Books.

Hanson, T. and Day, J. (eds) (1998) *Managing the Electronic Library: a practical guide for information professionals,* London, Bowker-Saur.

HEFCE (1993) *Joint Funding Councils' Libraries Review Group: Report*, London, HEFCE (The Follett Report).

Hooper, A. and Potter, J (2001) *Intelligent Leadership: creating a passion for change,* London, Random House Business Books.

Huczynski, A. and Buchanan, D. (2004) *Organisational Behaviour: an introductory text*, 5th edn, London, Prentice Hall.

James, S. (1994) A Review of Some General and Industrial Management and Their Relevance to Library Management, *Library Review*, **43** (1), 39–45.

John Fielden Consultancy (1993) *Supporting Expansion: a report on human resource management in academic libraries*, for the Joint Funding Councils' Libraries Review Group, London, HEFCE.

Jordan, P. and Lloyd, C. (2002) *Staff Management in Library and Information Work,* 4th edn, Aldershot, Ashgate.

Kubler-Ross, E. (1969) *On Death and Dying*, Toronto, Macmillan.

Lawes, A. (ed.) (1993) *Management Skills for the Information Manager,* Aldershot, Ashgate.

Lewin, K. (1951) *Field Theory in Social Sciences*, New York, Harper & Row.

Likert, R. (1961) *New Patterns of Management*, New York, McGraw-Hill.

Line, M. (1996) Needed: a pathway through the swamp of management literature, *Library Management*, **17** (3), 32–7.

Line, M. (2002) How Do Managers Learn to Manage? *Library Management*, **23** (3), 166–7.

Lynch, M. (1999) *Library Directors: gender and salary*, Chicago, IL, ALA Office for Research and Statistics, www.ala.org/ala/hrdr/libraryempresources/librarydirectors.htm.

McDermott, E. (1998) Barriers to Women's Career Progression in LIS, *Library Management*, **19** (7), 416–20.

Melling, M. and Little, J. (eds) (2002) *Building a Successful Customer-service Culture: a guide for library and information managers*, London, Facet Publishing.

Mintzberg, H. (1973) *The Nature of Managerial Work*, London, Harper & Row.

Morris, B. (1996) *First Steps in Management*, The Successful LIS Professional series, edited by Sheila Pantry, London, Library Association Publishing.

Moss Kanter, R. (1984) *The Change Masters – corporate entrepreneurs at work*, New York, Allen and Unwin.

Nankivell, C. (1992) *Equal Opportunity in the Library Profession*, London, Library Association Publishing.

Parsons, F. (ed.) (2004) *Recruitment, Training and Succession Planning in the HE Sector: findings from the HIMSS project*, Birmingham, The University of Birmingham.

Simon, J. (1995) The 'Double-glazed Glass Ceiling' in Australian Libraries, *Women in Management Review*, **10** (8), 19–29.

Simon, J. (1996) Success for Women Library Managers – But on Whose Terms? *Women in Management Review*, **11** (3), 12–19.

Toffler, A. (1970) *Future Shock*, London, Pan Books.

Urgo, M. (2000) *Developing Information Leaders: harnessing the talents of Generation X*, London, Bowker-Saur.

Usherwood, B., Bower, G., Coe, C., Coope, J. and Stevens, T. (2001) *Recruit, Retain and Lead: the Public Library workforce study*, Library and Information Commission Research Report 106, Sheffield, Centre for the Public Library and Information in Society, Department of Information Studies, University of Sheffield and Resource: the Council for Museums, Archives and Libraries.

Winston, M. D. (2001) *Leadership in the Library and Information Profession: theory and practice*, New York, Haworth Press.

Yukl, G. (2002) *Leadership in Organisations*, 5th edn, New Jersey, Prentice Hall.

3
People in organizations

Why do they work so hard? Why do they work when they do? Why, come to that, do they work at all?

(Handy, 1993, 29)

LEARNING OBJECTIVES

After reading this chapter you should be able to:

- demonstrate awareness of the concepts and theories that underpin understandings of how people work and interact within organizations
- appreciate the complexities and significance of the individual, groups and teams within the library and information context
- understand the nature of motives and motivation processes as influences on behaviour
- demonstrate an awareness of useful techniques and approaches with regard to the motivation of people
- apply relevant theories and models of communication to workplace scenarios
- be aware of career development issues and approaches for the library and information worker
- be aware of issues related to power, politics and conflict within the workplace.

Introducton

As Chapter 4 will highlight, the success of any organization depends on the

motivation, performance and commitment of its staff and the most common challenge for the library and information service manager is in dealing with people. This
is not simply about human resource management approaches and strategies, but is
interconnected with an understanding of how and why people behave and respond
as they do within the organizational context. Such understanding is key to motivating and leading staff, especially during periods of change. The answers to the
questions 'How can we influence behaviour?' and 'How can we engage staff at all
levels, ensuring ownership, commitment and motivation?' are fundamental to
effective information services management. The 'psychosocial environment'
within which people work is crucial and the manager must explore how to foster a
positive climate. Consequently, this chapter provides models to help us understand
organizational behaviour (and the individual within the organization); the manager
must engage with this environment and use such models as a basis for informed and
necessary intervention. As such, this chapter is also closely interlinked with Chapter
2, Management and Leadership, which develops the crucial theme of the required
management skills and roles necessary for a challenging and dynamic context.

There has been a noticeable shift in management thinking and approaches
from the 1990s onwards, towards a much more people-centred view of communication and consultation. This chapter discusses the cultures and values of organizations, the individual within their working context and issues of motivation,
then progresses to groups, teams and issues such as communication, power, conflict and stress. It concludes with reflection on career development, competencies
and techniques such as mentoring, coaching and job shadowing. The aim is to
develop an understanding of behaviour in an organizational context, with the
very nature and type of organization fundamental to building up a detailed understanding of its people.

An underlying theme is the impact of technology on organizational culture,
working practices, communication and groups. Rapid advances in information
and communications technology can be seen to be opening up new opportunities and modes of working and interaction yet also often causing additional stress
and challenges in the workplace.

Organizational behaviour

The understanding of organizations and the people within them derives from
several disciplines such as psychology, social psychology, sociology, economics
and political science as well as from history, anthropology and geography. As such
it is multi-disciplinary.

Organizational behaviour is recognized as a significant field of study with many practical applications, exploring the impact and interlocking elements of the individual, group and nature of the organizational context. Organizational behaviour is defined as 'the study of the structure, functioning and performance of organisations, and the behaviour of groups and individuals within them' (Huczynski and Buchanan, 2001, 2). To understand behaviour we must clearly place it within the context of the organization (see Chapter 1, Information Organizations), while recognizing that the term 'organization' can be difficult to define. Within any given organization there will often be inherent tensions between individual needs, aspirations and wants, and collective goals and objectives. The literature of organizational behaviour enables us to explore these tensions, leading to improved understanding and possible models to bring the two more closely together.

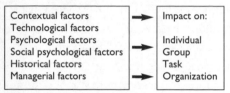

Figure 3.1 Influences on the organization and experience of work

The organization and experience of work itself is influenced by several, interlinking factors, illustrated in Figure 3.1.

Many writers on organization behaviour strongly suggest that modern organizational arrangements, methods (for example the need for flexibility, adaptability, constant change) and contexts (for example mergers, downsizing, competition) create pressures, stress and threat. This chapter explores how library and information services and their managers can identify such issues and minimize them within the workplace.

Organizational culture

Organizational culture has been a popular concept since the 1980s, providing an explanatory framework with which to analyse behaviour in an organization. Yet Ogbonna (in Billsberry, 1996) has suggested that there are as many definitions of culture as there are experts and there is no clear consensus as to its meaning. One useful definition is a 'collection of relatively uniform and enduring values, beliefs, customs, traditions and practices that are shared by an organisation's members, learned by new recruits and transmitted' (Huczynski and Buchanan, 2004, 643). A common theme is that culture is a dominant pattern of shared beliefs, something which is perceived and felt collectively. An awareness of the culture of their own organization is key for information service managers as it crucially impacts on their work, employees and performance. Figure 3.2 illustrates the multiple factors which both influence and are influenced by organizational culture.

Figure 3.2 Organizational culture: influences and impacts

But where and how do employees experience organizational culture? Schein's model of culture provides a useful starting point and is widely used; culture is viewed as the sharing of meanings and of basic assumptions among employees, working at three levels:

- *Manifestations*: organization-specific objects such as artefacts (furniture, appliances), ceremonials, jokes, language, mottoes, myths, slogans, symbols, norms (expected modes of behaviour, e.g. referring to colleagues as Mr, Miss or Mrs, a formal dress code).
- *Values and beliefs*: things that have personal or organizational worth or meaning; often unspoken they can mould behaviour. Values are seen as central by many theorists to organizational culture and development, providing guidelines and common direction. An interesting question is 'where do values come from?' Some see values as stemming from senior managers, or as representing organizational solutions to past problems. Organizational values are intrinsically linked to mission and objectives, and are explored further in Chapter 8, Strategy and Planning.
- *Basic assumptions*: these are assumptions that individuals hold about an organization and how it functions, and as such are invisible, e.g. 'Library assistants are never listened to', 'The department is really committed to staff development'.

Organizational culture is formed from a relatively stable collection of people with a shared history, yet within the modern working environment there is constant change and staff turnover; new members are therefore 'socialized'. Socialization is the way in which an individual's pattern of behaviour, as well as their values and attitudes, are influenced to conform with those of the organization. Socialization processes include the selection of staff, induction and instruction on behaviour and norms, and the reinforcement of desired behaviours. 'Signalling systems' also act as powerful influencers during socialization – these transmit the message 'Behave this way and you will be rewarded and/or promoted'. Reinforcement of desirable behaviours can be achieved by using such tools as mission statements, by articulating visions, and through performance review.

The concept of socialization naturally leads to an assumption that managers can (and must) control and change organizational culture in order to achieve objectives. For example, managers can aim to develop a customer-focused culture within an information service to meet specific customer satisfaction targets. In addition, writers suggest that strong cultures act as powerful levers for guiding workforce behaviour. However, this position is countered by the view that culture cannot be managed and that indeed it is not a 'known' entity. This can be represented as in Figure 3.3.

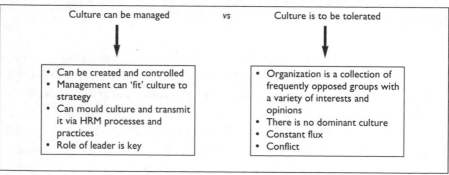

Figure 3.3 Views of organizational culture

It could also be argued that culture can be engaged with and negotiated (rather than more directly 'managed') over a period of time as cultures change slowly and sometimes imperceptibly. Socialization itself can be problematic as while strong organizations may have strong cultures this can prove difficult for the individualist who does not want to merely conform, resulting in conflict or poor motivation. As later highlighted, conflict can be viewed as healthy, ensuring that an organization doesn't stagnate; if all staff are 'owned' by the organization and fully socialized into its norms and values, such conflict may be rare.

Organizational cultures, if they can be said to exist at all, are the result of complex factors and influences and will vary according to the type of organization. They will also vary according to groups, and particularly professional groups who will have their own values, beliefs, and processes of socialization. It can be argued that the library and information profession has a particular set of values that are common across sectors and organizational types. However, these could also be dependent on the type of organizational context, for example corporate values will be very different to those of the public sector. A common set of information professional values could be said to include belief in:

- the value of information
- accessibility to information and services
- customer focus
- social inclusion.

(See values statement discussion in Chapter 8, Strategy and Planning.)

Reflection: *How would you describe your own values? How have these been influenced and developed?*

Learning organizations

A great deal has been written on organizational culture in relation to learning, with many authors seeing the development of a learning culture as vital to success and development. Learning theories have influenced a range of organizational practices and theoretical frameworks. The ability to learn (both individually and collectively) is recognized as having direct consequences for organizational ability to develop and survive as the external environment and users' needs continue to change. Learning can be considered at two discrete yet interlocking levels:

- *organizational learning* – understanding learning in an organization context
- *learning organization* – expanding the organization's capacity to learn.

Organizational learning – understanding learning in an organization context

One of the most important concepts of learning to emerge in the late 1980s and 1990s is that of experiential learning; this is a particularly valuable concept to apply to thinking about ongoing learning at work. It is predicated upon the principle that learning does not simply happen in formal settings but that we learn all the time from all our experiences of life. Kolb's model (see Figure 3.4) is useful in this context as it describes learning as the process whereby knowledge is created

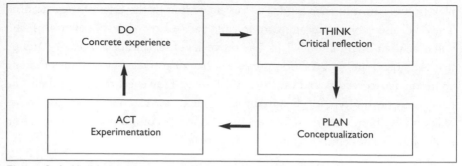

Figure 3.4 Kolb's learning cycle (adapted from Kolb, 1984)

through the transformation of experience. The sequence of do, think, plan and act begins with the individual experiencing some event or situation, moving to reflect critically on this (e.g. what happened and why, explanations, patterns, difficulties), then bringing in external perspectives to help conceptualize the issues and form an explanation. The fourth stage, 'act', leads to another experience where approaches or behaviour are modified in light of the previous experience. The cycle is continuous. An extension to this theory is that of learning styles, which suggests that we all have a preferred style of learning that corresponds to the stages of the learning cycle.

Reflection: Can you apply Kolb's learning cycle to your own experience of learning? Consider an example of when you feel this has worked particularly effectively, what you learned as a result, how you applied it and why you feel it worked well.

Learning organization – expanding the organization's capacity to learn

The learning organization concept derives from Argyris and Schon (1996) and Senge (1990) and supports the view that work must become more 'learningful' at all levels. A learning organization is one that learns continuously and transforms itself. Features of a learning organization have been described and analysed by various theorists in slightly different ways; Senge's summary of the 'Five learning disciplines' highlights the following:

- *Personal mastery* – aspiration, an understanding of what you as the individual want to achieve
- *Mental models* – reflection and enquiry, constant review, challenging assumptions
- *Shared vision* – collective vision, commitment to common purpose and goals

- *Team learning* – group interaction, collective thinking and action directed towards achievement of goals
- *Systems thinking* – understanding interdependency and complexity, constant feedback for development.

Many theorists believe that in order to survive and prosper an organization must cultivate a learning culture and this is a particular challenge for the information service manager.

People as individuals

It is important to consider people as individuals within organizations, and, more significantly, as *unique* individuals. Aspects of psychology such as personality, perception, communication and motivation, are closely inter-related and can contribute to our understanding of performance and behaviour at work. Personality is felt to be connected to job performance and career success; consequently personality tests (or psychometrics) are increasingly used as part of recruitment and selection processes. Ideally, an individual's goals and values should be aligned with those of the organization, tested during recruitment, then developed and managed once an individual is in post. Awareness of the importance of matching the person to the organization in relation to values is now leading to organizations 'hiring for the organisation, not the job' (Bowen et al., 1996), a system whereby employees are hired to fit the characteristics of the organizations and not just the specific job requirements. Jung's (1971) concept of personality types is a useful model for considering individual personality tendencies and is based on psychological preferences for extroversion or introversion, for sensation or intuition, for thinking or feeling, and for judging or perceiving. Jung's work was subsequently developed by Myers and Briggs (Myers, 1962) into the Myers–Briggs type indicator (MBTI) which is widely used as a personality assessment.

Reflection: What are the benefits of using personality assessments/psychometric tests as selection aids?

Eysenck's research (1970), following Jung, explored the key dimensions on which personality varies, believing that personality is based on genetics and biology. Table 3.1 demonstrates Eysenck's analysis of personality traits for extroverts and introverts.

Table 3.1 Eysenck's extrovert and introvert personality traits

Extrovert	Introvert
Activity	Inactivity
Expressiveness	Inhibition
Impulsiveness	Control
Irresponsibility	Responsibility
Practicality	Reflectiveness
Risk taking	Carefulness
Sociability	Unsociability

An additional useful model is Friedman and Rosenman's (1974) Personality Type A and B which identifies and clearly articulates two contrasting and extreme behaviour types. Type A personalities are characterized by ambition, competitiveness and impatience and are more likely to suffer stress related illnesses. Type B personalities, in contrast, are characterized by relaxation, calm and a leisurely pace.

Both these models provide insight into personality traits, formed through genetics, social conditions, learned behaviour, etc. and the Type A and B framework can be particularly helpful in the context of managing stress (see later sections in this chapter). The usefulness of such models could be challenged as individual personalities are extremely complex and our responses to situations are dependent on multiple variables, but they do highlight the need to be aware of differing personality types and traits and the need to both be knowing of ourselves and of those around us, whether in a work or social situation. A good understanding of individual personalities can also provide valuable insight into motivational factors.

Motivation and job satisfaction

Theorists and practitioners agree that having well-motivated staff is a significant influencer contributing to an effective and successful information service. Motives are major determinants of our behaviour; if the information service manager can understand an individual's motives they can potentially influence their behaviour and ultimately their performance within the workplace. Managers must understand their staff as individuals, recognize their differences, understand why they perform (un)satisfactorily, why some appear committed and others are often absent or unwell. People behave differently as the result of a wide range of very complex factors, from personality to experiences, to values and organizational cultures. The task of the manager is not to assume that everyone is the same and to attempt to understand what motivates and demotivates their staff.

Motivational theory is an extremely rich field of study and there is no single accepted answer to what motivates people at work; this section can only aim to illustrate key theorists and their work and their useful application within the information services context. Motivation theory is useful as a 'way of understanding how most individuals, *given who they are*, go about taking the short- and medium-term decisions in their life' (Handy, 1993, 53). The crucial point here is *given who they are* as motivation is intrinsically and uniquely individual.

Motivation theories can be divided into two categories:

- *'content'* approaches – based on the principle that people have definable needs and that managers must create roles and environments to satisfy these needs
- *'process'* approaches – based on the view that motives are neither predefined not universal and that our actions are less determined by needs and more by responses to opportunities provided at work.

Content approaches

Maslow's (1954) hierarchy of need has been extremely influential in developing understandings of behaviour dependent on a range of motives, for different individuals. Figure 3.5 illustrates the hierarchy in the form of a needs pyramid. Self-fulfilment and transcendence are the ultimate goals yet Maslow argues that they are rarely attained. What is crucial is the realization that behaviour depends on a

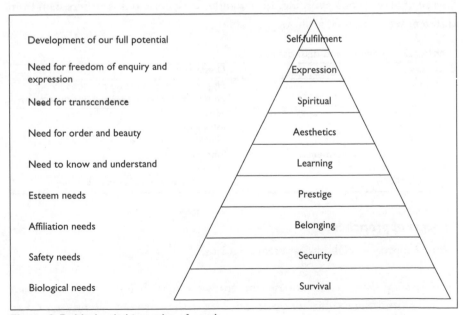

Figure 3.5 Maslow's hierarchy of needs

range of motives, that the basic levels are our priorities and that people have an innate desire to progress up the hierarchy. Interestingly, it must not be assumed that everyone needs all levels nor that they seek satisfaction for all needs in the workplace, as family, friends and outside interests can also all act as satisfiers. The principles underpinning this hierarchy of need provide insight into what motivates individuals, but also how the different stages are interlinked; a need is not an effective motivator until those lower down the hierarchy have been met, and a satisfied need is not a motivator. For example, a member of staff would not be motivated by the opportunity for skills development and learning if their job security was under threat.

Reflection: Consider Maslow's hierarchy in relation to your own needs. How many of the stages are currently met and in what ways?

Herzberg (1966) revealed factors which affected the ways in which people felt about work and suggested that if we aim to improve the factors classified as 'dissatisfiers' and increase the level of 'satisfiers' then individual performance will improve; crucially, both must be addressed in order to see improvements. In addition, each individual will value these factors differently depending on their personality, circumstances, etc., for example, training and development or more leisure time or flexible working. Importantly, satisfiers and dissatisfiers stem from different sets of factors, as shown in Table 3.2.

Table 3.2   Satisfiers and dissatisfiers

Satisfiers	Dissatisfiers
Motivators	*Hygiene factors* (must be provided by employer/manager to avoid dissatisfaction)
Achievement	Salary
Recognition from others	Job security
Responsiblity	Working conditions
Opportunities for advancement	Status
Interpersonal relations	Fringe benefits
The work itself	Company policy and administration

Process approaches

Process approaches fall into several categories:

* *Expectancy theory* – this is based on the view that an individual's behaviour stems from their subjective perception of reality. It consequently relates to how individuals perceive relationships between effort, performance and

reward, and the factors involved in stimulating them. This theory implies that individuals will only act if and when they have a reasonable expectancy that their behaviour will result in a desired conclusion and therefore will have an extrinsic (pay, status) or intrinsic (personal achievement, job interest) reward.

- *Equity theory* – this is based on the notion that individuals make comparisons with others in terms of inputs and outcomes in a work context, particularly in relation to rewards that are extrinsic.
- *Goal-setting theory* – this posits that motivation is driven primarily by goals that individuals set for themselves and the more demanding the goal, the better the performance.

Consequently, process approaches are interlinked with human resource management as they use techniques such as performance review schemes, performance-related pay and employee participation schemes to ensure motivation.

Considerable research has been undertaken on levels of job satisfaction (closely interlinked with motivation) among library and information services staff. Bundy found the satisfaction of subject librarians significantly greater than that of cataloguers while a survey of 'non-professional' staff in six UK academic and public libraries found that the most unsatisfactory aspects of their work were library policies, promotion and career prospects, treatment by managers, relationships with professional staff and lack of freedom of action (Jordan and Lloyd, 2002, 61). There is also an issue of motivation at lower-level jobs where there is less autonomy and flexibility, and often less involvement in the organization as a whole. Studies also show that staff in paraprofessional roles perceive a lack of status, recognition and appreciation. From such surveys it is clear that complex factors influence job satisfaction, particularly job design and the role and behaviour of managers – the complex 'interplay between the supervisor's management style, the organisational climate and the immediate work situation' (Jordan and Lloyd, 2002, 58). It could also be argued that distinctions such as 'professional' and 'non-professional' can act as demotivators and that a more inclusive, participative management style can reap rewards with regard to staff motivation and satisfaction (see Chapter 2, Management and Leadership, for more on management styles).

Motivation and the role of the manager

The role of the supervisor or manager is key to staff motivation, and it is their responsibility to find out what it is that motivates people. A manager must ensure, as far as possible, that they provide Herzberg's hygiene factors and eliminate dissatisfiers. Considering what motivates individuals, using the conceptual frameworks illustrated above, they can then approach the difficult task of maximizing motivation by a range of techniques. The inverse approach to motivation can be useful, i.e. highlighting demotivators to avoid; in general terms these can include:

• rigid structures and hierarchies
• unclear expectations and goals
• poor communication
• ignoring staff
• avoiding consultation
• negativity
• lack of recognition and reward.

Morris (1993) asks what the individual manager can do to make staff feel more committed while Jordan and Lloyd (2002) place great emphasis on a participative management style to meet staff needs. Figure 3.6 provides a checklist which includes their suggestions plus other practical methods drawn from a range of authors.

---

1. Begin with the job itself
   • Get the design right to begin with – consider the skills, variety, autonomy, significance.
   • Focus on job development via enrichment – delegation, job rotation, review job design.
   • Look at recognition and reward – feedback, praise, pay and promotion (although pay is often a dissatisfier rather than a motivator), involvement, responsibility.
   • Involve staff in objective setting and evaluating their performance.

2. Connect personally with your staff – be human!
   • Take an interest – 'management by walking about'.

   • Praise.
   • Help and support.
   • See and be seen.
   • Lead by example.
   • Take staff concerns and doubts seriously.

3. Encourage open communication and feedback, staff involvement
   • Seek involvement and advice/ consultation – push decision making down the structure.
   • Foster good communication – more informal, face-to-face, group and team meetings, lateral.
   • Nurture learning and development.

4. Maintain your own motivation and commitment (crucial – know yourself and ensure your own motivators are met).

Figure 3.6 Practical approaches to staff motivation

Specific information service approaches to alleviating problems associated with job satisfaction involve multi-dimensional strategies, for example:

- restructurings to reallocate work to the right levels and the right individuals, creation of new teams, flatter hierarchies, creation of new roles
- empowerment of staff – this has been particularly noticeable with regard to the rise of the 'paraprofessional' in academic and public libraries who has taken on duties previously associated with other roles such as enquiry work, branch management
- introduction of automation and increased self-service to reduce routine and free up resources to be used elsewhere across the service particularly in new projects, service innovation or key relationships with users
- review of the organization of work – introduction of different working practices and models such as flexible working, job sharing, career breaks, working from home (this links to work–life balance initiatives explored in Chapter 4, Human Resource Management)
- development of a team approach providing more involvement of staff, greater autonomy, increasing matrix management and project groups.

Motivation of staff is not easy and requires both a culmination of strategies addressing organizational, local and individual needs plus continual effort and adaptation. The impact of an individual's management style on staff morale and motivation cannot be overestimated (see Chapter 2, Management and Leadership). There are, however, problems in the application of motivation theories and strategies, highlighted by Jordan and Lloyd (2002) as cultural bias (national and professional cultures and their impact on attitudes to work) and the fact that work is only one facet of our lives and that our attitudes towards it are affected by such factors as personal relationships and domestic circumstances.

Reflection: *What techniques would you employ to motivate staff within a library and information service context?*

People within groups

From exploring people as individuals it is already clear that the individual cannot be considered in isolation from the group context. Many library and information services (in common with organizations generally) are developing increasingly team-based approaches to work in response to the 'need to devise structures which facilitate people working together towards shared goals' (Edwards et al., 1998, 13). Indeed, Bryson (1990) recommends that we view an organization as an interlocking network of formal and informal groups. The study of groups has merited a great deal of attention and a proper understanding of groups demonstrates how difficult they are to actually manage! As Handy (1993) highlights, individuals spend so much of their working lives in groups that once a manager has a clear understanding of how groups work, interact and are formed, they can better approach both the management of individuals and groups and the complex task of developing 'high-performance teams'.

The Human Relations School, based on Elton Mayo's research, emphasizes the importance of social processes at work. Mayo (1945) proposed a social philosophy which placed groups at the centre of our understanding of human behaviour in organizations and stressed the importance of informal groups to bring a sense of community and cohesion to the individual and the workplace. Likert (1961) echoes this approach, seeing the benefits as improved communication, increased co-operation and increased commitment. This has evolved into the concept of an organization being built around groups rather than merely including them, with writers such as Handy and Belbin advising that organizations should engender the right conditions to develop team approaches and structures.

Groups vs teams

There is some confusion and debate over definitions and distinctions between groups and teams. Vague definitions such as 'any collective of people who perceive themselves to be a group' (Handy, 1993, 150) are not necessarily helpful. From the organizational behaviour literature there is a clear distinction made between:

* *an aggregate group*, which is a collection of unrelated people who happen to be in close proximity for a short period of time, e.g. in a bus queue
  and
* *a psychological group*, which is a group whose members are aware of their membership and their interdependence as they work towards common goals, e.g. members of a football team.

Psychological groups can provide individuals with shared goals and a sense of identity and can also meet social needs, acting as great influencers and motivators. They can also constrain thinking, restrict freedom and affect behaviour.

Psychological groups can be described as *informal* or *formal*. Formal groups are consciously created to accomplish specific organizational goals and are task oriented and a part of the formal structure, for example a project team comprising a range of staff working on a library building refurbishment. Informal groups are collections of individuals who become a group when members develop interdependencies and influence behaviour, for example a group of staff who begin to meet over lunch to discuss their career development needs. Managers must not neglect informal groups as these can fulfil key functions related to motivation including a sense of identity, belonging and support. There is also the argument that informal groups can meet some of the higher-level needs in Maslow's hierarchy while the formal groups exist primarily to meet organizational objectives.

It can be argued that there is no difference between the formal psychological group and the team. However, Adair's definition of a team makes a significant distinction, seeing a team as not just a group of individuals with a common aim, but where 'the jobs and skills of each member fit in with those of the others' (Adair, 1986, vii).

Reflection: Think of a group that you belong to. Is it a formal group? What benefits do you gain from being a member? How does it influence your behaviour, thoughts and values?

Why encourage groups and teams?

As highlighted above, groups are recognized as fundamental to organizational success, individual motivation and job satisfaction. Extensive research demonstrates the power of the group to affect the behaviour of the individual member, both positively and negatively. Management research shows a continuing, worldwide trend towards teamworking – found to be beneficial to the organization and the employee – and the literature reflects this shift towards how staff can develop to both work in and lead teams. In the library and information service context, team approaches to work have been highlighted since the early 1990s with the Fielden report (John Fielden Consultancy, 1993) suggesting that new forms of teamworking were necessary to help build commitment to basic goals. Teamworking is seen as one way of raising both job satisfaction and involvement of staff at all levels of the organization, plus a more effective way of achieving goals. Consequently, team building and team development activities are now very common, with 'ability to work effectively within a team' often a standard person specification requirement in library and information services recruitment. The development of effective teams is a key challenge for the information service manager who should not assume that staff naturally possess the skills and competencies to function well in teams. As Levy (1997) summarizes in her research into the skills required for networked learner support in academic libraries, of all the skills required, teamworking is the most essential.

As highlighted in Chapter 1, structures have a major effect on organizational cultures, working practices, motivation and job satisfaction. Theorists such as Belbin and Handy argue that the future shape of organizations will be flatter and leaner and that the construction of small, self-managed and effective teams can outperform more hierarchical, top-heavy organizations. Consequently, managers need to consider their structures in relation to teamworking and how to foster team awareness and education. This approach to more team-based, flatter structures is now evident in many library and information services. A further factor in the rise of the team has been the increasing complexity of work and the rapid rate of change. Multi-skilled teams and cross-functional teams can also combine abilities and skills in a collaborative approach to tasks, e.g. in relation to e-learning where it is important to ensure that related areas are linked or work closely together to help synergy in working practices (Jenkins and Hanson, 2003). Whatever the type of group (see Table 3.3 for some examples), their purpose can be multiple but must always be overt and clearly communicated.

These multiple types of groups can fulfil a range of purposes, with most providing opportunities for consultation and participation in the wider organization. However, team approaches can be inappropriate to routine operations or very specialist work and they do require particular skills both from members and the team leader to make them work effectively. It is the role of the manager to provide conducive climates for group development (however formal or informal) and to consider approaches and techniques for their formation and success.

Group formation

The section 'Organizational Cultures' has already explored the development of norms, values and behaviours, and the socialization of individuals; these theories apply equally to groups as they do to organizations and are useful frameworks to develop our understanding of how groups form, develop and function. As previously noted, confusion around the use of terms such as groups and teams proliferates in the management literature. A useful model to help further our understanding is that of group formation, with Tuckman and Jensen (1977) providing a valuable model of five clearly defined stages of development, illustrated in Figure 3.7.

Table 3.3 Types of groups and teams in libary and information services

Type of group	Purpose	Example
Operational	Distribution of work Management and control Processing information Co-ordination and liaison	Circulation/lending services team of information assistants Enquiry services team Site/Branch team
Strategic	Problem solving Decision making Future direction Co-ordination and liaison	Management team Organizational senior strategic team
Cross-functional teams/ matrix management	Problem solving in relation to a specific issue or theme Co-ordination and liaison Consultation and participation – drawing on a range of staff from different areas within the organization	Project teams or working parties – use of themed, cross-area teams and groups in public libraries, e.g. to develop a new website, to develop new services for targeted groups of users
Multi-skilled or hybrid team	Similar to the cross-functional team, the emphasis is on drawing together staff with the right mix of needed skills, e.g. marketing, ICT, creativity. These teams can also draw on staff from outside the service itself.	Within higher education teams to develop e-learning would draw on learning technologists, academic subject librarians, educational developers.
Self-managing team/self-directed team	This type of team could apply to any of the team types included above; it is used to describe teams that work quite autonomously with little overt control from management. Such teams are felt to be more effective with staff more motivated and involved, and it could be argued that all teams should function in this way.	Could apply to any team activity.
Virtual teams	Work teams that either very rarely or never meet face to face but work via information and communications technology (e-mail, telephone, internet communication tools such as bulletin boards). This can be as a result of flexible working, remote site working, and/or organizational structures. Managers and team members must work hard to develop a sense of 'team' and effective communications and relationships.	Of particular relevance to electronic services and project teams that could be distributed across different organizations. Virtual teams could revolutionize the workplace with the advances in technology, the need for inter-organizational co-operation and people's desire to work more flexibly.
Networks and communities of practice*	Sharing of information Support and development Influence	An individual can belong to various networks and CoPs related to personal and professional interests that can be formal or informal.

* Communities of practice was developed as a concept by Wenger (1998) and has proved extremely influential in relation to learning: 'Communities of practice are everywhere. We all belong to a number of them – at work, at school, at home, in our hobbies. Some have a name, some don't.' CoPs are self-organizing systems and as such sit outside formal groups and have flexible boundaries. Technological CoPs which operate virtually have been explored by numerous authors and are seen as key to individual and group learning and development. It could be argued that networks and CoPs are interchangeable, and that they both bring the benefits of a sense of belonging, expertise, support and collective learning.

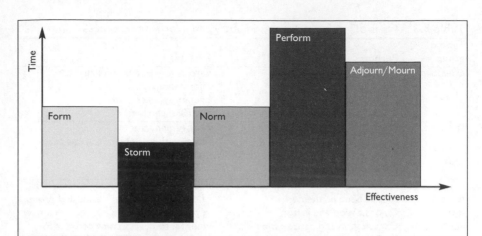

Figure 3.7 Five stages of group formation (adapted from Tuckman and Jensen)

Some groups don't develop through all stages, getting stuck at storming or never moving beyond norming. It is the information service manager's role to provide the conditions for effective team development and to see this process as cyclical rather than a finite evolution over a fixed period of time.

- During *forming* – the group is under-developed, beginning to organize itself to achieve common goals, but with a high level of anxiety and uncertainty. The role of the team leader is to establish goals and directions.
- During *storming* – the group is experimenting, gaining confidence, listening, exploring issues. Conflict may emerge, as may rebellion against the leader. The role of the leader is to resolve tensions.
- During *norming* – consolidation occurs, problems are resolved, and there is mutual support and group cohesions, personal relationships and interactions, clarification of tasks and agreement of objectives.
- During *performing* – we see successful performance and achievement of goals, openness, helpfulness, flexibility, co-operation and cohesion.
- Performing can naturally lead to *adjourning* as the task is completed or members of the group move on. This can lead to a period of mourning and anxiety about either moving on or change within the group. The role of the leader is to facilitate reflection, reassure and to ensure that the group moves back to forming if it is to continue with different members and new goals.

A group can be seen to be transforming into a team when it reaches performing; this has been described as a 'real team' as opposed to a 'work group'. The implicit assumption is that managers should strive to develop high-performance teams yet there will be occasions when other types of groups are adequate to the task. There has been a great deal of management interest, from theorists and practitioners, in designing and building effective teams. Clearly, multiple variables impact on a team's effectiveness, including the stages of its development as highlighted above. These variables can be summarized as:

- Establishing *the purpose* – A team's performance must be maximized by a clear definition and understanding of the task, plus defining and allocating workload responsibilities and authority.
- Establishing *the environment* and *group cohesion* – through developing norms and expectations, location, task (group and individual), size, communication channels and approaches. Groups are seen as society in miniature with their own rules, norms, traditions, hierarchies, goals and values.
- Establishing *effective group structures* – Group structures refer to the ways in which group members relate to each other. This is not fixed and works along several dimensions including: power, status, liking, communication, role and leadership. The process of group dynamics is often seen as key to effectiveness, encompassing how the individual member is behaving and relating to others.
- Establishing the *team members* including the size, the leader and *balanced group roles* – A team leader must ensure the right balance of skills and competencies for the task but also the right balance of team role types. Many theorists have developed their own taxonomies of team roles with Belbin's team role theory and model (1981) extremely popular and widely used. His nine team roles are seen as crucial for a well-balanced and performing team, with the manager's role being to ensure the makeup of the 'dream team' so that all the roles are represented, with no gaps. Consequently, the assessment (via a team role self-perception inventory or questionnaire), selection, placement and development of each team member can improve team effectiveness. Figure 3.8 illustrates the nine team roles; note the distinction between team roles and

Chairman/Co-ordinator – organizer, strong sense of objectives, disciplined approach, good at working with others
Plant or Innovator (ideas person) – creative input, source of ideas, knowledge
Resource investigator – explores ideas and resources outside the group, sociable with good networks
Shaper – drive, task focused, will push decisions forward and look for best course of action
Monitor-evaluator – analyses suggestions and evaluates their feasibility and practical value
Team worker – focused on feelings and needs of group, will be supportive and diplomatic
Implementer – practical organizer, will transform ideas into practical steps
Completer – attention to detail and follows things through, will be painstaking and conscientious
Specialist – brings a specialist expertise, skills or knowledge

Figure 3.8 Belbin's nine team roles

functional roles. It should also be noted that Belbin's model has also been crit-
icized as being overly psychological, with little recognition that performance is
affected by many diverse factors both at an individual and at a group level.
* Establishing *learning* – ensuring continual reflection, development and training
of all group members, facilitated by a learning culture.

Belbin and others highlight that the team should be greater than the sum of its parts,
with each player in a team game having a position and a specific responsibility but
the strength of the team dependent on how well the members interact. Many
authors also stress the importance of the role of leader: 'to help the group achieve
its common task, to maintain it as a unity and to ensure that each individual contributes his best' (Adair, 1986, 34). The role of leadership, covered in Chapter 2,
Management and Leadership, should not be underestimated in establishing and
maintaining team performance.

Communication

Through our explorations of organizational culture, learning, personality, motivation and team development, a common underpinning theme is that of communication. There are multiple reasons why information service managers
should study and be aware of communication in their organizational context:

* The effectiveness of communication is central to organization performance,
individual success and career progression.
* Very few people work alone and managers spend most of their time in meetings or conversation.
* Communication is recognized as central to individual and organizational performance yet many managers and staff regard it as a major problem. In addition, research findings in British libraries in the early 1980s highlighted that
'consultation and communication at all levels and in all types of library organisation appeared to be unsatisfactory' (Jordan and Lloyd, 2002, 76).
* New information and communications technology has brought about fundamental changes in how we communicate
* Employee communication has become increasingly important because of the
increased amount of information available and is also linked to a rise in
employee expectations to be kept informed.

Communication processes

Interpersonal communication is a complex process and typically involves more than the simple exchange of information. Commonly accepted models of the communication process present the 'transmitter' phrasing and expressing the message as a coding process, i.e. through choice of words, body language and how the message is expressed. The receiver must then successfully decode the message which is dependent on their understanding of language, emphasis, body language and so on. This model demonstrates the problems that can arise through the communication process, particularly as 'we can be careless coders and lazy listeners' (Huczynski and Buchanan, 2001, 183). The significance of non-verbal communication should not be overestimated as it is extremely rich and varied and often transmits feelings and emotions, for example through eye behaviour, facial expression, posture, tone and pitch of voice, distance.

The information service manager must be cognizant of the main barriers to communication and employ strategies for alleviating them. Barriers can include:

- *power difference* – staff may not find it easy to communicate honestly and openly with their superiors
- *emotional condition* – e.g. staff could feel intimidated, afraid, nervous
- *gender difference* – language, behaviour
- *physical surroundings* – how conducive they are to communication, e.g. noise
- *language* – variations in accents and dialect
- *cultural diversity* – norms and values of different cultures can lead to misunderstandings.

Enhancers to communication can include meeting face to face to use every channel of communication available, 'reality checks' to ascertain how messages have been interpreted, selecting the optimum time and place, and considering the other person's position and how they might see things. An added complexity within contemporary organizations, and particularly information services, is that communication occurs across multiple channels – face to face, via e-mail, telephone, networks – and managers and staff must become increasingly adept and flexible enough to communicate effectively in blended ways with each other (as well as with users and stakeholders).

As previously highlighted, organizational communication must be seen as a priority for all managers and is part of the channelling of employee behaviour to meet organizational goals. The information service manager must consider *what* they wish to communicate, *when*, *to whom* and *how*. Mechanisms and approaches for communication within information services can include:

- consistent communication of the mission, values and vision
- internal newsletters and regular bulletins
- notice boards – both physical and virtual
- conferences and seminars
- meetings – at different levels and for different purposes, e.g. cross-site meetings, assistant meetings
- team briefings to cascade information
- suggestion schemes
- open-door policies
- performance review system
- quality circles – where staff are brought together to look at solutions to specific issues, to constantly strive for quality improvement.

Of particular importance is the development of a climate or culture for communication that is open and two-way. Gibb (in Huczynski and Buchanan, 2001) developed the concept of the communication climate, characterizing an open and supportive communication climate as contrasted with a closed and defensive communication climate, presented in Table 3.4.

Table 3.4   The communication climate (adapted from Huczynski and Buchanan, 2001)

Open, supportive communication climate	Closed, defensive communication channel
• Descriptive: informative rather than evaluative communication	• Judgemental: emphasis on apportioning blame, making people feel incompetent
• Solution oriented: focus on problem solving	• Controlling: conformity expected
• Open and honest: no hidden messages	• Deceptive: hidden messages, manipulation
• Caring: emphasis on empathy and understanding	• Non-caring
• Egalitarian: everyone valued regardless of role or status	• Superior: status and skills differences emphasized
• Forgiving: errors seen as inevitable, focus on minimizing them	• Dogmatic: unwillingness to accept views of others or compromise
• Feedback: positive, essential	• Hostile: needs of others given little importance

Interestingly, the features of an open communication climate are all conducive, and related, to approaches taken to improve motivation and job satisfaction. The library and information service manager must recognize that organizational communication (in climate and mechanisms) is not neutral, but rather constructed (either consciously or subconsciously) in an attempt to manipulate the attitudes and behaviours of the staff, and as such is a powerful influencer and motivator.

Power, politics, conflict and stress

Organisations are not machines. … They are communities of people, and therefore behave just like other communities. They compete amongst themselves for power and resources, there are differences of opinions and of values, conflicts of priorities and goals.

(Handy, 1993, 291)

Position power	reward power	being able to grant favours or benefits to someone
	coercive power	through punishment, threats or control
	legitimate power	through authority of your status/role
Personal power	expert power	through your skills and competencies
	referent power	through being attractive to someone else who wishes to please you

Figure 3.9 Bases of power

Power, politics and conflict are givens in any organization and within any group; the library and information service manager must harness that energy and develop an understanding of the politics within their own context and how power is distributed. Power is the potential of one unit to influence another. French and Raven (in Bryson, 1990) defined five different bases of power, as shown in Figure 3.9.

Successful managers use all types of power to some degree depending on the circumstances. As Bryson (1990, 1999) comments, power and influence are closely related to political behaviour and politics. Organizational politics can be defined as the ways in which individuals 'acquire, develop, and use power and other resources to obtain one's outcome in a situation' (Bryson, 1990, 251). Individuals engage in politics for numerous reasons – to further their own ends (ambition, status), protect themselves, further organizational or team goals, and to acquire power. It can be argued that politics has increased within organizations as a result of increasing change, uncertainty and competitiveness. Politics is often seen as a negative but can be equally viewed as necessary at a personal level, a decision-making level and at a structural level within organizations, as it engenders competition and can lead to change. Moreover, St Clair (1994) strongly advocates the acquisition of power and influence by the information service manager, whatever their organizational context, as they must actively demonstrate the value of services and staff to ensure the provision of resources. Consequently, the manager must act politically, understanding the organizational culture in order to influence and obtain power. Power and influence can be seen as crucial in a climate of scarce resources and competition. St Clair suggests several useful strategies for turning superiors, peers, staff and stakeholders into advocates.

Differences are essential if organizations are going to continue to adapt, change and develop. As Handy highlights, 'Change is a necessary condition of survival ... and differences are a necessary ingredient in that change' (1993, 291). Competition and conflict are closely linked to politics as they often arise out of quests for power, leading to differences in values and opinions and conflict over priorities and goals. They can lead to pressure groups, cliques, rivalry, alliances and factions. Intergroup conflict can be common between departments as it arises when members perceive that they are being prevented from achieving their group goal by the actions of another group; conflict between hierarchical levels can also be common. The benefits can be increasing productivity as a result of competitiveness, and greater cohesion within teams as they focus on a common 'enemy'. However, competition can be damaging and managers need to be aware of their own and others' political behaviour and to manage this appropriately.

Networking and communities of practice have already been briefly alluded to. Individuals will become members of different (formal and informal) networks that can act as power bases or influencers. Networking can occur both within the parent organization, within the library and information profession and with members of external groups and organizations, e.g. suppliers, politicians, stakeholder groups. Benefits of networks include political alliances to further goals and increase influence, support and development for the individual, information sharing and benchmarking.

Conflict and stress

Managing conflict and stress is often viewed as highly problematic, and associated with what can be termed 'dealing with problem people' (see Chapter 4, Human Resource Management, for more on this). Conflict is inevitable, a fundamental force in human life, and should not necessarily be viewed as negative. Without difference and conflict organizations can stagnate, but if not handled appropriately conflict may be destructive. Conflict can bring issues to the surface and the main outcome is usually change. Sources of conflict within information services can include:

- territories
- contrasting goals and ideologies
- expansion – mergers, convergence with different services, power struggles

- resources – ownership issues, struggle for additional or scarce resources
- role expectations
- divisions between staff groups – e.g. non-professional and professional, library and IT staff
- external environment – uncertainty and complexity, impact of external changes and drivers on structures and skills requirements, e.g. technological change.

A manager must therefore recognize, acknowledge, manage, resolve – and even at times, stimulate – conflict, turning it into a positive force for organizational change. Approaches to managing conflict begin with early recognition of a conflict situation and an understanding of individual or group behaviour and its source. Methods for early detection of conflict are important and can usefully include observation, ongoing feedback models, suggestion schemes and exit interviews. Three approaches presented by theorists and practitioners for resolving conflict are:

- *win–lose* – authoritative, coercive, doesn't lead to change
- *lose–lose* – no one is happy, compromise
- *win–win* – acceptable to all, superordinate goals are established that are greater than the individuals' own goals. Consensus and commitment to objectives are gained.

Clearly, a manager should aim for a win–win result and their style in managing conflict will play a crucial part in a positive outcome. Different styles in conflict resolution can be summarized as:

- *avoidance* – ignore that there is actually an issue and that conflict is occurring
- *smoothing* – attempt to smooth over the problem without exploring the issues or resolving the conflict
- *forcing/competing* – authoritatively impose a solution that may be of benefit to the manager
- *compromise* – find a compromise that may or may not be acceptable to all parties
- *collaborative* – find a solution together with all involved.

Management of conflict is related to the skills and abilities information service managers need now and for the future – including negotiation, mediation and facilitation. These are explored in more detail in Chapter 2, Management and Leadership, but it should be stressed here that managers must be flexible and capable of moving between styles depending on the situation and the individuals involved.

Another key feature in the study of people in organizations is stress and its effective management. Stress has been defined as 'the response that the human system makes in adjusting to demands or activating life events' with the life event known as 'the stressor' (Jordan and Lloyd, 2002, 303). Theorists agree that stress is not necessarily unhealthy as it can stimulate and motivate, and that stress tolerances differ between individuals with some more easily able to control or manage their responses. This is foregrounded by the previously discussed Type A and Type B personality theory. The information service manager must recognize their own stressors and responses and develop coping strategies while also remaining sensitive to the stressors of their staff. Stress can be an organizational problem or an individual problem (or often a combination of the two). Within the library and information context, surveys on the causes of stress are illuminating and can help managers avoid certain pitfalls; most highly rated stressors include workloads, users, prospects and working environment. A holistic approach to the effective management of stress is reflected in Figure 3.10.

Identifying stressors (causes)	Recognition of different types of stress
Typical organizational stressors Inadequate physical environment Poor job design Poor management style Poor relationships Job uncertainty Conflict	Episodic stress – linked to life changes and specific problems (time limited) Chronic stress – constant stress with no alleviation **Recognition of symptoms** Organizational – e.g. high staff turnover, poor performance, conflict, absenteeism Individual – e.g. sickness, emotional difficulties
Individual stressors Issues of confidence Individual skills gaps Personal issues (e.g. family problems, bereavement) Personal conflict in the workplace Harassment or bullying	**Stress management strategies** Organizational problem-focused e.g. job redesign or enhancement, HRM processes, improved communication, development of supportive working relationships, improvements to physical working environment Individual emotion-focused e.g. coping strategies to include time management, relaxation and 'self-care'

Figure 3.10 The management of stress

Reflection: Can you diagnose your stressors? How could you alleviate them?

There is growing evidence that workplace stress is on the increase; consequently its alleviation is a major challenge for the information service manager, particularly given the legal framework and obligations that they work within.

People and careers

It is widely recognized within the information profession and beyond that there are no longer jobs for life and that an individual is responsible for managing their own career. Continuing professional development approaches are explored in Chapter 4, Human Resource Management; this section will briefly encompass roles and career opportunities within information services and the mechanisms to ensure a developmental and supportive process.

Library and information services have, historically, been rather conservative and hierarchical organizations, particularly in relation to career paths and progression. Qualifications at either undergraduate or postgraduate level provide an entry to professional posts, although more flexible routes are currently under consideration in the UK. While a linear and traditionally hierarchical progression remains true across many services, there is a definite shift towards increasing flexibility, opportunities and movement both within and across organizations and, indeed, now across different sectors.

The types of roles now available to information professionals have diversified, as too have the skills and competencies required, with transferable skills and abilities opening up opportunities outside the traditional sphere. For example, the impact of converged services in higher education on career opportunities (see Abbott, 1998) with information professionals moving into the management of diverse teams and services encompassing ICT, media, etc., the development of broader educational roles and the impact of clinical governance within the NHS leading to new roles such as the clinical librarian. The types of roles are varied and numerous but can be categorized and summarized as in Table 3.5.

As many authors have stressed, career development and progression should be a supportive process within organizations. Many organizations have introduced techniques and mechanisms to help support people both within their roles and their careers. These approaches have significant benefits for the individual and the organization and include:

* *Mentoring* – professional and personal development through a one-to-one relationship, it may be formal and planned by the organization or may develop informally. Schemes within information services are now well-established in many organizations. They can be particularly useful for the newly qualified, for staff working in very small departments and for those at key points in their career.

Table 3.5 Roles of information professionals

Type of role	Example
Entry level	Information or library assistant
Paraprofessional	Help desk adviser, counter supervisor
First professional post	Subject librarian, assistant librarian, reference librarian
Project role/specialist	Electronic resources specialist, project adviser, web developer, archivist
Team co-ordinator	Collections team leader, special collections co-ordinator
Management	Branch manager, customer services manager, deputy
Director level	Head of service/division
Leadership beyond the library and information service	Senior roles in universities, businesses, local government, national government policy making, European and international organizations

Note: At different points an individual could move outside the traditional library and information services sphere to a role in another profession that requires their transferable skills, e.g. web designer, learning support adviser, while individuals from different professional backgrounds (e.g. in marketing or finance) could move into specific information services roles.

- *Coaching* – a one-to-one relationship with the purpose of developing within the individual a new skill or enhancing performance in some way. Coaching is about helping individuals take responsibility for their own development, with a quite specific focus, and is therefore different to mentoring which takes a more generalist and holistic approach to development.
- *Job shadowing* – the shadowing, over an agreed period of time, of an individual where there are opportunities for on-the-job learning, self-reflection and review. Bruce and Roberts (2003) provide insight into the experience from the host and shadow's perspectives, emphasizing the benefits for all involved, while also stressing the importance of selection, planning and the management of expectations.

Linking back to organizational cultures and considerations on how people and organizations learn, all these approaches highlight that 'People may learn best not from conventional training, but from engagement, discussion and experience' (Bruce and Roberts, 2003, 38).

Summary and conclusions

The study of people within organizational contexts encompasses the complex interaction between individuals, groups and cultures, often with no clear defini-tions and no agreed solutions. The information service manager must be aware of key concepts and approaches from a contextual point of view (including organizational culture, organizational learning) and in relation to the individual (motivation and how people work in groups). They must also consider the impact of their own management style and techniques in order to influence and motivate their staff, peers and superiors. Many authors strongly advocate that organizations can only survive in a culture that encourages empowerment, employee involvement and trust, and that this can be engendered through self-directed teams and flatter structures. Managers must then take on different roles, including coaching and development, and participative leadership. As illustrated here, there are multiple synergies between organizational culture, the communications climate, individual and team motivation and performance, management style and leadership. The challenge for the information service manager is to maximize these synergies and adapt their own style and techniques to ensure that individual staff can achieve their own goals by directing their efforts towards the success of the organization.

REVIEW QUESTIONS

1 What is organizational behaviour and why should the information service manager study it?
2 What are cultural norms and values, and how are they formed?
3 What are possible uses for personality tests?
4 How could Maslow's higher needs be met within the information service context?
5 Is there a clear distinction between definitions of a group and a team?
6 Why should library and information service managers want to develop team approaches to work?
7 Detail key barriers and enhancers to communication at work.
8 What are the main characteristics of an open communication climate?
9 What are the positives and negatives associated with conflict in the workplace?
10 Consider possible stress management strategies.

CASE STUDY

Team roles
Referring to Figure 3.8, consider the two team profiles below, analysed using Belbin's team type model, and discuss the following:

- Are there any team roles missing? How could the team accommodate these missing roles?

- How do you think each team will work together?
- How likely are they to work successfully and why?
- What could the manager do to maximize their effectiveness?
- What could the team do to maximize their effectiveness?

Team A A senior management team within a large public library

Team types	Additional information
Alice – Chairman/Co-ordinator	Very good at directing others, can be rather inflexible
John – Shaper	Is extrovert and passionate, can be impatient with others
Rachel – Teamworker	Extremely supportive but can be sometimes quiet and indecisive
Mark – Chairman/Co-ordinator	Strong personality, goal oriented
Lindsey – Resource investigator	Identifies resources needed, can lose interest in projects quickly

Team B A project team for a new library management system in a workplace information centre

Team types	Additional information
Ruth – Teamworker	Extremely collaborative, dislikes making decisions
Coral – Monitor–evaluator (also Co-ordinator tendencies)	Evaluates feasibility of ideas and systems, can at times be critical
Mandy – Implementer	Great at organizing others, highly motivated, can be inflexible
Liz – Completer	Will get the job done, attention to detail, a worrier

CHALLENGES

1 Can organizational culture be managed and formed to ensure strategic objectives are met?
2 Can managers really influence and 'control' people within the workplace?
3 How could multiple channels of communication affect teamworking within an information service context? What might be the barriers to effective communication?
4 Will the 'flat organization' and self-directed teams ever become the norm in information services? Would we want them to?
5 How can managers balance the loss of control and hierarchies with the need to empower and involve staff?

References and additional reading

Abbott, C. (1998) Personal Career Development in Converged Services, *Librarian Career Development*, **6** (3), 28–35.

Adair, J. (1986) *Effective Teambuilding: how to make a winning team*, London, Pan Books.

Argyris, C. and Schon, D. (eds) (1996) *Organisational Culture II: theory, method and practice*, Cambridge, MA, Addison-Wesley.

Belbin, R. M. (1981) *Management Teams: why they succeed or fail*, London, Heinemann.

Belbin, R. M. (1996) *The Coming Shape of Organisation*, Oxford, Butterworth-Heinemann.

Billsberry, J. (ed.) (1996) *The Effective Manager: perspectives and illustrations*, London, Sage Publications in association with The Open University.

Bowen, D., Ledford Jr., G. and Nathan, B. (1996) Hiring for the Organisation, Not the Job. In Billsberry, J. (ed.), *The Effective Manager: perspectives and illustrations*, London, Sage Publications in association with The Open University, 139–50.

Bruce, L. and Roberts, S. (2003) Job Shadowing: shaping tomorrow's leaders, *Library + Information Update*, **2** (9), (September), 36–9.

Bryson, J. (1990) *Effective Library and Information Centre Management*, Aldershot, Gower.

Bryson, J. (1999) *Effective Library and Information Centre Management*, 2nd edn, Aldershot, Gower.

Edwards, C., Day, M. and Walton, G. (eds) (1998) *Monitoring Organisation and Cultural Change: the impact on people of the electronic library*, The IMPEL2 Project, London, Library Information Technology Centre, South Bank University.

Eysenck, H. J. (1970) *The Structure of Human Personality*, 3rd edn, London, Methuen.

Friedman, M. and Rosenman, R. F. (1974) *Type A Behaviour and Your Heart*, New York, Knopf.

Handy, C. (1993) *Understanding Organizations*, 4th edn, London, Penguin Books.

Herzberg, F. (1966) *Work and the Nature of Man*, New York, Staples Press.

Huczynski, A. and Buchanan, D. (2001) *Organisational Behaviour: an introductory text*, 4th edn, London, Prentice Hall.

Huczynski, A. and Buchanan, D. (2004) *Organisational Behaviour: an introductory text*, 5th edn, London, Prentice Hall.

Jenkins, M. and Hanson, J. (2003) *A Guide for Senior Managers*, LTSN Generic Centre e-Learning series No 1, York, Learning and Teaching Support Network.

John Fielden Consultancy (1993) *Supporting Expansion: a report on human resource management in academic libraries*, for the Joint Funding Councils' Libraries Review Group, London, HEFCE.

Jordan, P. and Lloyd, C. (2002) *Staff Management in Library and Information Work,* 4th edn, Aldershot, Ashgate.

Jung, C. G. (1971) *The Collected Works of C. G. Jung, Vol. 6: Psychological Types,* Princeton, NJ, Princeton University Press (first published 1923).

Kolb, D. (1984) *Experiential Learning: experience as the source of learning and development,* London, Prentice Hall.

Lawes, A. (ed.) (1993) *Management Skills for the Information Manager,* Aldershot, Ashgate.

Levy, P. (1997) Continuing Professional Development for Networked Learner Support: progress review of research and curriculum design, *2nd International Symposium on Networked Learner Support,* 23–24 June 1997, Sheffield, www.netskills.ac.uk/reports/conferences/netlinks97/levy.htm.

Likert, R. (1961) *New Patterns of Management,* New York, McGraw-Hill.

Maslow, A. (1954) *Motivation and Personality,* New York, Harper & Row.

Mayo, E. (1945) *The Social Problems of an Industrial Civilization,* Cambridge, MA, Harvard University Press.

Morris, B. (1993) Motivation of Staff. In Lawes, A. (ed.), *Management Skills for the Information Manager,* Aldershot, Ashgate, 26–39.

Myers, I. B. (1962) *The Myers-Briggs Type Indicator Manual,* Princeton, NJ, Education Testing Service.

St Clair, G. (1994) *Power and Influence: enhancing information services within the organisation,* London, Bowker-Saur.

Senge, P. (1990) *The Fifth Discipline: the art and practice of the learning organization,* New York, Doubleday Currency.

Tuckman, B. C. and Jensen, M. A. C. (1977) Stages of Small Group Development Revisited, *Group and Organizational Studies,* **2** (4), 419–27.

Wenger, E. (1998) *Communities of Practice: learning as a social system,* www.co-I-l.com/coil/knowledge-garden/cop/lss.shtml.

4 Human resource management

There are no poor staff, only poor managers.

(Peters and Harvey-Jones in Lawes, 1993, 35)

LEARNING OBJECTIVES

After reading this chapter you should be able to:

- define human resource management (HRM) and related concepts
- be aware of the HRM lifecycle
- appreciate the challenges of HRM within the library and information context and the skills required
- apply HRM theories and models to workplace scenarios
- reflect on role and skill requirements for the current and future library and information workforce.

Introduction

Within any organisation, whatever the sector and whatever the business, success depends upon the performance, commitment and motivation of its staff. For the library and information service manager the majority of their working life will be spent working with and through people; indeed, a basic definition of management is 'getting things done through people'. Many new managers find this aspect of managing the most daunting and difficult to master and are often ill prepared during the early stages of their careers. Staff management, personnel management or human resource management (whatever terminology we choose to use) is all pervasive in translating an organization's goals into reality and as such is central to the role of any manager at any level.

Management theorists now talk of 'human assets' and 'human resources' – people as a commodity that needs maintenance, management, effective deployment and utilization like any other resource. As Handy (1993) highlights, the application of economic and financial terminology to the management of people is now the norm and has led to a whole body of methods, systems and procedures for the maintenance, control and planning of these assets. This shift to a formal approach to managing staff, underpinned by management theory, stems from a recognition of their significance in organizational success and the imperative not to leave their effective management to chance. This chapter explores some of these methods and theories while also retaining an emphasis on the 'human' element of human resource management. A recurring theme is that of individuality with a reminder that humans are not as predictable and manageable as machines.

Contemporary HRM is a rapidly changing field of study; this chapter aims to provide a foundation and key concepts from the management literature that can be usefully applied within the library and information context, without attempting to cover every aspect in depth. This chapter must also be read with reference to Chapter 3, People in Organizations, and Chapter 2, Management and Leadership, as theories of management and concepts such as motivation, leadership, teamworking and communication interlink and overlap with concepts and models of human resource management.

What is HRM?

The term human resource management (HRM) emerged from the USA and became fashionable in the mid-1980s, replacing the concepts personnel management and industrial relations (although such terminology is still in use and personnel specialists often still remain committed to the term 'personnel'). Interestingly, the adoption of the term and concept varies according to national, regional and sectoral contexts and is by no means a given. Many management theorists and practising managers remain sceptical over the distinction between HRM and the older terms, while others feel that there is an essential difference. The distinction is definitely one over which there is much debate and uncertainty with some authors seeing significant differences. Figure 4.1 highlights definitions of HRM and personnel management, articulating this ambiguity and conflict.

HRM = 'resource-centred', directed mainly at management needs with an emphasis on planning, monitoring and control. Underpinning view that the management of human resources is an integral part of general management and should be within the role of the line manager, not a specialist function. The HRM literature often stresses the proactive, developmental management of people as a major resource for achieving organizational goals.

Personnel management = 'workforce-centred', directed at the organization's employees, sometimes seen as personnel specialists mediating between the workforce and the management. Sometimes viewed as reactive, emphasizing industrial relations and welfare. Underpinned by the idea that people should be treated as people and that their job-related personal needs are important and should be met.

Figure 4.1 HRM vs personnel management

It can be argued that this distinction is overly simplistic and that the two terms can co-exist and are interconnected; or that approaches to managing people have simply evolved and that the terminology is also evolving but does not represent a distinct split between approaches and concepts – 'As the function has evolved it has added new dimensions without shedding those developed in earlier periods' (Torrington and Hall, 1998, 7). Tellingly, Torrington and Hall's definition of personnel management has many similarities with other writers' definitions of HRM:

> A series of activities which: first enables working people and the business which uses their skills to agree about the objectives and nature of their working relationships and, secondly, ensures that the agreement is fulfilled.
>
> (Torrington and Hall, 1998, 20)

Human resource development (HRD) is another term often used within the management literature and refers to the 'integration of learning and development processes, operations and relationships' (Redman and Wilkinson, 2002, 108). It aims to enhance organizational effectiveness through the development of the workforce. Again, there is ambiguity and debate around the term and concept as some writers view HRD as one element of HRM while others would argue that it is separate.

What is clear is that concepts and approaches to the management of people have evolved and become more complex, systematic and holistic. A strong central theme emerging from the key works on HRM theory is that of linking people management and development to business strategy and organizational goals, thus taking a more strategic and integrated approach. The varied perspectives in relation to human resource management are all valuable and valid, and illustrate the tensions that library and information managers must work with. Organizational cultures will favour different approaches and managers need to respond in a way that is consistent. Above all, human resource management deals with people, consequently managers must plan for what is acceptable within organizational culture and structures as well as for what is feasible.

Reflection: *Reflecting on the debate around definitions of HRM, your own further reading and experience of human resource management in practice, what difference do you think it would make in practice to be considered and treated as a 'resource' or as a 'person with a set of skills'?*

The HRM professional

A whole profession has developed around the concept that people must be managed in the same way as non-human resources. The role of the HR professional and their relationship with managers and staff has changed significantly over recent years and it is important for library and information service managers to develop an awareness of the parameters of the relationship both generically and within their own context. Management theorists have highlighted the shift from the HR/personnel manager as experts to help with absence, discipline, performance management, etc. to HR specialists as advisers and consultants to provide frameworks for line managers to work within. Responsibility for human resource management within departments is now more likely to be left 'to the line', resulting in the need for line managers to develop more awareness and knowledge of HR issues, policies and procedures as well as the softer skills of communication and motivation. Within the literature and the workplace we can also find diametrically opposed views on HR departments, their significance and usefulness within organizations and to managers. It is important to explore the relationships between the manager, their staff and the HR department within an organization and the difference in roles and function. It can be argued that HR departments, and HRM itself, is required to systematize, order and ensure consistency; however, this can be perceived as added bureaucracy and an overloading of procedures and forms. In contrast, the HR professional and department can provide valuable guidance, advice and support to the library and information manager, particularly at the early stages of their career.

Reflection: *Consider the differences between the role of the HR professional and the library and information manager in relation to the human resources function in an organization. What factors might contribute to the development of an effective relationship?*

The HRM cycle

HRM should not be viewed in a vacuum: it begins with the mission and objectives of the organization and is a product of the context of the organization's needs and objectives. Managers and organizations need to select, develop and reward their staff as well as to structure and design their work. Consequently, there is a range of approaches and methods that form a holistic HRM cycle:

• HR strategy
• HR planning – workforce planning/job analysis and design
• recruitment and selection
• performance management
• staff development and training
• reward and recognition.

These are underpinned by ongoing organizational development and can be seen as a portfolio of inter-related activities. Torrington and Hall (1998) proffer a similar model of the personnel/HR process built around the strategic core or strategic objectives of the organization. All elements of the cycle must be incorporated to result in effective human resource management, yet this strategic approach to the HRM cycle is rather impersonal. Taking an individual member of staff and tracking their HR lifecycle from the moment they are recruited to when they leave the role or organization illustrates the different phases in their working life, many of which are cyclical and interconnected. Figure 4.2 illustrates this lifecycle within the context of a library and information service.

Reflection: *Consider your own experience of the staff lifecycle in Figure 4.2 (overleaf). What were the strengths and weaknesses of this experience? How would you improve on this?*

Such frameworks can at times feel like a labyrinth of information but they are central to ensuring standardization, equality of opportunity and legal compliance, and will also aid in the prevention of problems such as underperformance,

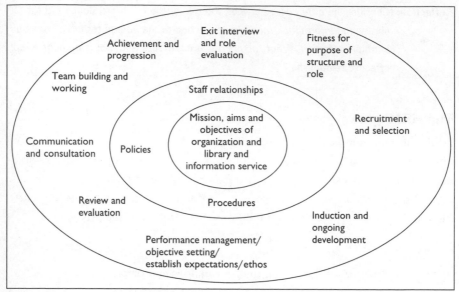

Figure 4.2 The staff lifecycle

harassment, grievance, capability and disciplinary issues. The framework will consist of an array of policies, procedures and guidance notes that are cognizant of external factors such as equal opportunities legislation, competencies and qualifications standards, and developing HR practice within the organization. These could include:

- *absence management* – policies in relation to the proactive management of absence (caused by sickness, stress, personal problems)
- *performance review* – policies, procedures and guidelines for the standardized and effective annual review of staff performance including objective setting and monitoring
- *capability procedure* – invoked when a member of staff is considered to be performing below agreed standards or where there is a failure to meet the contractual requirements of the role
- *grievance and harassment procedures* – invoked where a member of staff makes a formal allegation of bullying, harassment or grievance against another member of staff
- *maternity, paternity and adoption* – policies in relation to staff rights and legal requirements
- *redundancy procedure* – in the case of redundancy a procedure could provide a

framework to ensure that legal obligations are met, in addition to fairness, equity, support and consultation

* *regrading procedure* – utilized where staff and/or their manager feel that the role has developed and warrants a review of the grading and salary.

The legal framework

The legislative framework relating to HRM is constantly developing and only a summary of significant areas of employment law can be covered here. It is the library and information manager's responsibility to remain up to date and aware of obligations and to adapt approaches and practices as necessary. Key areas of legislation (UK examples) include:

* Employment Rights Act 1996 – law relating to unfair dismissal, permitted reasons for dismissal
* Data Protection Act 1998 – right of employees to be informed about (and to see) personal data held by their employer
* Discrimination – plethora of legislation in relation to race, gender and religious beliefs
* Disability Discrimination Act 1995
* Health and Safety at Work Act 1974 and Management of Health and Safety at Work regulations 1992
* Working Time Directive – statutory rights to paid holidays, rest periods, length of working week
* Flexible Working Time regulations 1998 (with amendments 2003) – the amendments focus on the right of employees with young or disabled children (under 6, or under 18 if disabled) to request to work flexibly, and employers must seriously consider any request; plus the extension of maternity, paternity, adoptive parents' and carers' rights.

The library and information service workforce

The library and information service workforce will vary in size, types of roles, skills and culture, depending on the organization, sector and structure. However, certain characteristics and trends are evident within the 21st-century context that will be common across many organizations. Library and information services are now described as hybrid, combining electronic resources and services with 'real' services and physical facilities and materials. This has undoubtedly impacted upon roles, leading to new configurations, titles and skills. Examples of this rapid change include the introduction of the People's Network and the provision of access to ICT training in the UK public library service, and the convergence of library and information services with other services such as learning and teaching development and computing in academic institutions. Such sweeping changes have their consequences for human as well as non-human resources (see Chapter 7, Finance and Resources, for more on this). In general terms the library and information manager is also asking themselves a range of critical questions in this context:

- How can we improve our performance by making more effective use of resources?
- How can we develop a positive and flexible approach to change?
- How can we evaluate the impact of our services to demonstrate their importance?
- How can we engage staff at all levels in the work of the service and organization?
- How can we ensure ownership, commitment and motivation among our workforce?
- How can we develop our workforce to work in more flexible and user-needs-driven ways?
- How is ICT transforming the role of services and consequently the workforce requirements and strategies to manage this?

Another common workforce characteristic is the changing balance between 'core' (i.e. full-time, permanent) and 'peripheral' workers. This often-used distinction is now unhelpful as the peripheral are becoming an increasingly large and important group, including: permanent and temporary part-time staff, job share, homeworking, term-time only, staff working in a consultancy or freelance basis, outsourcing, volunteers. The widespread use of a range of contracts is tied to the demands of managing variable workloads, to providing cover at key times, retaining staff and providing flexibility, and to the need to draw into the service specific areas of expertise. With these benefits also come management challenges, especially with regard to communication, recruitment and inclusivity to ensure that such staff are managed effectively and equitably and that they are integrated fully into the organization. This is highlighted effectively by White and Weaver (2004). Further examples of change impacting on the workforce include convergence with other services and functions such as information technology, dispersed/virtual services and staff, and the increasing need for multiskilling and rapid skills development.

The working context is constantly shifting and as a result the major challenge for the information service manager is the management, motivation and development of their staff to enable them to respond to changing demands.

Undoubtedly the challenges will differ according to context but the ones explored here are prevalent across sectors within a profession that continues to experience the impact of new technologies, restructures, changing customer expectations, new relationships with other groups, and the need to empower staff to respond proactively to change. A snapshot of other suggested challenges would include:

- diverse range of staff backgrounds, expertise, skills
- rapidly changing environment
- changing expectations of users and staff
- distributed teams and different cultures
- inclusive approach to part-time and temporary staff (research shows significant use of these types of staff in a library and information context)
- equality of access to staff development and training
- reward and recognition
- retention – for example, the Public Library Workforce Study (Usherwood et al., 2001) identifies serious concern with the ability of public libraries to retain quality staff).

Skills

From this context arises the need for specific skills development. Research is continually influencing our understanding of the skills sets required to operate in the library and information environment. Those required by the generic library and information workforce have been extensively researched and discussed; Pantry and Griffiths' (1999) comprehensive list encompasses:

- oral communication skills
- interpersonal skills
- writing skills
- time management skills
- management skills
- project management skills
- knowledge management skills

- marketing and publicity skills
- skills to work independently or as part of a team.

Other literature (Fowell and Levy, 1995; Edwards et al., 1998; Oldroyd, 2004) has highlighted additional skills sets, or variations on Pantry, including:

- teamworking and team leadership (project based as well as functional)
- learning and teaching/educational role (especially but not exclusively with reference to academic library and information services)
- management and leadership
- influencing and persuading (political skills)
- technological aptitude (the application and impact of technologies rather than the 'hard' technical aspects)
- project management and development
- ability to work across structures and conventional boundaries.

The challenge for the library and information manager is not only to develop their workforce in accordance with the changing skill requirements but to also encourage flexibility. The latter is another common theme within the HRM literature, both for employers and employees. From the employees' perspective, there has been a great deal written on 'work–life balance' with the European Working Time Directive (2003) now providing support for certain groups of staff to request more flexible working conditions. From the employers' perspective, flexibility is also desirable; Bramham's eight forms of flexibility (1994), represented in Figure 4.3, effectively identifies the types of flexibility that could be needed in any workforce and is particularly relevant in the context of library and information work. The majority relate directly to the individual employee while numbers and wage costs refer to the workforce as a whole. This emphasis on individual adaptability highlights both the imperative to recruit staff who have a positive

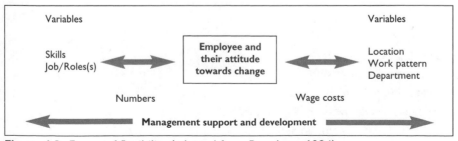

Figure 4.3 Forms of flexibility (adapted from Bramham, 1994)

attitude towards change and also the role of the manager in supporting and developing them through such change. However, the needs of the employee and employer may not always be in line, which may result in conflict.

Reflection: *Reflecting on the skills required of library and information staff as identified in the lists above, evaluate your potential performance in your first management post. What are your strengths and weaknesses?*

HR strategy and planning

The HR strategy should be seen as a central component of a business strategy, linked to corporate goals, mission and vision. The main purpose of a HR strategy is to integrate policies and practices into a coherent whole, ensuring the dovetailing of HR developments with organizational developments and needs. A strategy must provide a coherent view on how to deal with changing contexts and demands. According to Bryson (1999), an HR strategy is generally behaviour based with an analysis of types of employee behaviour required to fulfil business objectives and then the identification of policies and practices to bring about and reinforce that behaviour. Possible themes to be included in a strategy could be:

- quality
- learning and development
- teamworking and development
- customer care and focus
- motivation and involvement
- leadership
- flexibility and commitment
- technologies.

Of particular relevance to a rapidly changing working environment is a strategic approach to personal and professional development. Writers such as Corrall (2000) and Jordan and Lloyd (2002) agree that the development of staff needs to move beyond job-specific skills to building a more general capacity for flexible responsiveness in evolving roles. This is reflected in 'Learning and Development' below. Depending on the size and nature of the organization, a library and information manager will either respond proactively to an organizational HR strategy or will need to develop their own distinct strategy, or possibly a combination of the two.

Like other service and knowledge-based industries, library and information work is highly labour intensive with salaries usually the highest budget expenditure. Consequently, library and information service managers need to plan consciously for the most effective and efficient use of staff. This concern and focus has led to the adoption of various models and methods under the umbrella of 'workforce planning' or its more recent metamorphosis, 'human resource planning'. Human resource planning (HRP) covers a range of activities designed to ensure a balance between supply and demand and is concerned with questions such as: what kind of roles, what kind of people with what skills, and how many, are needed now and in the future.

Human resource planning at a macro level

As Bryson (1999) demonstrates, effective human resource management is planned and executed at a macro (strategic) and micro (operational) level. Macro refers to human resource planning and forecasting, transforming organizational objectives into specifics associated with procurement, development and utilization. Micro refers to activities such as role evaluation, developing job descriptions, recruitment and other processes that relate to the individual. At the macro level a systems approach to HRP can provide a valuable framework This begins with an assessment of environmental influences both internal and external:

- external factors
  — government legislation and policies
  — legal framework
  — unions
  — economic conditions
  — labour market
- internal factors
  — size and nature of organization/department
  — health of organization (projected growth? decline?)
  — organization's objectives
  — culture
  — technology
  — existing staffing base
  — structures.

Several models and approaches exist to assist the library and information service manager in scanning and interpreting their own environment (see Chapter 8,

Strategy and Planning, for further information). Reflection on the context should influence the human resource planning process and forecasting, for example the number of staff, the level and skills required, shifts of staff from one area to another where there is real or projected growth, decline in the need for some groups or types of staff e.g. cataloguers, patterns of hours required with extended or amended opening. The stages following environmental analysis can be summarized as:

1 Determine human resource needs based upon environmental analysis and especially the organization's and service's goals.
2 Assess the human resources currently available.
3 Identify any gaps between the projected needs and the current status (either a 'match', 'excess' or 'deficit').
4 Identify actions to be taken, e.g. recruitment, redeployment, development, redundancy, changes to structures or hours of work.
5 Monitor and evaluate feedback, especially with regard to performance and the objectives set.
6 Review and redesign human resource plan as appropriate.

The usefulness of human resource planning has been questioned as it can prove difficult to make concrete predictions in a turbulent environment. However, the systematic approach can provide a useful framework for the library and information manager in considering their current and future workforce.

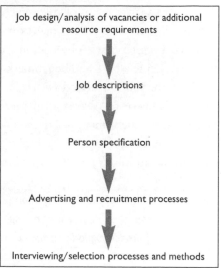

Figure 4.4 The stages in recruitment and selection

Human resource planning at a micro level: recruitment and selection

The micro approach to HRP, as previously highlighted, relates to the interface of individuals with their roles and as such involves a number of processes, illustrated in Figure 4.4.

Role analysis and job design are crucial in helping to match the role with the organization's objectives and to attract the right kind of person. Before embarking on recruitment in rapid response to a vacancy, a manager should ask themselves a number of questions:

- Why has the vacancy or need for additional resources arisen? (Return to environmental scanning and objectives.)
- Need the post be filled at all? Are there priorities within other parts of the service?
- Should it be changed in any way? For example, is it at the right level, what hours are required, who should it report to?
- Does the existing structure effectively support the work and role?
- What skills are required?

Role analysis can help provide answers to these questions; it is the process of studying and collecting information relating to the functions and responsibilities of a specific role or set of roles (it does not have to occur in isolation and often it is desirable to analyse teams or role sets, e.g. all library assistants, the team providing enquiry desk services). The collection of qualitative and quantitative data can be achieved by interviews, observations, daily diaries or time logs, questionnaires, statistics, user feedback and benchmarking (both internal and external).

Often the job is analysed with a 'task-oriented' approach that breaks down a role into units or tasks. A second approach is 'worker oriented' where the units of analysis are the human behaviours needed for the post. Within role analysis it is important to consider not only the functions and tasks but the underpinning abilities and aptitudes needed to successfully undertake the work.

Reflection: *As a library and information service manager with a new vacancy arising from the retirement of a long-serving member of your team, how would you approach exploring if the current post needed to be filled?*

Following the job analysis a job description and person specification can be developed. Interestingly, job descriptions are not a legal requirement but they are imperative in human resource planning and staff management.

- *Job description*: a descriptive, factual statement of the duties and responsibilities of a specific job including its objectives, accountability and super-visory/management duties.
- *Person specification*: describes the attributes of the person doing the job, e.g. qualifications, experiences, skills, abilities and knowledge.

Uses of job descriptions include:

- recruitment and selection
- performance review (or appraisal)
- induction
- objective setting
- assessing training and development needs
- ongoing job evaluation.

Given the changing nature of library and information work and roles, job descriptions do need to allow for ongoing review and should now incorporate an element of flexibility. A well-designed and clear job description should include: an understandable job title, the department, who the post is responsible to and for what, who the post is responsible for and for what, grade and salary band, key tasks and responsibilities, and any other relevant information including the pattern of working hours.

A person specification should emerge organically from a job description and is a key tool in the recruitment and selection process. Its purpose is four-fold: to specify clearly the criteria the interview panel will be looking for in the ideal candidate (and to provide this guidance to potential candidates), to describe the qualifications, experience, knowledge, skills and abilities of the person required to perform the job effectively, to distinguish what is essential and what is desirable, to reduce the risk of subjectivity and ensure equality of opportunity.

Recruitment and selection

Within a competitive job market attracting the right candidates is crucial. The library and information manager needs to be aware of the range of methods to attract suitable candidates; these can include:

- internal advertising
- secondments
- external advertising (via local, national and professional press, and the internet)
- specialist recruitment agencies (Aslib Professional Recruitment Ltd, INFOmatch, Sue Hill Recruitment and Services Ltd, TFPL Recruitment Ltd).

Job advertisements convey powerful messages, not just about the role but about the organization, department and the type of person required. A job advertisement should provide the following information:

- name of the organization
- title of the post with a brief explanation
- salary and grade
- main purpose and duties
- essential qualities required
- specific conditions, e.g. evening working, flexible working, cross-site working.

Reflection: *Using one of the online recruitment websites below consider two advertisements from two contrasting organizations and evaluate them from the perspective of a potential candidate, using the following checklist:*

- *What are your first impressions of the advertisement?*
- *Does it provide all the essential information you would need?*
- *What messages does it convey about the organization and department?*
- *What key words or phrases are used to 'sell' the job and organization to you?*

www.lisjobnet.org.uk/jobs/query.htm
www.aslib.co.uk/recruit/sys/jobs_main.php

As Jordan and Lloyd (2002) emphasize, 'the ability to recruit staff successfully is one of the essential skills that a manager needs' (127) and each organization will have clear procedures that should adhere to relevant legislation, especially in relation to equal opportunities. The application form and interview form the cornerstones of the selection process in most organizations but there are a variety of other methods that can result in a wealth of valuable information and a more productive process for both candidates and recruiters.

Shortlisting is based on the written application or CV and the shortlisting panel must ensure that candidates are shortlisted from the information on these sources alone and that the person specification should be used as a guide as to which criteria must be met. Criteria for rejecting candidates should be agreed, the information recorded for possible feedback, and equal opportunities and other appropriate legislation should be adhered to.

The aim of the interview and any related tests, presentations or exercises is to find a candidate who could and would do the job, and to enable the candidates and interviewers to explore all elements of the role in a relaxed and conducive environment. The latter is particularly important to enable the candidates to present themselves in the best positive light. HRM literature does question the reliability of the formal interview primarily because of a tendency for interviewers to talk more than candidates. In addition, there is the criticism that interviews are artificial and benefit people who interview well. However, with a focused approach, a clear structure, skilled interviewers and the use of additional methods, the interview can be a productive selection method. In planning for a successful interview process, the library and information manager should consider:

- The formation and constitution of the interview panel – How large should it be? A good starting point might be to include a member of human resources and/or an external person.
- The environment.
- The structure of the interview – Begin with an ice breaker question, allocate groups of questions to each panel member, have a panel chair to co-ordinate the interview.
- The questions – These should be preplanned and open rather than closed with follow-up questions as necessary.
- The behaviour of the panel – Good practices include active listening, note taking, encouragement and a relaxed atmosphere.

The final decision should be based upon the information gathered during the selection process evaluated against the person specification. Informing candidates as to the outcome depends yet again on the policies and procedures of the organization but it is advisable to be prompt and clear and to offer feedback to unsuccessful candidates to enable them to reflect on the experience and their performance.

The processes of recruitment and selection are time consuming and complex and will require adequate training and development for the manager to ensure a positive experience for all involved and a fair and open approach that is consistent with policies and procedures.

Managing performance

From a new member of staff's first day, the management and support of their performance is crucial and a key responsibility of their line manager. Performance management is a concept that originated in the USA and has particularly influenced the widespread adoption of performance review or appraisal. Both performance management and review are central to the day-to-day management of staff and the cyclical review of performance. There is a clear distinction to be made between:

- *Performance management*: systems, approaches and attitudes which help organizations to plan, delegate and assess their operations in relation to employee performance.
- *Performance review (or appraisal)*: systematic and regular review of an employee's performance, typically undertaken by their line manager.

A principal feature of performance management is the connection of the organization's objectives and strategic goals to the work of the individual employee. Consequently, there is a need to develop HRM processes which ensure that all managers (and all staff) aim for and achieve what the organization requires. This need to integrate the objectives of the individual and the organization is a major challenge for any manager. Management by objectives (MBO) was a model that focused entirely on objectives and was popular in the 1970s. This has since been overtaken by increasingly holistic approaches to performance management. A standard performance management system would incorporate:

- a shared vision of the organization's objectives communicated to all employees (via different channels, e.g. mission statement)
- individual performance targets which are related to the team/service and also to the wider organizational objectives
- regular meetings to review progress towards objectives
- a review process which identifies training and development needs
- reflection and evaluation on the effectiveness of the whole process and its contribution to overall organizational performance by all parties involved.

Performance management has been developed to co-ordinate several features of HR management – goals/targets, performance review, training and development, reward systems – to deliver effective performance in a role. Other central elements include probationary review and feedback – which ascertains if a member of staff can be confirmed in post – codes of conduct, coaching and mentoring.

The lynchpin of the whole process is commonly agreed to be the performance review, although it should be stressed that performance management is more than this and is interlinked with staff motivation and the creation of a conducive working environment and relationship plus many other factors that contribute to staff motivation and achievement. The Human Relations School of Management in the USA in the 1920s recognized the importance of people within the work process. Motivational theories and practical methods of motivation must be of central concern to the manager in managing performance and are discussed more fully in Chapter 3, People in Organizations.

1. Evaluation – of performance against set goals which could then be related to reward if appropriate. Note: with regard to salaries and rewards, pay is viewed as a motivating agent yet very few organizations use it deliberately, particularly outside the private sector
2. Auditing – to discover the work potential of individuals and departments
3. Succession planning
4. Identification of training and development needs
5. Motivating staff
6. Developing individuals by providing advice, information, guidance and feedback
7. Improving standards and performance
8. Checking the effectiveness of procedures and practices
9. Enabling the effective management of change
10. Developing effective relationships between staff

Figure 4.5 The purpose of performance review: ten-point checklist (adapted from Randall, 1984)

Performance review

Performance review originates from the desire to be systematic, formal and ultimately more equitable, in the setting, monitoring and evaluating of objectives, usually in a yearly cycle. In addition, it should provide a framework for discussions between employee and employer on achievements, job satisfaction, motivation, barriers to success, team relationships, aspirations, training and development and future career plans and opportunities. Management theorists and practitioners hold varied views on the advantages and disadvantages of such an approach with sceptics seeing it as too bureaucratic and formal, and supporters seeing it as the foundation for effective management, development and role progression. Figure 4.5 highlights the key purpose of performance review, drawn and adapted from Randall (1984).

The performance review is now a commonly used tool across all library and information sectors and should ideally be available to all staff. It should be viewed as an integral part of performance management, linking to regular review/update meetings and continuing professional development, contributing to the evolving relationship between a manager and their staff. The performance review 'event' itself remains central and needs to be prepared for and managed effectively to ensure a positive experience for all involved. The manager should consider the following issues when preparing themselves and their staff for performance review:

- *Evident commitment* of the organization, management and staff.
- *Individualization* – Performance review is a very personal and individual experience and can be seen as stressful by many staff. As the literature highlights, the relationship between the manager and member of staff will fundamentally affect the whole experience and its productivity.
- *Promotion of the benefits to staff* – Proactive promotion to allay staff fears and suspicion that performance review is simply a management tool or a way of controlling staff. The benefits could be identified as recognition, guidance, increased motivation and commitment and career development.
- *Structure and framework* – The process should be clearly articulated to all involved with a structure, procedures and accessible, user-friendly forms.
- *Training for all involved* – As with recruitment and selection, performance review requires a skills set for both manager and employee. In addition, all involved must ideally come to the process in a spirit of openness and honesty.
- *Ownership and self-appraisal* – The concept of ownership is crucial and self-appraisal is one way of developing this. Questions such as 'How well have I achieved my objectives?' and 'How well have I contributed to my team?' should be incorporated.
- *Objectives* – These should be SMART (see page 223), linked from the individual to the organization and translated into agreed action plans that are under ongoing review.
- *Feedback* – A key element of the process is providing feedback on an individual's performance; this is a core management skill and requires sensitivity, openness and often a balance of praise and constructive criticism.

An effective performance management system that is owned and understood by managers and staff, and a commitment to developing open and honest working relationships, should provide a preventative approach to performance issues that if allowed to develop unchecked can lead to capability, disciplinary and grievance cases. Additional benefits of such an approach include contributing to the effective management of change and to the development of the individual.

Reflection: *Consider the strengths and weaknesses of performance review systems. How could you ensure that performance review was of benefit to both employer and employee?*

Learning and development: supporting the individual in a changing environment

Learning and development have become a lifelong task with individuals changing over time, developing new skills, adapting to change and taking on new roles over the course of their working lives. This is particularly crucial within a rapidly developing employment market with emerging roles and new technologies. The importance of developing staff within the HRM cycle cannot be overemphasized or overvalued and it must form part of an integrated, systematic and forward-looking approach to HR management. In addition, there has been a shift in emphasis with regard to responsibility for development; it is no longer seen as wholly organization led but also driven by the individual who has responsibility for their own continuous development over their career(s).

The library and information literature has recently focused on workforce development planning and capacity building, echoing a serious concern for future workforce needs especially with regard to leadership and the need to develop staff to deal with ongoing change. Oldroyd (1996) highlights the principle that training staff for their current roles and developing them for future roles is central to present and future levels of organizational performance. Consequently, the development of the individual is widely recognized as a key HRM function within library and information work, although not necessarily across all organizations. However, learning and development should not simply be viewed at an individual level. The concept of the *learning organization* (explored in more detail in Chapter 3) is now accepted as critical to future organizational success.

From staff development to continuing professional development

Theories of learning have greatly influenced concepts of staff development. Whether at an organizational or individual level, development is seen as a broader process than training, being concerned with motivation, attitude, personal qualities, skills and ethos. Within the management literature, and reflected in professional standards (such as those of CILIP and the Chartered Institute of Personnel and Development), 'training and development' has been replaced by 'learning and development', highlighting the importance of continuous learning that can be achieved through a wide range of activities and processes.

Continuing professional development (CPD), or continuing professional and personal development (CPPD), has at its heart the recognition that learning is ongoing and that this is the cornerstone of professional practice, both within the library and information profession and across other professions. As CILIP emphasizes in the UK, 'The dynamic and rapidly changing environment of the library and information sector requires library and information professionals to remain up-to-date, flexible and responsive to change' (2003, 17). Examples of other professional bodies that have CPD policies include the Law Society, the Royal College of Nursing and the Chartered Institute of Personnel and Development. CPD encourages staff and their managers to consider development in its broadest terms and to look for opportunities outside formal training. Useful summary concept definitions include the following:

- *Staff development and training* together 'encompass all the means by which staff are enabled to do their present jobs effectively and to prepare themselves to meet changing needs' (Oldroyd, 1996, xi).
- *Experiential learning* is 'insight that is gained through the internalisation of our own or observed experiences' (Beard and Wilson, 2002).

Continuous professional development stems from the belief that skills and competencies soon become outdated and that the individual must be involved in a process of continuous development post-qualification.

Opportunities for development and learning can arise in many contexts and forms, planned and ad hoc, formal and informal. Three major methods of individual learning have been identified as:

- formal education and training (accredited and non-accredited courses, short courses, on the job training)
- Group Action Learning Sets (a way of problem solving in the workplace using learning in small groups – or sets – that meet to discuss real issues and possible actions; see Revans (1998))
- planned experience (job shadowing, work experience).

A focus within the library and information profession has often been on formal education and training, yet staff development literature has highlighted limitations in this as the major strategy for development. It can be argued that formal training is more relevant where clear job requirements and definitions are in place from the outset. Learning can be as powerful, if not more so, through experience and modelling. Experiential learning is explored further in Chapter 3 in relation to individual and organizational learning and learning cultures. Models for CPD now focus on self-development and experiential learning rather than formal courses. The following examples demonstrate the wide variety of CPD tools available:

- professional reading and updating
- coaching or mentoring
- job exchanges or job shadowing
- conferences
- open or distance learning
- training others
- meetings
- networking
- learning from others.

For the library and information manager, learning and development is both a key tool in performance management and a significant lever in the management of change. Managers must ensure that training and development needs are identified through the performance review and by such tools as training needs analysis.

The future of CPD: models and mechanisms

The library and information profession is also developing new approaches to CPD to reflect the changing demands of the working environment, the need for flexibility and the recognition that the more traditional and formal forms of development are not always the most appropriate nor most successful. Such new modes include online learning, either as online courses or as online networks and communities of practice. At a basic level e-mail lists and specialist groups function as online communities exploring issues and sharing practice, but this is being developed further through the use of virtual learning environments (VLEs) with tools such as discussion fora. Technology is providing new solutions for increasingly complex CPD needs and is bringing different communities and groups together in new educational spaces.

Future issues for human resource management in the library and information context

Multiple challenges have been explored throughout this chapter; such challenges will continue to shape strategies, approaches and thinking within the library and information service HR context. The challenge of recruiting and retaining quality staff with a flexible approach to change will remain a constant, especially given that marketable skills (and more importantly, personal attitudes and behaviour) will no doubt remain in high demand. HR management skills will become increasingly crucial, hopefully leading to further professionalization, self-reflection and self-development in this aspect of the library and information professional's role and identity. In order to meet changing and growing demands from diverse user groups, working practices and roles will continue to develop and adapt, potentially increasing virtual and distributed individuals and teams (not necessarily located in a physical library or information unit) and leading to increased blurring of roles and increasingly converged services or new partnerships.

One area where many of these impact factors converge is that of e-learning and e-services. This is a crucial cross-sectoral issue for the future as networked technologies are dramatically changing services, education, training and development, and working practices, roles and conditions. As Allan (2002) and others highlight, library and information professionals in a range of contexts are becoming increasingly involved in e-learning whether as facilitators, designers and developers or supporting learners. Allan's thought-provoking chapter on implications for the library and information provision considers a number of new opportunities that are extremely relevant to human resource management at both strategic and operational levels:

- implications of e-learning for the library and information professional
- new learning opportunities
- new employment opportunities
- working in new teams and partnerships
- development of new skills
- new roles and responsibilities
- teleworking
- life–work balance via increased flexibility
- involvement in the development of new services or extended services to meet user need.

What Allan fails to explore is that with the opportunities also come threats; other professions also see e-learning as providing new possibilities, boundaries between functions and responsibilities are blurring, and the need for accelerated skills development grows. The information service manager needs to predict such threats and opportunities, develop strategies and plans accordingly and involve and prepare their staff at all stages.

Summary and conclusions

Human resource management is of crucial importance to the library and information manager. This chapter has introduced key concepts and models and suggested approaches to navigate the complexities of developing and managing a workforce that faces continuous change. Information service managers must be aware of every aspect of the HRM lifecycle, at a micro and macro level, and ensure effective management of human resources at every stage – from recruitment to performance and continuing professional development. This chapter also advocates an institutional/organizational approach to management theory which provides fitness for purpose and matches methods and approaches to the environment, tasks and people. Despite the plethora of concepts, theories and management techniques, the manager must question the basic traditional assumption that 'There is one right way to manage people – or at least there should be' as this is 'totally at odds with reality and so totally counterproductive' (Drucker, 1999, 17). As Handy surmises, 'individuals are different, so are organisations. There can and should be no one grand design or theory, but rather a plethora of possibilities from which to choose' (1993, 252). An integrated and holistic approach, with the individual at the centre, and a skilled and flexible manager, should enable a constantly evolving human resource cycle to meet organizational and individual goals.

REVIEW QUESTIONS

1 What is human resource management and why is it important to the library and information manager?
2 Why can human resource planning in the library and information context prove difficult?
3 What are the key elements of the HR lifecycle?
4 How has the generic skills set for the library and information professional changed? What are the important current skills as identified by the literature?

5 What are the different stages of recruitment and selection? Why is it important to carefully consider recruitment needs?

6 What are the factors that will aid a successful interview process?

7 What is the difference between performance management and performance review?

8 Why is continuing professional development key to the future of the library and information profession?

9 How can a manager support CPD and by what methods?

10 What are the potential impacts of e-learning and e-services on the library and information workforce?

CASE STUDY

Job description design

Analyse the job description below and consider whether it addresses the following:

- responsibilities of the role/key objectives
- accountability
- what a prospective employee might expect with regard to working patterns, salary, etc.

Discuss the person specification that would relate to this job description.

Human Resources

It is important to note that this job description is a guide to the work you will be required to undertake. It may be changed from time to time to meet changing circumstances. It does not form part of your contract of employment.

Job description for the post of:
Information Assistant – Collections

The postholder will be responsible to:
Collections Manager

The post
The post will normally be based at the Leigh site, but may be asked to work at any service point at any Library and Information Service site. The postholder will be

Continued on next page

---

required to work flexibly, including evenings and weekends if required. Duties and working patterns may vary according to service needs.

Main purpose of the job

1. To provide assistance and support at the issue desk
2. To provide administrative support within Collections Management.

Specific duties and responsibilities

1. Issue desk support

- To perform circulation desk duties, including issues, returns, renewals, reservations and other relevant transactions
- To participate in service opening/closing procedures
- To handle cash for fines, sales, etc.
- To operate the security system and deal with security incidents
- To register new users and issue replacement cards
- To deal with enquiries relating to circulation of loans and locating library material
- To liaise with staff in Library and Information Services.

2. Collections Management

- To maintain all aspects of the Collections Management processes providing a fast and efficient service which responds to variable departmental spending patterns throughout the year.
- Bibliographic checking via the library management system and other bibliographical sources to verify accuracy of information sent to suppliers
- Inputting orders for stock ensuring correct transfer of supplier, budget and quantity information. Telephoning and faxing of urgent orders. A high degree of accuracy and attention to detail is essential.
- Receipt of new stock including checking delivery noted against goods and following up any queries, calculating single copy price for input and recording invoice details.
- Updating order information via book reports from suppliers, and filing copy invoices and other documentation.
- To be aware of current demands on stock and where necessary order additional copies liaising as appropriate with librarians to ensure appropriate loan categories and latest editions are selected.
- To support the rolling programme of stock maintenance including weeding, relocation, repair and withdrawal.
- To administer all processes involved in sending books for binding.

Continued on next page

- To monitor on a daily basis casual assistants undertaking stock maintenance and processing duties and to report on progress to the Collections Administrator.

3. Other duties
- To contribute to the maintenance of a secure and tidy environment.
- To be familiar with the operation of library equipment, recognize, rectify or report equipment faults.
- To participate in work related training and staff development.
- To participate in light stock and equipment moves.
- To collect statistical data.
- To participate in stock maintenance including processing etc.
- To participate in shelving stock and shelf-tidying.
- To participate in staff meetings and service reviews.

Hours of work: 37 hours per week. Evening working may be required.

CHALLENGES

1 Assessing your own human resource management skills against those explored in this chapter, are you prepared for the demands of HRM?
2 Can the HRM concepts and models always be applied to the local library and information context? How might they be adapted?
3 How might the manager maintain the 'human' in HRM given the need to be systematic and rigorous and to standardize approaches?
4 Can the manager plan for the future workforce in such a turbulent environment?

References and additional reading

Allan, B. (2002) *E-learning and Teaching in Library and Information Services,* London, Facet Publishing.

Beard, C. and Wilson, J. P. (2002) *The Power of Experiential Learning*, London, Kogan Page.

Berry, J. (2002) Managing your Career, *Library + Information Update*, **1** (2) (May), 48–9.

Bramham, J. (1994) *Human Resource Planning*, 2nd edn, London, Institute of Personnel and Development.

Bryson, J. (1990) *Effective Library and Information Centre Management*, Aldershot, Gower.

Bryson, J. (1999) *Effective Library and Information Centre Management*, 2nd edn,

Aldershot, Gower.

Bryson, J. (1999) *Effective Library and Information Centre Management*, 2nd edn, Aldershot, Gower.

Chartered Institute of Library and Information Professionals (CILIP) (2003) *CILIP Framework of Qualifications: consultation document on the proposed new framework of qualifications to be introduced in Spring 2005*, London, CILIP.

Corrall, S. (2000) *Strategic Management of Information Services: a planning handbook*, London, ASLIB/ Information Management International.

Drucker, P. (1999) *Management Challenges for the 21st Century*, Oxford, Butterworth-Heinemann

Edwards, C., Day, M. and Walton, G. (eds) (1998) *Monitoring Organisation and Cultural Change: the impact on people of the electronic library*, The IMPEL2 Project, London, Library Information Technology Centre, South Bank University.

Fowell, S. and Levy, P. (1995) Developing a New Professional Practice: a model for networked learner support in higher education, *Journal of Documentation*, **51** (3), (September), www.aslib.co.uk/jdoc/1995/sep/4.html.

Handy, C. (1993) *Understanding Organisations*, 4th edn, London, Penguin Books.

Jordan, P. and Lloyd, C. (2002) *Staff Management in Library and Information Work*, 4th edn, Aldershot, Ashgate.

Lawes, A. (ed.) (1993) *Management Skills for the Information Manager,* Aldershot, Ashgate.

Oldroyd, M (ed.) (1996) *Staff Development in Academic Libraries: present practice and future challenges*, London, Library Association Publishing

Oldroyd, M. (ed.) (2004) *Developing Academic Library Staff for Future Success*, London, Facet Publishing.

Pantry, S. and Griffiths, P. (1999) *Your Successful LIS Career: planning your career, CVs, interviews and self-promotion*, Successful LIS Professional series, edited by Sheila Pantry, London, Library Association Publishing. Second edition re-titled *Your Essential Guide to Career Success*, published 2003, Facet Publishing.

Randall, G. (1984) *Staff Appraisal*, London, Institute of Personnel and Development.

Redman, T. and Wilkinson, A. (eds) (2002) *The Informed Student Guide to Human Resource Management,* London, Thomson Learning.

Revans, R. (1998) *ABC of Action Learning*, London, Lemos & Crane.

Sharpe, D. (2003) Cross-sectoral Staff Development, *Library + Information Update*, **2** (8), (August), 51.

Thomson, R. (1997) *Managing People,* 2nd edn, Oxford, Butterworth-Heinemann, Published in association with the Institute of Management.

Torrington, D. and Hall, L. (1998) *Human Resource Management*, 4th edn, Harlow,

Essex, Pearson Education Limited.

Usherwood, B., Bower, G., Coe, C., Coope, J. and Stevens, T. (2001) *Recruit, Retain and Lead: the public library workforce study*, Library and Information Commission Research Report 106, Sheffield, Centre for the Public Library and Information in Society, Department of Information Studies, University of Sheffield and Resource: the Council for Museums, Archives and Libraries.

White, S. and Weaver, M. (2004) Lifelong Learning at Work: staff development for the flexible workforce. In Oldroyd, M. (ed.), *Developing Academic Library Staff for Future Success*, London, Facet Publishing, 113–28.

5 Marketing and user relationships

Marketing is a social and managerial process by which individuals and groups obtain what they need and want through creating and exchanging products and value with others.

(Kotler et al., 2002, 5)

Librarians and information professionals will need to recognise that developing effective marketing strategies is more difficult today, not because of the digital revolution, but because of a society in which customers are becoming more sophisticated and knowledgeable, maybe even cynical, about marketing activities.

(De Saez, 2002, 3)

LEARNING OBJECTIVES

After reading this chapter you should be able to:

- understand the essence of marketing, and its application in information organizations
- discuss the concepts of customer and customer/user relationships
- analyse the way in which the 'marketing mix' defines the offer to customers
- reflect on the nature of 'product' and 'brand' for information organisations
- identify the components of the marketing communications process
- appreciate the importance of marketing strategy and planning.

Introduction

Information organizations and professionals have sometimes been reluctant to embrace the concept of marketing, preferring to rely on the quality of their services and their reputation. In addition, identifiable budgets for marketing are often modest, and the impact of any marketing communications campaigns may be delayed and difficult to measure. Marketing is indeed a mix of persuasion, with all of its associated ethical issues, and information. Taking the above definition from Kotler et al. (2002) as a point of departure, this chapter takes the position that marketing has moved on from its emphasis on products to focus on the delivery of customer value, and benefits that the customer appreciates. Key aspects of this perspective on marketing are:

- Marketing is a social and managerial process, and is about people and communication.
- Marketing is an exchange process through which individuals, groups and organizations obtain benefits and value, defined in their own terms.
- Marketing is a process through which relationships with customers or users can be developed.

The stance that is developed throughout this chapter is that marketing is about everything that an organization does or says. Actions and words are both important; marketing is concerned with communicating to others what you are about, and using their response to that message to evolve what you are and what you do. Because an organization involves numerous product and service exchanges, and communication episodes, enacted through many different individuals, marketing needs to intervene to align and integrate these processes across an organization.

In summary, then, marketing is a process in which customer's needs for information and knowledge are met through matching these against appropriate information resources and services. This involves:

- researching and understanding customer's needs and other factors in the marketplace
- selecting and defining the customer or client groups that the information service will serve
- defining the offering, in terms of products, and associated elements of the marketing mix, and doing this with reference to the potential value that offerings can deliver to the customer
- ensuring communication and engagement with the user community
- establishing strategic direction and making plans that support this continuing engagement.

This chapter starts by examining customers and ways in which their needs, interests and concepts of value can be understood. It moves on to discuss the concept of the marketing mix, the marketing offer that the information organization makes to its customers, in terms of both what the offer is, and how it is communicated to customers. This provides a platform for further exploration of two aspects of the marketing mix, product and promotion. 'Product' is a word for the offer made to the customer, but particularly in the service environment it is important to appreciate how the customer experiences, values and responds to that offer. 'Promotion' describes the marketing communication process. This section identifies some of the actions that organizations may take in seeking to communicate their 'offer', and raise awareness of and engagement with their service.

Reflection: *Explain what you understand by the statement 'marketing is a social process'.*

Customers

This section focuses on customers or users and approaches to thinking about the relationship with customers or users. It starts with an important exploration of the nature of 'customer' or, as some would prefer, user or stakeholders for information organizations. The concepts of customer value and relationships are important in understanding the process of knowing customers, and, the next section on market research introduces some of the approaches to learning about customers. Collecting data and information on customers provides a basis for forming groups or segments of customers, so that it is possible to consider their different expectations, needs and value sets and to respond accordingly.

Identifying customers

Many information organizations have several stakeholder groups, including local government officers, the electorate, local and national businesses, political parties and pressure groups, in addition to the end-consumer, their families and friends. Each of these stakeholder groups has a different experience of the service, and all have different roles in service definition and the evaluation of service quality. For example, in education, although all stakeholders are concerned with the 'end product', they are concerned to varying extents with the process associated with the creation of the product. Employers and society in general are concerned primarily with the 'product' of the system, whereas students and arguably their families will also be concerned with the process.

Also, many information services are offered as part of the wider service provision of their parent organization. For example, college libraries offer a component of the total service experience that a student undergoes in a college. The quality of the information service that teaching staff receive may indirectly affect their service delivery to the students. The provision of a service to such customers and the quality of relationships with them is, then, often central to efficient and effective operations within the organization, and accordingly customer service delivered by other parts of the organization.

Another useful distinction is that between citizen, customer and consumer:

- Citizens generally have rights of access to public service, and may be vociferous through political channels and pressure groups in ensuring that appropriate services are available.
- Customer is the generic term for any stakeholders, individuals or groups for whom the organization in some way provides a good or service.
- Consumers are the users of the service.

There is clearly overlap between these groups, and members of one group will influence the attitudes and behaviours of members of other groups through word of mouth across family and social networks. Consumers for public sector organizations are generally a subset of customers. Most customers are citizens, but, because of geographical boundaries and other factors, they may not always have right of access to the public services over which they have some influence.

Table 5.1 suggests some terms for customers you may encounter in different contexts. However, the complexity in understanding the nature of the 'customer' for many library and information services makes it difficult to give a definitive answer to the question of who customers are. Information service managers need to reflect carefully on which stakeholder or customer group they are seeking to reach with a specific service or communication. A process described as 'stakeholder mapping' can be helpful in identifying the key groups of stakeholders for information services. In terms of users, different groups of users have different needs and expectations, and these change over time. One of the factors that shape

Table 5.1 Some terms for customer

Context	'Customer' term
Public library	Readers, Borrowers
Academic library	Users, Readers, Learners
Bookshop	Buyers
Website	Surfers, Visitors
Newspaper	Readers
Workplace library	Clients
Professional body information service	Members
Journal	Subscribers

needs and expectations is their experience of the service, but this experience is delimited by their expectations. Marketing communication has an important role in shaping and challenging assumptions and expectations. This role extends to non-users and potential users. Pateman (2004) suggests that in order to tackle social exclusion public libraries need to attend to their service to non-users, and passive/lapsed users.

Reflection: Which labels would you use to describe yourself as a customer of an information service?

Customer value, satisfaction and relationships

Customer value is the customer's evaluation of the difference between the benefits and costs of a marketing offer, relative to those of competing offers. Customers form expectations about the value of various marketing offers on the basis of past experiences, the opinions of friends, and marketing and competitor information and promises.

A key contributing factor to customer value perceptions is customer satisfaction. Customer satisfaction is based on the products' perceived performance relative to a buyer's expectations. Marketing can influence satisfaction by communicating appropriate expectations; in other words, it is important not to promise what can not be delivered. Service agents such as library staff can influence expectations and performance, and thereby contribute to shaping customer satisfaction. The issues of service quality and customer satisfaction are revisited in Chapter 6, Quality Management.

Loyal customers are important for organizations (Kotler, 2003). They are more likely to continue to engage with the organization, through additional purchases, or regular usage. In addition, since they have a positive attitude towards the organization, loyal customers will promote the organization to others (known as word-of-mouth promotion). In the last decade organizations have increasingly recognized the importance of customer retention. This has led to the development of the marketing paradigm known as relationship marketing, where the central focus for marketing shifts from encouraging customers to engage in a series of individual transactions, to building long-term sustainable relationships.

Established relationships with library and information service users, whether these are through face-to-face or digital channels build experience with the service. This experience can lead to learning on the part of the customer. They may be able to frame more precise questions to extract information from an online help-desk, or they may become more competent users of electronic journal collections. This in turn is likely to build customer satisfaction, and commitment to the service.

Successful product or service delivery depends upon organizations managing relationships:

- between departments within their organization, through their value chain (see Chapter 6, Quality Management), and
- with a range of internal and external stakeholders, including the organization and its supporting stakeholders: customers, employees, suppliers, distributors, retailers, consultants and agencies. (Christopher, Payne and Ballantyne, 2001).

Organizations therefore need to consider and build their relationships internally, and through their supply chain, as well as with customers. Marketing is one of the strategies for building those relationships.

Learning about customers

Organizations need to learn about and arguably with and through their customers. They achieve this through the application of a variety of processes that, taken together with monitoring competitors, and other environmental factors, are known as *market research*. The collection of data about customer behaviour is a significant element of market research. Customer-based market research allows the organization to learn about the customer's response to its offer, what customers value, customer satisfaction, customer reactions to new products and customer aspirations for future products. Such data informs segmentation, targeting and positioning discussed in the next section, new product development and strategic choices.

Data can be collected through the use of any of the tools described in Chapter 6 under 'Listening to Users'. These include the collection of customer response as part of service delivery, and engagement in quality management processes, as well as specific questionnaire-based surveys, focus groups and interviews. The choice of data collection method for any specific purpose may depend on whether the key objective is to monitor response to existing service, trial a new service or develop longer-term strategic visions and plans. Data may be collected on an ongoing basis, on a regular cycle, or as a one-off process. However the data is collected, and whatever its purpose, information organizations need to be clear about the questions to which they want answers, in order to analyse and interpret the data to inform strategy and policy making, and specific service or marketing communications initiatives.

Digital environments offer opportunities for tracking and profiling user search behaviours. Intelligent agents can create a profile of customers' search interests on the basis of their previous choices and searches, and thereby support their search for information on the web. Such tools allow data about customers to be used to customize the service delivered to the customer.

Creating customer groups and profiles

Services are generally delivered to customer groups and many, but not all, of the opportunities discussed in the previous section for learning about customers treat customers in groups. Generally it is more resource-efficient to create a service for a group of customers, rather than to develop services that are customized to individual needs. So, for example, if a library is considering its opening hours, it will be interested to assess not which individual users, but which groups of users might be affected by the change, the size of those groups and the impact on the value of the information service to those groups. Equally, a leaflet about, say, a new business database is likely to be addressed to the group of potential users. On the other hand, many aspects of information service provision impact on most of the user community. The design of a website, or the efficiency of a self-service circulation control system, affects most users.

On those occasions on which it is useful to divide customers into groups in order to tailor either the 'offer' or marketing communications to suit specific groups, the information service manager needs a process for defining those groups. This is described as market segmentation:

- *Market segmentation* is a process whereby an organization divides its market into distinct groups with distinct needs, characteristics or behaviour, that might lead to these different groups being best served or reached by different product or marketing mixes.

The key characteristic of any segmentation approach is that it should reflect what customers value. Figure 5.1 lists some of the characteristics that might be used for segmenting users of information services.

Segments need to be of sufficient size to be viable in commercial or service resource utilization terms. Once a set of segments has been identified, an organization:

- selects the segments for which it will make a 'marketing offer', and
- defines the specific 'market offer' for each segment.

This process is known as *targeting*. Many information organizations may have little choice but to offer services to all potential user groups, but they do have choices concerning the nature of the 'offer' or service, the allocation of resources to support value creation for specific groups, and the approaches taken to market communication. This implicitly means that many information services practise multi-segment marketing, in which they have to achieve a careful balancing of their responses to sometimes conflicting customer needs and expectations.

Once specific market segments have been identified, marketing is concerned with understanding the competitors in that market, or perhaps the other options available to customers in that segment. For example, a digital health information service might seek to understand the range of options open to the general public for health information and to consider what their service has that is unique, and will make the people with, say, babies use them, rather than some other source. This assessment should lead to market positioning. *Market positioning* seeks to 'position' brands within the consumers' minds in a specific sector. A product's position is the way that the product is defined by consumers, relative to, for example, competing products. Public libraries are being offered the opportunity to re-position themselves as agents in lifelong learning, social inclusion, and e-citizenship. Figure 5.2 illustrates the relationship between market segmentation, targeting and market positioning.

The conventional focus for segmentation activities is on the consumer. Sometimes other stakeholder groups also need to be segmented including, for example, citizens, potential consumers, or non-users or lapsed users. Any stakeholders who may affect funding or business opportunities should not be overlooked. If these stakeholders are non-users, the segmentation of such customers

<table>
<tr><td>

- Age
- Location, and convenience of access
- Frequency of use
- Day and/or time of use
- Ability or willingness to pay
- Job function or status
- Subject interest
- Preferred Information delivery mechanism
- Purpose of information use

</td><td>

</td></tr>
</table>

Figure 5.1 Some variables for segmenting information service customers or users

Figure 5.2 Market segmentation, targeting and market positioning

is not relevant to service delivery, but its purpose is to inform the design of marketing messages addressed to this group. Many of the marketing messages for this group will be embedded in management information, and reports on successes and progress. All management information conveys a marketing message!

Reflection: *Discuss how the variables in Figure 5.1 on page 134 could be used to define specific customer groups for an academic library.*

The marketing mix

The 'marketing mix' is one way of profiling the offering that an organization seeks to make to its chosen customer groups. The marketing mix is frequently described in terms of the combination of four major tools of marketing, product, price, promotion and place, known widely as the 4 Ps. For services the extended marketing mix adds people, process and physical environment (the 7 Ps).

Product is the aspect of the marketing mix that deals with the creation, development and management of products. Product decisions are important because they directly involve creating products that satisfy customers' needs and wants. An organization needs to maintain a satisfactory set of products; this involves introducing new products, modifying existing products and eliminating products that no longer satisfy customers or yield acceptable profits. Products have both functional characteristics and psychological characteristics; psychological characteristics are captured by the brand.

Price relates to activities associated with establishing pricing objectives and strategies and determining product prices. Price represents the agreed value of an exchange. Price may be used as a competitive tool and it is one of the marketing mix variables that can be changed relatively quickly to respond to changes in the environment. Price plays both an economic and a psychological role. From an economic perspective price is closely associated with costs and profits. From a psychological perspective, price may be used as an indicator of quality. In the service sector, the psychological role of price is magnified because consumers must rely on price as the sole indicator of service quality, as the intangible nature of services means that other quality indicators are absent. Libraries have a long tradition as a free service, and this has been extended to much of the digital information to which they provide access. This approach informs expectations of free information and ambiguous messages about the value of information.

Products must be available at the right time and at a convenient location. *Place* is concerned both with consumer service delivery points such as retail outlets and libraries, but also with the distribution network that ensures that products make their way from the producer or creator to the user or consumer. Delivery channels are significant factors within an industry and involve a complex web of organizational relationships, in which collaboration and competition are equally important.

Distribution involves making products available in sufficient quantities to satisfy as many customers as possible and keeping the total inventory, transport and storage costs as low as possible. Distribution, in the sense of offering the right service at the right time and in a convenient location, is particularly essential for services, where value may be viewed as transient. Libraries, both academic and public, are usually situated centrally to their target market, occupying central locations on university campuses and city centre or shopping centre locations. The chief difficulty arises from the fact that some of these locations were chosen in excess of 50 years ago, and may no longer be central to the target market. Additional branch libraries and mobile libraries may seek to alleviate this situation, but do not offer complete resolution. Digital delivery of documents and information can be to home or office. Developments in mobile technology promise delivery to the location that the person occupies.

Promotion or marketing communication relates to activities used to inform one or more groups of people about an organization and its products. Promotion can be used more generally to increase public awareness of an organization and of new or existing products, or alternatively it can be used to educate consumers about product features or to maintain public awareness of existing products. Promotion includes advertising, public relations, personal selling and direct marketing. Promotion is one element of the two-way communication with customers that forms the basis for customer relationships.

Promotion of services presents specific difficulties because of their intangible nature. The intangible element is difficult to depict in advertising, so service advertising needs to emphasize tangible clues, such as physical facilities or other concepts that project an image that reflects services (Jobber, 2001). Tangible clues are embedded in the environment, such as the building and service points occupied by a library building, or the professionalism of the appearance of staff, but may also be used in picture form on publicity and websites. Personal selling is potentially powerful in services because this form of promotion allows customers and sales persons to interact. Customer contact personnel therefore have an important promotional function.

Most services use *people* in service delivery, often creating and delivering the product in interaction with the customer. The quality of the interaction between the service agent and the customer is a major influence on satisfaction. In services where the level of contact is high, as in dentistry or physiotherapy, the customer needs to feel comfortable with the service agent, to trust them and to develop a rapport with them, probably over a service relationship that comprises several service episodes. Even where the service is less intimate, as in a shop or a library, the attitude and responsiveness of the staff can make a difference to the acceptability of the service experience, and the customer's evaluation of service quality.

Services are manufactured and consumed live, and because they involve an interaction between two people, it is more difficult to exercise control and ensure consistency. The service *process* needs careful design; it may include queuing arrangements, processing customer details and payment, as well as elements of the core service delivery. For example, call centre operators and help lines may have a standard set of questions that they ask each caller. Once a customer has experienced a service process once, they will start to learn 'the script'; this helps them to feel more comfortable with the process. In self-service environments such as, for example, with a public access kiosk, the customer is taken through a process by the prompts on the computer screen.

Physical evidence is concerned with the physical surroundings from which a service is delivered and other tangible elements in a service episode. Physical evidence is important in service delivery, because it is usually the only tangible clues that the customer has about the quality of the service experience. Thus information services should pay attention to presentation of staff, atmosphere, ambience and image, and to the design of premises.

These final 3 Ps are explored in more depth in Chapter 6, Quality Management, and Chapter 3, People in Organizations. Product and promotion are discussed further in later sections of this chapter.

The marketing mix is an important tool in creating and maintaining an offering that is of value to customers. Successful marketing depends on 'the right mix'. In other words, a product that lacks visibility among the potential customer group will fail. A marketing message that is not consistent with the value that customers perceive the product to offer will mean that the promise does not match the delivery; this will lead to dissatisfaction, and may damage customer's attitudes to the organization or the brand. All elements of the marketing mix are interdependent and must be consistent with one another. The most appropriate marketing mix depends upon the customer and is influenced by the marketing environment. An organization needs to design and combine elements of the marketing mix in such a way as to create an offering that differentiates it from its competitors and creates a competitive advantage.

The elements of the marketing mix can be changed. However, changes to most of the elements of the marketing mix are constrained by the organization's existing resources (including its existing customer base), and the rate of change that is possible may at times be frustratingly slow. For example, libraries often occupy specific buildings; these are not always in the best locations to ensure the optimum level of visits, but a new building must be negotiated over many years and through complex political processes.

Information products and brands

Most library and information services offer a range of products or services. Figure 1.2 on page 8 lists some of the offerings from a public library service. Typically information organizations offer a range of services. Before considering issues such as promotion, it is important that library managers have a clear view of the offering that their service is using as the basis for their engagement with customers. In addition, it is important to acknowledge that, as with many complex services, each user has a different experience of a library depending upon which of the services and products on offer they use. The consumer has scope for personalizing the service, and the benefits that they derive from an information service are unique to their needs, the route that they choose to satisfy those needs and their success in travelling their route.

This section briefly explores the nature of information service, through the three-level model of product, and the new product development process which ensures a dynamic and evolving product portfolio. A final section explains the role of brands.

The three-level model of product

Products have multiple levels. One simple model is offered in Figure 5.3. This shows products as having three levels: the core product, the actual product and the augmented product.

The *core product* is what actually meets the consumer's needs. In this case, the core product is always information. In most cases the user seeks information on a specific subject and to fulfil a specific purpose (leisure, education, writing a report, undertaking a market research exercise).

The *actual product* is what is actually delivered to the consumer. For information products this will be the various different ways in which information can be packaged into products such as books and journals, or into service, such as database access. In the case of information products the actual product may have structuring, indexing, quality, presentation, design, style and physical character-istics. For example, an entry in an encyclopedia in print form may contain simi-lar information to the same entry in electronic form, but layout, presentation, ways in which the information can be manipulated may all be very different. In addition, the digital version may have other multimedia elements, such as a video clip which allows a more multi-dimensional expression of the information.

The *augmented product* embraces the other features that make up the product and add value. For an online search service, the actual product might be database access through a user-friendly interface. The augmented product might embrace a document ordering and delivery option, an SDI service and training seminars. Elements of the augmented product may be charged for, and others may be avail-able free.

The boundaries between core, actual and augmented products are not fixed for all time and are in any case more difficult to draw for services (and probably digital information products) than for physical products. Organizations in the same marketplace all share the same core product. They differentiate themselves on the basis of the actual product or the augmented product.

Reflection: *How might a subject gateway on the web augment the databases to which it provides access?*

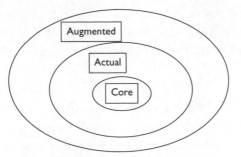

Figure 5.3 The three-level model of product

Reflection: *What are the core, actual and augmented products offered by an academic library when it makes a collection of electronic journals available to its users?*

Dynamic product portfolios

The range of services or products offered by an organization is referred to as its product portfolio. Often the specific products in a product portfolio are grouped together into product lines that might be designed for different customer groups. A public library, for example, may have groups of products that are intended for schools – their schools' product line.

The success of the overall product portfolio, specific product lines and specific items within those lines should be under regular scrutiny. Intelligence on customer satisfaction, competitors and other aspects of the marketing environment leads to the identification of proposals for development and change in the product portfolio.

The development of new products or services or significant step-changes in the design of existing products or services requires a specific product development process (often called the new product development process). A simple model of such a process would embrace the following stages:

1 Identification of need, and drivers for change or development.
2 Development of a product concept to respond to the identified need or drivers.
3 Design of the new service, taking into account the details of the nature of the service, the target customer group, staffing and other necessary resources, and the implementation process.
4 Testing of the new service, possibly with a pilot run, in one location, for a limited period of time. The testing must conclude with an evaluation that may make recommendations that impact on the eventual implementation of the product.
5 Launch and promotion of the new service, including any staff training, changes in staff roles, developments in information systems and promotion through any appropriate elements of the marketing communication mix.
6 Evaluation of the new service after an appropriate period of time (see Chapter 6).

Such developments often have consequences for the activities and skills expected of staff. Effective negotiation of the implementation of a new service will require attention to change management. (see Chapter 3).

Finally, resources will not be used to maximum effect, and will often not be available for the development of new services, if existing services do not come under continual review. The outcome of such review may lead to minor enhancements or major proposals for new services as discussed above. Alternatively, such review will on occasion lead to recommendations to withdraw services. This process also needs to be managed, so that customers who are committed users of such services can be supported in transferring to alternative services or routes to fulfil their needs.

This evolution of products and services is modelled in the product lifecycle. The stages in the product lifecycle are introduction, growth, maturity and decline. In any product portfolio there will be products that are at different stages in their lifecycle.

Brands

> A brand is a name, term, sign, symbol or design, or a combination of them, intended to identify the goods or services of one seller or group of sellers and to differentiate them from those of the competitors.
>
> (Kotler, 2003, 418)

A brand can be viewed as the seller's promise to consistently deliver a specific set of benefits, values or attributes to the consumer. A brand, then, facilitates the communication process between the producer and their customers. It may take the form of a name, term, design, symbol or any other feature that identifies one seller's good or service as distinct from those of other sellers. Organizations typically seek to brand their products and thereby to create images and expectations in the minds of the consumer. These expectations may have a significant effect on the product or service selection and, in the case of services, the development of the service interaction.

Branding is designed to facilitate the acquisition and retention of a loyal customer base and is integral to the building of customer relationships. In this context, brand can be viewed as an expression of a relationship between the consumer and the product.

There are a number of different approaches to branding. Branding may relate to individual products or groups of products, or to the organization or company name. Although service sector industries may on occasions seek to brand their products, in general there is significant emphasis on branding the company, or in other terms, creating a corporate identity and seeking to influence the corporate image:

- *Corporate identity* is how the company or organization sees itself, in terms of achievements, values, mission and aspects of products such as product range, price and quality
- *Corporate image* is how the customer or potential customer or other target audience perceives the organization, in respect of some or all of the above features.

Thus, for a library and information service, corporate identity might emerge from general professional concerns associated with public service, customer care and accessibility to a wide range of different information sources in both electronic and print media. Corporate image, in the eyes of the customers, may, at the worst be associated with shelves of dusty and dry books, inconvenient opening hours and the need for silence.

Image, then, in common with the expectations that may colour customers' quality judgements, is shaped to a considerable extent by previous experiences of a specific service point or of the category of service in general. The challenge is to align corporate identity with corporate image. This needs to start with an assessment of both identity and image, and the development of a vision of potential identities and images. Thereafter, marketing communications should contribute to the creation of strong, appropriate and positive brand and corporate images, and establish the positioning of the brand.

Reflection: *Examine the web page in Figure 1.2 on page 8, and other web pages shown in this book, and discuss how these organizations are using branding.*

Marketing communications

Promotion or marketing communications is concerned with the approaches that organizations adopt to communicate with their customers and audiences. As discussed earlier, communication is all pervasive and is embedded in actions as much as in explicit promotional ventures. Nevertheless, the formal marketing communications process has much to contribute with its focus on audiences, objectives, messages and media. This section discusses the stages in that process, and then moves on to focus on three tools that are likely to be particularly important for information organizations: public relations, advertising and websites.

Designing marketing communications

Figure 5.4 summarizes the stages in the design of marketing communications.

| Identify target audience |
| Determine communication objectives |
| Design the message |
| Select communication channels |
| Establish promotional budget |
| Decide on promotional mix |
| Evaluation |

Figure 5.4 Stages in the design of communication strategies

Identification of target audience

The first stage is to characterize the target audience. This target audience may include the complete market segment for the product or the organization, or a specific promotional strategy may be targeted more narrowly at a niche within the broader segment. Messages and channels may be selected accordingly, but care must be taken to ensure that other groups in the market segment are not alienated by the messages that might be associated with a niche strategy. The characteristics of the audience need to be understood. Segmentation might be applicable here, but in addition it will be important to garner an understanding of the types of marketing messages to which the audience is likely to be susceptible.

Determining communication objectives

In designing communication strategies is important to identify whether the objective is to increase awareness, form opinions and attitudes or to encourage action. A simple model of consumer behaviour identifies three stages in the consumer decision making process. Marketing communication may be designed to intervene at any of these stages:

- the *cognitive* stage during which potential customers become *aware* of products
- the *affective* stage during which customers *form opinions and attitudes* concerning products
- the *behaviour* stage during which customers *take action* (such as making a purchase) on the basis of their experiences in the first two stages.

Even in non-purchase situations these stages assist in the definition of marketing communications objectives.

Reflection: *Pick up a leaflet on library and information services. What is its target audience? To what extent is it designed to: increase awareness, form or change opinions and attitudes, or provoke action?*

Designing the message

Each communication strategy must have a message that is consistent with its communication objectives. The message will often strongly reflect the *unique selling proposition* (USP) of the products. The USP is the unique set of benefits which the producer believes are provided by their product, and which will be of interest to their customers. Where promotion focuses on a brand or corporate image or identity, this will form the basis of the marketing message. Another factor that needs to be taken into account is message consistency between different marketing communication activities. An organization needs to promote a consistent, if evolving, image through all of its separate communication activities, otherwise the audience will become confused and the overall clear message will not be communicated.

Selecting communication channels

Communication channels can be divided into personal communications and non-personal communications.

Personal communications channels are those in which two or more people communicate with one another, and *word of mouth* is the primary means of communication, although other media such as e-mail are growing in significance. There are three types of personal communication channels:

- *advocate channels*, such as company sales people
- *expert channels*, such as independent experts, including software and CD-ROM reviewers
- *social channels and consultants*, such as friends, professional colleagues and professional networks.

Exhibitions are an important arena in which advocate channels such as salespeople can come into contact with customers. These are widely used in promotion to organizations. In this context, as in many others, personal conversation will be supplemented by leaflets, posters and possibly videos and samples (such as sample discs).

Non-personal communication channels are those in which communication is through some medium other than person to person. These include:

- *The press*, including national and regional newspapers and magazines but, most significantly for the information industry, trade, professional and technical journals. Appropriate professional journals or newsletters can be very effective in reaching targeted professional groups.

- *Television*, including satellite, cable and digital television. The expensive nature of this medium means that it is only an option for major advertisers.
- *Radio* offers a wide range of competitively priced promotional options. In general it is deemed to have less potential impact than television since there is no visual image.
- *Posters* can be placed in a wide variety of different environments from billboards at the roadside, to the Underground rail network and other public places, to libraries and notice boards within organizations.
- *Leaflets and publicity* are important 'takeaways' that can act as reminders of products and contact points.
- *Websites* are increasingly important for marketing as well as service provision, as information services are increasingly accessed remotely.

Establishing the budget

The available budget has a significant effect on the range of communication activities that can be pursued. For many libraries marketing budgets are extremely limited, but commercial organizations in the information marketplace will have marketing budgets which are consistent with (if not sufficient for!) the market segments with which they need to establish and maintain communications. Some channels are more expensive than others, and some incur only hidden cost, such as those associated with staff time. Information service managers need to be aware of the costs of communication activities, even when they do not generate a separate invoice, and to continually monitor the value and impact associated with marketing communications activities.

Deciding on the marketing communications mix

The choice of elements in the marketing communications mix is determined by:

- The nature of the service and, specifically, how much personal support is needed in the decision-making process associated with the choice to use the service, and other factors that determine the need to establish a relationship between the customer and the provider. In many information environments, the user needs support and training in the use of products, and in service contexts a relationship is important in encouraging repeat visits and continued patronage.

- Target audience at which the communication is aimed, and the medium through which they can most easily be reached.
- Stage of the lifecycle of a service or product. Promotion for new products is concerned with raising awareness; later in the lifecycle, sustaining relationships and fending off competition might require different media channels.
- Marketplace situation and, in particular, the degree and nature of the competition, and the promotional channels used by competitors.
- Available budget.

The *media plan* should be one outcome of this selection of communications media. This needs to specify the exact media and times and dates of appearance of advertisements.

Three important elements in the marketing communications mix for libraries are public relations, advertising and websites; these are discussed in greater detail below.

Measuring promotion results

Promotion involves considerable investment. It can frequently be difficult to differentiate between the effect of promotion and the other elements of the marketing mix. Nevertheless, it is important to monitor the effects of promotion, by looking at use figures and any other measures of reputation that are available. This data can then be used to inform both future service provision and any further marketing activities.

Reflection: *You are engaged in the development of a new service for teenagers in a public library. Identify: (a) communication objectives, (b) message, (c) media or channels.*

Public relations

Public relations or PR deals with the quality and nature of the relationship between an organization and its publics. The objective of PR is to generate communication between an organization and these publics, and thereby to influence attitudes and opinions, and to achieve a mutual understanding between the organization and its publics. This may include:

- the creation and maintenance of a corporate identity and image
- the enhancement of the organization's standing in the community

- the communication of the organization's philosophy and purpose
- the establishment and maintenance of relationships with the media, and in various political arenas
- attendance at trade exhibitions.

Public relations may use any of the following: press releases and press kits, sponsorship, speeches and presentations, annual reports, library brochures, information service newsletters, leaflets on specific services or targeted toward specific customer groups, assorted other publications, community relations initiatives, lobbying in political and other arenas, sponsorships, launches and other events.

Public relations achieved through relationships with the media are more attractive than advertising because:

- *Credibility* – Editorial comment carries more authority and credibility; readers expect adverts to be partisan.
- *Reach* – PR may reach wider or different audiences, including managers and community leaders and other stakeholders, who may or may not be users or customers. PR can lend sponsors good publicity and leave a positive image with others who have influence in political and financial arenas.
- *Cost* – No advertising costs are incurred, although PR is not free. Effective PR requires commitment to and resources for a planned programme.
- *Excitement* – PR is, by definition, news, and must be written in such a way that it will attract reader interest.

The major disadvantage of PR is its uncontrollability. Editors control what is published and it is not always the case that all publicity is good publicity!

Reflection: *Identify an interesting activity undertaken by an information organization known to you and write a brief press release to tell other people about it.*

Advertising

Advertising can be defined as any paid form of non-personal promotion (Kotler et al., 2002). Advertising reaches communities and individuals beyond those with whom the organization already has a relationship, or others where there are other factors which make direct contact difficult or expensive. Examples of the sort of information organizations for whom advertising may be beneficial include:

- information organizations with large target audiences (such as public libraries)
- information organizations who do not know the name of the person to contact in an organization
- information organizations that need to widen their marketplace, perhaps for one particular service or product, e.g. a subject gateway or public access to the internet.

In these contexts advertising is good for:

- communicating simple messages, such as announcing the launch of a new service, an open evening or extended opening hours
- establishing and reinforcing brand image and loyalty, through bringing the product or organization to the audience's attention
- visibility in the marketplace, especially if competitors do not advertise
- selling specific items, such as a new service, or publication.

Most advertisements in the information marketplace are placed in magazines and newspapers, and on notice boards, websites and bulletin boards. Although such media are less glamorous than broadcast media, they have powerful advantages. With such media, people have selected what they will read, have an interest that they are actively pursuing, and pay attention to and absorb what they read. Print media are also often circulated to other readers and may be retained for later reference.

Reflection: List all of the media through which an information service might 'advertise' itself.

Websites

Information services are increasingly interacting with customers remotely. This means that both service delivery and marketing communications, the two elements of interaction with customers that can contribute to building customer relationships, are mediated through remote communication. Information services need to understand and clearly differentiate the complementary roles of face-to-face communication and e-communication.

Information service websites can have a number of different functions:

- creating brand, product and corporate awareness and image, and continually bringing these to the customer's attention

- providing product and other information
- delivering content, such as electronic journals, databases and other digital documents
- customer service handling, training, help, customer complaints, queries, suggestions and establishing two-way dialogues
- establishing customer/user communities who are loyal to the information service and also interact with each other to their mutual benefit (Chaffey, 2003).

While many commercial websites would place the first of these as a top priority, many public sector information services often overlook this objective and do not accord sufficient significance to considerations of audience, message, and image and identity.

Web pages do not allow much scope for communicating messages as well as information about an organization and how to start navigating a site. Not only is the overall screen size for a home page relatively limited, but web pages need to be designed to accommodate the different generations of technology that might be available to individual users. The answer is to enlist all of the components of the website in marketing communication, to make the brand message integral rather than an add-on (Rowley, 2003). This means attending to the elements identified in Figure 5.5.

- Brand mark or logo
- Graphics, including pictures, logos and other images
- Text and copy, including content and style
- Currency and news, suggesting dynamism and activity
- Colours and consistency of colour palette
- Shapes, including: shapes of pictures or graphics, shapes of buttons, and shapes of menu option displays
- Layout and combination of images, including any use of metaphor

Figure 5.5 Website elements important in marketing communication

Marketing strategy and planning

Marketing strategy and planning draws together the range of operational marketing concerns that have been explored earlier in this chapter and sets them in a strategic and longer-term context. Because marketing strategy and planning is a key element of corporate strategy and planning, many of the tools and concepts that are important in the former are also often used to inform the latter. These are therefore described in more detail in Chapter 8, Strategy and Planning. This short section explores the specific nature of market strategy and planning, and contextualizes it within the context of the wider strategic planning framework for the organization.

Marketing planning takes place within a wider strategic and planning framework in any organization. Most organizations divide their operations into 'strategic business units' (SBUs), possibly, but not always, aligned with departments. Each of these SBUs will typically be charged with a strategy development process that is likely to lead to a strategic planning document, to act as a framework for operations within that SBU for the duration of the planning period. As such, an information service is likely to be expected to create a strategy document. One element of that strategy document should outline the principles of marketing strategy. The purpose of such a marketing strategy is encapsulated in the following defintion:

- The *marketing strategy* of an organization indicates the specific markets towards which activities are to be targeted, and the types of competitive advantages that are to be developed and exploited. It may be concerned with issues such as customers and customer relationships, and the establishment of appropriate marketing mix strategies.

Depending on the role of the information service within an organization, the information service's marketing strategy may be used to inform the corporate marketing strategy. It should certainly form the basis for the development of a marketing plan:

- The *marketing plan* focuses on the operational detail, converting strategies into implementable actions. It is a detailed statement, which specifies target markets, marketing programmes, responsibilities, timescales, resources to be used, and budgets. Market strategy considers all aspects of an organization strategy in the marketplace, while a marketing plan is more normally focused on implementing marketing and promotional strategies, in the context of specific target markets and the marketing mix.

In practice, information services may not always differentiate between a marketing strategy document and a marketing plan, and may produce a plan that is an amalgamation of the two. Figure 5.6 summarizes the sections in such an integrated plan. It includes sections that report on audit, identification of objectives and the specification of strategies, and focus on setting direction. Final sections on marketing programmes and implementation, marketing budget and evaluation may embed more operational detail. These various sections reflect the

1. Executive summary
2. Introduction
3. Marketing audit
4. Marketing objectives
5. Marketing strategies
6. Marketing programmes and implementation
7. Marketing budget
8. Evaluation

Figure 5.6 Sections in a marketing plan

stages in the strategic planning process outlined in Chapter 8. Different models for the structure of the marketing strategy and planning process and any associated documents will be appropriate in different circumstances. The most effective approach will be influenced by the size of the organization, the scale of its marketing activity, the strategic planning process, market structure and opportunities, and the extent of the marketing orientation of the organization. The key message is that there must be a plan.

Summary and conclusions

Marketing is concerned with the development of relationships with customers, users and other stakeholders. Segmentation of customers and users into groups, and the targeting of specific groups with specific offerings or services, enhance customer relationships and customer value. The market offering, often defined in terms of the marketing mix of product, price, place, promotion, people, process and physical evidence, needs to be designed to suit specific client groups. Information products and services can be described and experienced at different levels: core, actual and augmented. The range of products or services offered by a library and information services needs to be dynamic and evolving, and the process of change needs to be managed through the stages of a new product development process. Brands and corporate images position the product in the minds of consumers; organizations engage in branding in order to influence these perceptions. Marketing communications or promotion is concerned with the design and delivery of planned communication with users or customers. This involves consideration of target audiences, communication objectives, messages, communication channels and media, budgets and evaluation. Marketing needs planning and organizing, through a marketing plan. Marketing planning must be linked to corporate objectives and strategy.

Finally, all aspects of service delivery communicate an image to customers. Signage, condition and ambience of the building and furniture, reliability of computer equipment, whether telephone calls are answered promptly and even cleanliness of the toilets will all have an impact on the perceptions that users have of the organization. Ultimately, marketing messages must be reinforced by and consistent with the customer's experience. This leads neatly into the next chapter.

REVIEW QUESTIONS

1 What is marketing and why is it an important element of library and information service management?

2 Discuss the nature of customers and stakeholders for library and information services.

3 Explain how library and information centres can segment their customers or users. Why is segmentation useful?

4 Describe and illustrate the elements of the marketing mix.

5 Use the three-level model of product to explain the nature of information services as products.

6 What are the elements of the marketing communications mix? What factors determine the most appropriate mix for an information organization?

7 Explain the stages in the design of marketing communications.

8 Discuss the role of public relations for a specific type of information organization.

9 What factors should be taken into consideration in website design to ensure that a website is an effective marketing communications tool?

10 Why is marketing planning important? What are the elements of a marketing plan?

CASE STUDY

The British Library

Answer the questions on the basis of the web page extracts or, if you prefer, by visiting the British Library site at www.bl.uk.

1 Describe the way in which the British Library is segmenting its customers. Are there any other approaches that the library might have taken?

2 Choose one segment and describe the services that the library is suggesting might be of interest to members of that segment. Are some of these services also useful to other segments?

3 What does the British Library want to project as its corporate image? Are there any inherent tensions in the core message? How does it achieve this positioning? Do you think that it is successful in achieving this positioning?

4 Compare the pages from the British Library website with those from the Stockport Libraries website (www.stockport.gov.uk/content/leisureculture/libraries). Which website has the most marketing impact? Examine the components of the website in detail and explain your preference.

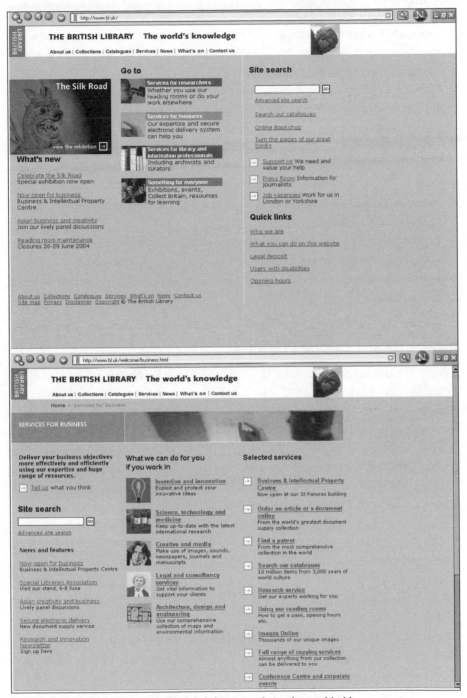

Figure 5.7 Extract from the British Library website (www.bl.uk)
By permission of the British Library

CHALLENGES

1 Outline the range of different ways in which an information service can manage relationships with customers. What are the consequences in, say, a public or academic library context of shifting customer groups?

2 Remote access to information services provides a different range of opportunities for communication with customers and users. What are the consequences of these changes and how might they be managed?

3 Discuss the concept of 'value' in relation to one or more information services. What are the challenges associated with defining the concept of value in this context?

4 What factors and processes need to be embraced in an integrated approach to marketing communications?

5 Explain why branding is both necessary and difficult for information services. What is the relationship between branding and marketing communications?

6 In what sense does the marketing of information services differ from that of goods and services?

References and additional reading

Adcock, D., Halborg, A. and Ross, C. (2001) *Marketing Principles and Practice*, Harlow, FT Prentice Hall.

Bickerton, P. (1996) *Cybermarketing, Oxford,* Butterworth-Heinemann.

Brassington, F. and Pettit, S. (2000) *Principles of Marketing*, 2nd edn, London, Prentice Hall.

Bryson, J. (1999) *Effective Library and Information Centre Management*, 2nd edn, Aldershot, Gower.

Chaffey, D. (2003) *E-business and E-commerce*, London, FT Prentice Hall.

Christopher, M., Payne, A. and Ballantyne, D. (2001) *Relationship Marketing*, 2nd edn, Oxford, Butterworth-Heinemann.

Christopher, M. and McDonald, M. (1995) *Marketing: an introductory text,* London, Pan Books.

Coote, H. and Batchelor, B. (1997) *How to Market Your Library Service Effectively,* 2nd edn, London, Aslib.

Davies, M. (1998) *Understanding Marketing,* London, Prentice Hall.

De Chernatony, L. and Dall'Olmo Riley, F. (1998) Defining a 'Brand': beyond the literature with experts' interpretations, *Journal of Marketing Management,* **14** (5), 417–43.

De Chernatony, L. and McDonald, M. (1998*) Creating Powerful Brands in Consumer,*

Service and Industrial Markets, 2nd edn, Oxford, Butterworth-Heinemann.

De Saez, E. E. (2002) *Marketing Concepts for Libraries and Information Services*, 2nd edn, London, Facet Publishing.

Dibb, S., Simkin, P., Pride, J. C. and Ferrell, J. (2000) *Marketing: concepts and strategies*, 4th European edn, Boston, MA, Houghton Mifflin.

Doyle, P. (1998) *Marketing Management and Strategy*, 2nd edn, London, Prentice Hall.

Gabbott, M. and Hogg, G. (1997) *Contemporary Services Marketing Management: a reader*, London, The Dryden Press.

Gupta, D. and Jambhektar, A. (eds) (2003) *An Integrated Approach to Services Marketing: a book of readings on marketing of library and information services*, Mumbai, India, Allied Publishers Private Ltd.

Hart, K. (1999) *Putting Marketing Ideas into Action*, London, Library Association Publishing.

Jobber, D. (2001) *Principles and Practice of Marketing*, 3rd edn, New York, McGraw-Hill.

Kotler, P. (2003) *Marketing Management*, 11th edn, London, Prentice Hall.

Kotler, P., Armstrong, G., Saunders, J. and Wong, V. L. (2002) *Principles of Marketing*, 3rd European edn, Harlow, FT Prentice Hall.

Lancaster, G. and Massingham, L. (2001) *Essentials of Marketing*, 4th edn, New York, McGraw-Hill.

Lovelock, C. H. (2003) *Services Marketing*, Upper Saddle River, NJ, Prentice Hall.

Pateman, J. (2004) Developing a Needs-based Service, *Library + Information Update,* **3** (5), 34–7.

Rowley, J. (2002) *Information Marketing,* Aldershot, Gower.

Rowley, J. (2003) Branding Your Library Web Site, *Library + Information Update*, **2** (2), 45.

6 Quality management

LEARNING OBJECTIVES

After reading this chapter you should be able to:

- discuss the nature of quality, quality assurance, quality enhancement and quality management
- understand the concept of service quality and the value of tools such as SERVQUAL and LibQUAL
- evaluate the different approaches for listening to customers and eliciting feedback
- identify the key elements of a total quality management (TQM) approach
- evaluate the contribution that benchmarking can make to quality management
- discuss the nature of performance management and measurement
- explore the role of accreditation schemes such as Charter Mark and IiP.

Introduction

Sometimes it can seem that quality management is an industry in itself. The multiple external quality regimes relating to the information service, various specific projects, elements of service, co-operative ventures and the sector within which the information organization exists can sometimes feel like a never-ending set of hurdles, all demanding management attention. Such external regimes imposed by funding and accrediting bodies need to be matched with and used creatively to support the manager's concern with managing, and where possible enhancing, the quality of the information service. This chapter seeks to explain the elements of quality management processes, and to illustrate this discussion with reference to a selection of the approaches that are used in information organizations.

The chapter starts with some generic quality management topics. First and foremost, it is important to understand that quality has multiple meanings, and to understand the relationship between quality management, quality assurance and quality enhancement. Armed with definitions of quality, it is possible to explore approaches to measuring service quality, through customer satisfaction surveys and other means of listening to users. Such approaches both provide a 'measurement' of quality and provide suggestions for service improvements. Quality management and enhancement systems propose frameworks and best practice in relation to the management of quality. Total quality management is a much discussed theoretical approach to quality management that is embedded in accreditation schemes, such as the European Foundation for Quality Management. Charter Mark and Investors in People are more specific quality management and accreditation models. Benchmarking has become very popular in both private and public sector organizations in recent years to set quality standards. Benchmarking data needs to be collected through surveys, which are likely to cover customer satisfaction as one of the measures of performance. Performance measures or indicators are elements of most quality management, and strategic planning frameworks. Information organizations have to decide which measures are appropriate to their vision, mission and objectives.

Perspectives on quality

A good place to start is with a definition of *quality*. Unfortunately this is no easy task. Each of the major contributions to the quality debate has offered their own unique contribution on the nature of quality:

- The *exceptional* view sees quality as something special. Quality refers to something distinctive and elitist, and is linked to notions of excellence or high quality that is unattainable by most.
- Quality as *perfection* sees quality as a consistent or flawless outcome. This democratizes the notion of quality such that if consistency can be achieved then quality can be attained by all.

- Quality as *fitness for purpose* views quality from the perspective of fulfilling a customer's requirements, needs or desires.
- Quality as *value for money* sees quality in terms of return on investment. If the same outcome can be achieved at a lower cost, or a better outcome can be achieved at the same cost, then the customer has a quality product or service.
- Quality as *transformation* is a classic notion of quality that sees it in terms of change from one state to another.

Library and information services are services and therefore the literature on service quality is of particular significance in establishing models of quality. Writers on service quality have tended to focus strongly on customer requirements and customer experience. This tends to emphasize the fitness for purpose view of quality, although the value for money view may also play a role.

Quality management is also a complex concept. Later in this chapter we explore concepts such as customer surveys, total quality management (TQM), benchmarking, performance measurement, standards and customer charters. These activities are all part of quality management. Quality management in this book is used to describe all of the processes, activities and measures that contribute to the management of the quality of the products, service or other outputs from the organization. Quality management then involves:

- processes, to measure or improve quality
- measures, to set targets, and monitor progress.

Organizations need to set objectives, with precise targets, commit resources to achieving those targets, measure whether they have met targets, and review targets. In a service environment, data on customer response to services is a key element of feedback that indicates whether or not quality targets have been met. Quality management systems are designed to monitor whether this cycle is occurring appropriately. Target setting may also be informed by external standards or benchmarks. Very often a library and information service operates within the quality management regime that applies to its specific sector. Thus, library and information services in higher education are obliged to respond to processes and systems defined by the Quality Assurance Agency, the National Health Service and Ofsted. Libraries in further education colleges respond to targets and processes established by Ofsted and the Learning Skills Council, and public libraries have to meet benchmarks set by the Department of Culture, Media and Sport.

There are two related concepts that also need definition. *Quality assurance* is a widely used term that refers to the processes associated with ensuring that quality adheres to some externally or internally set standard. Through quality assurance, the organization and external stakeholders can be assured that the performance of the organization is of an appropriate standard. In higher education, external examiners contribute to quality assurance when they compare standards of marking between one organization and another. In the UK National Health Service, NHS trusts may be given targets for waiting list reduction. The processes whereby the organization collects the data to demonstrate that these targets have been met are quality assurance. Quality assurance requires standards of performance to which organizations must aspire, often, but not always, articulated as quantitative performance measures. Such performance measures are often based on the collection of benchmarking data from across a sector.

Quality enhancement focuses attention on those processes associated with enhancing or improving quality. Again performance measures are a necessary representation of quality; organizations will not only seek to make improvements, but will also want to be able to monitor that improvements have been made. Quality enhancement programmes may also embrace standards and targets and the various other elements of quality assurance, but improvements are not constrained by or restricted to achievement of these targets. In addition, the focus is on the processes that lead to quality enhancement, such as staff development (see IiP below) and customer focus (see TQM below).

All organizations should be committed to achieving the best quality possible within the available resources. A quality culture should be embedded. In other words, quality enhancement, with a view to the strategic aims of the organization and customer views and requirements, is always to be preferred to quality assurance. The exception is where quality assurance processes encourage an organization to respond to targets to which it might not otherwise aspire and thereby provoke enhanced excellence. This is the objective of many recent UK government benchmarking initiatives. For example, university and college information service managers may benchmark their spend per student against national statistics in order to negotiate with management for a baseline spend that is aligned with that of their benchmarking or competitive group.

The real tension between quality assurance and quality enhancement in public sector organizations arises from the fact that both performance measures and standards and the internal processes of quality assurance and management in those organizations are dictated by government bodies for specific sectors. There is also considerable truth in the view that organizations and governments exhibit an enhanced interest in quality in times of change or reduced resources. It is often the case that public sector organizations are expected to respond to elaborate bureaucratic dictates in terms of data to be reported to funding bodies and quality assurance frameworks to be adopted to monitor the delivery and development of services, with no additional resource allocation to cover the work involved in such processes. The creative public sector manager needs to work at interpreting both processes and management information reported to the funding body so that they can be used to drive quality enhancement that is relevant and appropriate for the unique characteristics of their organization.

Another important tension between externally set quality assurance measures, targets and processes and quality enhancement within organizations is generating the kind of ownership of externally imposed quality agendas that leads to innovation and creativity. As is discussed in the section on total quality management below, quality enhancement depends on commitment to quality throughout the organization. This means that quality processes need to embrace all levels in the organization, and hierarchically structured organizations need to define a *hierarchy of quality management* or a series of linked quality enhancement, assurance, and monitoring processes, with associated targets or performance measures at each level. For example, in discussing customer satisfaction, broad-based surveys generate an overarching impression of issues and problems that might inform planning at the top strategic level and dialogue with funding bodies. Customer satisfaction surveys relating to specific services of, say, digital library initiatives for remote users will be more limited in scope. At the most detailed level the evaluation of, say, the design of a new user interface is still relevant to user satisfaction and is part of the quality management processes of the library and information service, but the information collected is more likely to lead to enhancements in the design of the interface than to any major strategy decisions affecting the funding or future direction of the information service. Similarly performance indicators and benchmarking can operate in relation to different units of analysis.

Reflection: *Discuss the match between quality management approaches and organizational levels in an organization known to you.*

Understanding and measuring service quality

Service quality is an elusive concept. As summarized in Figure 6.1, services are essentially intangible and therefore it is difficult to propose objective concepts of quality. In addition because the customer is involved in the service experience

Intangibility	Services cannot be evaluated in advance of use.
Perishability	Stocks of the service element of the service package cannot be held and services need to deal with demand and capacity directly.
Simultaneity	The customer must be present before the service can take place.
Heterogeneity	There is inherent variability in the service offered.

Figure 6.1 The fundamental characteristics of services

(simultaneity) the customer can influence the outcome of the service experience, which in turn contributes to the inherent variability in the service as experienced (heterogeneity).

Service quality is defined in terms of customer perceptions and expectations in relation to the value of a service experience, viz:

Quality = Customer's perception − Customer's expectations

This leads to a model of the measurement and management of service quality which is crucially dependent on customer identification and their evaluations; the diversity of stakeholders for information services (see Chapter 5, Marketing and User Relationships) suggests that such data needs careful interpretation.

Another important concept is that of customer satisfaction. One model regards satisfaction as the outcome of one service episode while service quality develops over a number of service episodes.

Service organizations have long recognized the need to be able to measure service quality. Such organizations frequently produce questionnaires and use them to assess customer satisfaction and service quality. Although each of these is valuable, they tend to reflect the special features of the individual organization. In addition there is recognition that the elusive and abstract nature of service quality can make it difficult to measure. Parasuraman, Zeithaml and Berry (1988) sought to design a general instrument for measuring service quality known as SERVQUAL. SERVQUAL is a multiple-item scale encompassing expectations and perceptions concerning a service encounter. SERVQUAL has been recognized as a valuable tool and has been widely used, commented upon and adapted.

Work on SERVQUAL has led to the identification of service quality dimensions or attributes; they are those attributes which contribute to consumer expectations and perceptions of service quality: These are:

* *tangibles* – the appearance and functioning of physical facilities, equipment, personnel and communications materials
* *reliability* – the ability to perform the promised service dependably and accurately

- *responsiveness* – willingness to help customers and to provide prompt service
- *assurance* – the knowledge and courtesy of employees, and their ability to inspire trust and confidence
- *empathy* – the caring individual attention provided to users.

Reflection: *Discuss how these dimensions could be translated into questions in a customer satisfaction survey for a library.*

Knowledge of these dimensions and the ability to measure them can help to yield an insight into more effective ways of improving service quality, but for the purposes of most library and information services these dimensions are very generic. They do not provide the detailed profile of which services are well received and which are not, and why. They do not easily lead to a plan of action that can lead to quality enhancement.

One significant piece of work that has tailored the work on SERVQUAL by developing an instrument that is specifically targeted to the evaluation of customer response to information service is LibQUAL. LibQUAL, a joint research and development project of Texas A&M University and the Association for Research Libraries (US) has emerged as both a process and a tool that enables institutions to address service quality gaps and to enhance responses to user needs. The application was developed gradually, through annual cycles, from 2000 onwards; in 2002 it was delivered in and data was collected from 164 different library and information service settings. The web-based instrument with 25 items, which cover both traditional and digital library settings, is useful to libraries for collecting customer data; in addition the database is used to provide a rich seam of benchmarking data. The dimensions of the LibQUAL tool are:

- *affect of service* – the human side of the enterprise, encompassing traits of empathy, accessibility and personal competence (e.g. willingness to help users)
- *personal control* – the extent to which users are able to navigate and control the information universe that is provided (e.g. website enabling them to locate information on their own)
- *access to information* – an assessment of the adequacy of the collections themselves and the ability to access needed information on a timely basis regardless of the location of the user or the medium of the resource in question (e.g. comprehensiveness of collections and convenience of business hours)
- *library as place* – comprising variously, according to the perspective of the user, utilitarian space for study and collaboration, a sanctuary for contemplation and

reflection or an affirmation of the primacy of the life of the mind in university priorities.

There are numerous other reports of the development of instruments that embed dimensions or factors that are expected to affect the perceived quality of library and information services. For example, Majid, Anwar and Eisenschitz (2001) identify the following factors for agricultural scientists: the provision of current literature; the adequacy of the library collections; the involvement of the respondents in selecting material for the library; the adequacy of library equipment; the adequacy of the physical facilities in the library; library skills of the users; frequency of library visits; the location of the library; the adequacy of the library promotion; the availability of needed materials; and availability of library assistance. Snoj and Petermanec (2001) identify five categories of factors that affect perceptions of the quality of library service in the context of Slovenian academic libraries: the physical surroundings and ambience of the library; its equipment and information technology; the library collection; the information and library services; and the library staff.

Questions that collect data on customer views of information services may also feature in more general surveys. For example, the Student Satisfaction surveys conducted by many UK higher education institutions often include questions on access to learning resources, because this is viewed as one of the key aspects of the student learning experience.

The LibQUAL instrument has worked towards the incorporation of measures appropriate for measuring the performance of digital libraries (Heath et al., 2003). Work on e-service quality (Zeithaml, Parasuraman and Malhotra, 2000) from the e-commerce perspective also has relevance. In the digital library context this has led to considerable discussion of the nature of the e-service experience and relevant quality or performance metrics, as discussed in the section on performance measurement. Choudhury et al. (2002) report on work towards the development of a framework for evaluating digital library services. One of the real challenges in this process is to integrate concerns of website usability into measures of service quality, without allowing these to dominate (Morse, 2002) over other concerns. The other challenge is to develop tools that adequately reflect the service quality of a service delivered through multiple channels, including face-to-face, internet, telephone and post/mail.

Finally one of the aspects of digital and traditional library service is that there is an element of self-service. The more experienced the user, the better the service that they will experience when they search a library or other website.

How can this dependence on learning be factored into assessments of the service experience?

Reflection: *Explain what you understand to be the self-service elements in the delivery of library and information services.*

Listening to users

Research and practice on service quality measurement as described above privileges the quantitative approach and offers considerable insights into the design of questionnaires, together with some generic perspectives on the factors that affect customer evaluations of quality. These processes yield useful profiles but they are limited in their ability to lend qualitative insights into customer experience and response to services and to suggest future innovation. Talking and listening to users are also important. Information organization staff may meet with users in a variety of different forums and contexts. Some approaches are used to investigate response or gauge support for specific projects or initiatives or to resolve issues, whereas others may be part of the routine quality management processes of the information service and its parent organization. They can be used to respond promptly to specific concerns as and when they arise, but also need to monitor and profile user satisfaction over the longer term, in order to develop an awareness of achievements and failures. Typically information services listen to customers through:

* An *annual user satisfaction survey*, designed to give all users the opportunity to express their opinions. This survey is often questionnaire based, and may take into account many of the questionnaire design issues touched on in the previous section. The questionnaire may be delivered by post, personally administered, or delivered over the internet.
* *Questionnaires* can also be used at other times to gauge reaction to a specific service, such as a new service for distance learners. Questionnaires can either be used to conduct a wider survey than might be possible with other methods, or to collect subjective data such as user attitudes that customers might not be prepared to discuss in a person-to-person situation. If users are scattered and it is impossible to conduct interviews, a questionnaire may elicit a quick response from a large number of people. Questionnaires may also be used to identify 'key' individuals, so that interviews can be focused on these individuals. Questionnaires provide quantitative data. This means that analysis

is likely to involve at least some basic statistical processing. The nature of these analyses must be determined at the questionnaire design stage, and not after the data has been collected.

- *Liaison staff* – In academic libraries, liaison staff have responsibility for providing an active link between the library and specific academic departments. In addition to providing service and advice, which may elicit informal feedback, the liaison librarian will also probably be a member of course committees, in which issues of concern to staff and students will be raised.
- *Suggestion schemes*, either boxes, or electronic channels, which allow users to make suggestions regarding improvements in service.
- *Complaints schemes* and processes, designed primarily so that users can express their complaints and these complaints can then be dealt with, thus promoting a dialogue between the user and the service. Analysis of complaints received also supports the identification of specific issues, and may provide indications of directions for improvement.
- *Individual interviews* – The two-way communication that is a feature of interviews should provide a more multi-dimensional analysis of the situation, yielding qualitative data concerning not only what a user does but also why they do it. Interviews can be conducted in person, over the telephone, or through an e-mail dialogue. Interviews can be structured to a greater or lesser extent, depending upon whether the priority lies with comparing data, or discovering the unknown.
- *Focus groups* provide an arena for group discussion in which group members exchange attitudes, experiences and beliefs. The advantages of focus groups are:
  — respondents experience a sense of safety in numbers and therefore greater willingness to express insights and greater spontaneity
  — the process highlights the possible range of different attitudes and behaviours in a relatively short time
  — the group can be observed with the aim of yielding data on reactions, vocabulary and perceptions
  — group discussion triggers counter responses, which might not surface in individual discussion.
- *Online focus groups* often follow a bulletin board or discussion group form where different members of the focus group respond to prompts from the focus group leaders. Such groups eliminate the need to bring customers together.

- *Informal communication and observation* can be a feature of day-to-day interactions with users. LIS staff can learn a lot about user habits and activities by watching or discussing issues as they arise. Observation may, for example, be useful in the evaluation of a new OPAC interface. Cognitive information such as attitudes, beliefs and motivation or perceptions cannot be observed. One way of gathering this information is active observation, where the subject is asked about their actions after the observation episode.
- *Weblogs* – Transaction logs that reveal the search strategies and use of digital documents are a further means of observing user behaviour in digital environments. There has been considerable work conducted to establish the most appropriate statistical measures and how to generate meaningful information from such data. Like all observation such statistics are limited in that they only monitor activity and do not provide any insights into the underlying factors influencing behaviour, or how users might behave in the future.

Reflection: *Make a table to compare the relative strengths and weaknesses of individual interviews and focus groups as means of collecting data on customer satisfaction.*

Total quality management (TQM) and the European Foundation for Quality Management

Total quality management is a philosophy that had its origins in Japanese management, and has been widely developed and adopted across organizations. Its central tenet is that the entire organization should be managed to achieve excellence in all dimensions of products and services which are important to the customers. Excellence in a TQM organization is defined by customer requirements and needs (Rowley, 1998).

Library and information services managers have long recognized the need for the customer orientation that is inherent in the TQM philosophy and some have sought to implement TQM or have been involved with TQM initiatives elsewhere. In addition, customer care and other customer-focused programmes have been used in training those library staff who are in direct contact with the public.

The main elements of TQM are:

- *Quality is customer defined* – Quality is defined in terms of customers' perceptions and expectations. Such customer focus requires not only an attention to internal processes, but also an awareness of the external marketplace, and achievement of a match between the two.

- *Internal and external customers* – The only way to ensure that customer orientation permeates the organization, including those not in direct contact with the external customer, is to encourage each employee to identify those to whom they provide a service and to view those people as their internal customers.
- *Employee involvement* – Everyone must understand that they contribute equally to quality and can only succeed through co-operation and support. In order for this to be achieved the organization needs a culture which encourages this behaviour.
- *Error-free processes* – The focus of TQM is on prevention to eliminate waste, reduce costs and achieve error-free processes. The traditional approach to TQM in a manufacturing environment involved a strong focus on process quality control. Service managers also need to focus on service processes.
- *Performance measurement* – Performance measurement needs to be based upon timely measures of, and feedback on, performance through superior quality information systems.
- *Continuous improvement* – Continuous improvement must be seen as the responsibility of everyone in the organization. This is developed through training, education, communication, recognition of achievements and teamwork.

TQM can have a significant impact on an organization. Effective TQM is dependent upon senior management commitment and may lead to changes in structure, culture, teamworking and management and leadership style. Implementing TQM requires:

- *Establishing quality as a strategic issue* – This implies acceptance of the importance of customer requirements throughout the organization, the identification of continuous improvement as a key organizational objective and the introduction of meaningful performance indicators. Top management commitment is vital.
- *Organizational structure* – Organic structures are much more likely to foster the central elements of TQM in respect of responsiveness to customer requirements, participative and creative problem solving and team ethos. This implies structures that make effective use of project teams, taskforces and the matrix approach to management (where staff and managers are accountable to more than one manager or team).

- *Organizational culture* – Success with TQM requires a culture that actively promotes response to customer requirements, continuous improvement, creative problem solving, strong team ethos and a people-centred approach to management.
- *Agreed definitions and measures of quality* – Teams, departments and individuals need to be assisted in identifying definitions and measures that are appropriate in their context. This includes developing an understanding of 'who our customers are' for each team, and the most appropriate approaches to data collection for the measurement of quality.

The *European Foundation for Quality Management* (EFQM) provides a widely accepted general framework for quality management. Founded in 1988 and building on the principles of TQM, the EFQM sought to develop a European framework for quality management, to enable businesses to make better products and to improve services through the effective use of leading edge management practices. Specifically, process improvements were designed to make organizations become more efficient and effective, to secure competitive advantage and to gain long-term success. The EFQM was designed as a European framework for quality improvement to parallel the Malcolm Baldridge Model in the USA and the Deming Prize in Japan. The EFQM currently has over 700 member organizations in over 50 countries.

The EFQM Business Excellence Model is used to assist organizations in self-assessment and as the basis for judging entrants to the European Quality Award. All UK government departments are required to use the model to improve their businesses. Within the UK the model is promoted, and organizations are assessed on their performance in terms of the model, by the British Quality Foundation.

The model is based on the nine criteria for excellence shown in Figure 6.2. The five 'Enabler' criteria relate to what the organization does, and *how* it runs. The four 'Results' criteria relate to *what* the organization is actually achieving in the eyes of its stakeholders (i.e. customers, employees, the community and funders). Enablers lead to the Results, or, in other words, excellence in terms of performance, customers, people and society is achieved through leadership, policy and strategy, people, partnerships and resources, and processes. Innovation and learning drive and improve the Enablers to produce improved Results.

Enabler criteria

1. *Leadership* – Leaders develop and facilitate the achievement of the mission and vision. They develop the organizational values and systems required for sustainable success and implement these via their actions and behaviours. They identify and champion organizational change.

2. *Policy and strategy* – Is based on the present and future needs and expectations of stakeholders, information from performance measurement, research and learning. Policies, plans, objectives and processes are developed and deployed to deliver the strategy. Strategy and policy are developed, reviewed and updated.

3. *People* – People are involved and empowered, rewarded, recognized and cared for. People resources are planned, managed and improved, with people's knowledge and competencies being identified, developed and sustained.

4. *Partnerships and resources* – External partnerships, finance, buildings, equipment and materials are all managed.

5. *Processes* – Processes are designed, managed and improved in order to fully satisfy, and generate increasing value for, customers and other stakeholders.

Results criteria

6. *Customer Results* – Organizations use perception and performance measures with respect to customers.

7. *People Results* – Organizations use perception and performance measures with respect to their people.

8. *Society Results* – Organizations use perception and performance measures with respect to society.

9. *Key performance results* – Organizations use perception and performance measures with respect to key elements of their policy and strategy.

Figure 6.2 Characteristics of EFQM award winners

Benchmarking

Benchmarking can be described as: 'improving ourselves by learning from others' (www.benchmarking.gov.uk). Benchmarking both sets standards for the organization to aspire to and also provides insights into the processes that need to be enacted in order to achieve those standards. Standards may be derived from comparison with other organizations or from comparison with some nationally set standards, such as those emerging from the various benchmarking activities discussed below or from national collections of standards such as the LISU annual library statistics (Creaser, Maynard and White, 2003), and other reports available at www.lboro.ac.uk/departments/dils/lisu.

In practice benchmarking usually involves:

- regularly comparing performance (including function and processes) with standards or best practitioners
- identifying gaps where performance falls seriously below standards and comparators
- seeking out different approaches that can achieve improvements in performance
- implementing improvements
- monitoring progress with improvements and reviewing the benefits.

Benchmarking has been widely promoted within the public sector in recent years in pursuit of improvements in the cost of quality of service. In this arena, benchmarking has been used to:

- establish nationally recognized benchmarks of good practice that can be used to assess the performance of managers and the overall effectiveness of their organizations
- encourage the sharing of good practice and the adoption of best practice in pursuit of excellence.

Benchmarking is promoted as an approach that can achieve quantum leaps in performance. Benchmarking provides:

- an effective 'wake-up' call and supports the case for change
- insights into and models for ways in which step changes in performance can be achieved through learning from others who have already undergone comparable changes
- the impetus for seeking innovations and a drive towards a culture that is receptive to, and welcoming of, new approaches and ideas
- opportunities for staff to be fully involved in any transformation process
- opportunities to share knowledge and learning, and in general to increase collaboration and understanding between organizations.

There are a number of different types of benchmarking that can be used to meet a range of requirements for improvement. The Public Sector Benchmarking Service (UK) describes the following types of benchmarking:

- *Strategic benchmarking* is used when organizations are seeking to improve their overall performance. It involves the study of the long-term strategies and general approaches that have enabled high performers to succeed, and is likely to focus on core competencies, innovation, change capabilities and market competence.
- *Performance benchmarking* or competitive benchmarking involves organizations in examining the performance characteristics of their key products and services. Benchmarking partners are drawn from the same sector.
- *Process benchmarking* focuses on improvements in specific critical processes and operations. Benchmarking partners are drawn from best practice organizations that perform similar work or deliver similar services. Process maps are used to

facilitate comparison and analysis of processes. Such benchmarking offers short-term improvements.

- *Functional benchmarking* or generic benchmarking is used when organizations benchmark with partners from different business sectors or areas of activity to find ways of improving similar functions or work processes. This may lead to radically different ways of working and innovation.
- *Internal benchmarking* involves benchmarking with partners, such as other business units within the same organization. Such processes are often implicit in the change processes associated with re-structuring, but can also be adopted at other times. Internal benchmarking may avoid confidentiality issues, may operate within standardized systems, data and cultures, and may require less time and resources, but outcomes are less likely to be radical than with external benchmarking.
- *External benchmarking* involves benchmarking with outside organizations that are known to adopt best practice.
- *International benchmarking* is used where partners are drawn from other countries, because best practice is seen to be located in organizations outside of the home country.

Wang, Wu and Wu (2000) describe an interesting functional benchmarking process in which they visited shopping centres and banks, to inform the implementation of a quality service strategy for Shanghai Library, China.

The *Public Sector Benchmarking Service* (PSBS) is a UK government body whose role is to promote effective benchmarking and sharing of good practices across the public sector. The Service provides a range of information, advice and guidance on benchmarking and good practice to UK organizations who wish to deliver better public services. Membership of the PSBS offers access to their good practice database, The Knowledge Bank, and a notice board, news groups and discussion forums for member interaction and sharing. There is also a help-desk, a newsletter and guidance books and leaflets.

Service First Quality Networks are informal benchmarking schemes, supported and co-ordinated by the UK Cabinet Office. They are run by groups from all areas and levels of public service, with the objective of sharing information on best practice, comparing progress in areas of common interest, building partnerships between public service organizations and encouraging problem sharing and solving. The Networks are largely self-financing, but the Cabinet Office plays a strategic planning and co-ordinating role, and trains Network leaders.

The *Beacon Council* scheme was developed by the UK government to help local authorities to learn from those other authorities that have developed centres of excellence and quality service. Each year the UK government chooses a theme for the Beacon scheme and authorities are invited to apply for Beacon status on the basis of their practice related to the scheme. Only three or four Beacon Councils are selected each year and these Councils have to plan and deliver a programme of dissemination activities during the year that will promote the sharing of learning.

Performance measures and measurement

Benchmarking and other approaches to quality management rely on performance measures. In benchmarking, these performance measures can set standards and act as the basis for comparisons between services. The statistics or data upon which performance measures are based are often collected as part of a study. For example, Ruthven and Magnay (2002) report a benchmarking study of 100 Australian libraries in the context of interlending operations. Data was collected on the four characteristics of interlending: turnaround time, fill rates, unit costs and patron satisfaction. Summary statistics from this data can be used to benchmark the performance of individual library interlending services. The LibQUAL instrument described above is used by member libraries of the Association of Research Libraries (US). Analysis of the data not only generates user satisfaction measures for individual libraries, across the dimensions covered by the survey, but also generates comparative data that can be used in the benchmarking process. The work conducted by the Innovatie Wetenschappelijke Informatievoorziening (IWI) consortium which manages a benchmarking project for university libraries in the Netherlands, further illustrates that performance measurement is part of a wider quality framework. This project designed a set of performance indicators that libraries could use to measure their service, to develop policy instruments and to periodically compare performance of the libraries using these indicators. The indicators are founded on a quality model that was used as a framework for the project. Performance indicators were derived for library resources, library facilities, process efficiency and library use. The project also supports libraries in the collection of data and the use of the benchmarking process in practice (Laeven and Smit, 2003).

Performance measurement involves a number of stages:

1 Selecting appropriate performance measures that align with the objectives of the organization. In the evaluation of the interlending service cited above, the measures were turnaround time, fill rate, unit costs and patron satisfaction.
2 Establishing challenging but attainable targets in respect of each of the

measures. For example, for the measure turnaround time in interlending, an average time of three days might be selected as a target.

3 Examining the factors and processes that can be changed to enhance performance.

4 Putting strategies in place to effect the enhancement.

5 Establishing record-keeping/data-gathering and analysis systems so that performance against measures can be monitored.

6 At intervals, and preferably through some consultative or committee process, examining the match between actual performance and targets.

7 Adjusting targets on the basis of performance and other changes in the environment.

8 From time to time reviewing the performance measures in order to ensure that they continue to align with organizational objectives.

Much of the theoretical and modelling building discussion in the context of performance measurement is concerned with the selection of appropriate performance measures. A good general purpose model is the Balanced Scorecard of Organizational Goals (Kaplan and Norton, 1996; Table 6.1). The Balanced Scorecard embeds a number of key themes for quality management:

Table 6.1 The Balanced Scorecard of Organizational Goals (adapted from Kaplan and Norton, 1996)

Goals	Measures
Financial perspective	
Survive	Cash flow
Succeed	Quarterly profits
Prosper	Return on investment
Recognition	Share price
Process perspective	
Technological	Competitive benchmarking
Manufacturing excellence	Productivity
Time to market	Benchmarking
Quality	Total quality
Customer perspective	
Satisfaction	Customer surveys
Responsiveness	On-time deliveries
Loyalty	Repurchases
Market share	Share growth
Internal perspective	
Employees	Satisfaction surveys
Internal growth	Sales growth
Innovation	Number of new products
Development	Training days

- Performance measures must be linked to organizational goals or objectives.
- Performance measures that are designed to support the evaluation of the strategic development of an organization can be divided into four quadrants, relating to the financial, process, customer and internal perspectives, respectively.
- Performance measures can be quantitative, such as average response time to requests, or qualitative, such as comparison of level of innovation between two libraries, derived from a benchmarking process.

Performance measures need to be relevant indicators of the performance of the information service and therefore the most appropriate measures are dependent on the mission and objectives of the service. These measures may relate to the overall performance of the service, such as the standards and measures proposed by the UK Department for Culture, Media and Sport for public libraries (DCMS, 2001; see Figure 6.3), or to other aspects of the service. Table 6.2 is a selection of a few assorted standards that information services may take into account in designing and judging aspects of service quality and performance. It illustrates the range of different standards that are potentially relevant, and the range of different organizations who are engaged in the drafting of such standards.

• Library authorities must enable convenient and suitable access for users of libraries.	• Library authorities must encourage the use made of the public library service.
• Library authorities must provide adequate opening hours of libraries for users.	• Library authorities must ensure user satisfaction with the service provided.
• Library authorities must enable electronic access for library users.	• Library authorities must provide choice in books and materials made available to users.
• Library authorities must ensure satisfactory services for the issuing and reserving of books.	• Library authorities must provide appropriate levels of qualified staff.

Figure 6.3 DCMS framework for standards for public libraries (from DCMS, 2001)

E-metrics

As libraries change, so their relevant performance measures change. In the digital environment, libraries have been concerned to develop additional measures that support the evaluation of the performance of digital library environments and the related issue of service for distance learners (Gadd, 2002). There are a number of projects working on performance indicators for digital library environments, otherwise known as e-metrics. The US Association of Research Libraries (ARL) has developed a set of metrics which include accessible electronic resources (books and journals), expenditures for networked resources, use of networked resources and services, and library digitization activities (www.arl.org/stats/newmeas/emetric/index.html). Young (2001) proposes a model for electronic

Table 6.2   Assorted standards for information services (selected from Weeks and Mason, 2003)

Standard	Responsible organization	Topic
Guidelines for secondary school libraries	CILIP	Management of secondary school libraries
Guidelines for UK Government websites	Office of the e-Envoy	Usable and accessible website design
Matrix Quality Standard	The Employment NTO	Essential features of successful delivery of information, advice and guidance services
Web Content Accessibility Guidelines	World Wide Web Consortium	Making web content accessible to those with disabilities
Assorted guidelines	Council of Europe	Information policy and legislation in Europe
Guidelines for digitization projects for collections and holdings in the public domain	International Federation of Library Associations and Institutions	Conceptualization, planning and implementation of a digitalization project
The Disability portfolio	Resource	Inclusive service and practices

service measurement that includes measures of network technology infrastructure, information resources content, extensiveness and efficiency.

There remain some key questions concerning the selection and application of e-metrics to which there are no easy answers:

- What is the purpose of e-metrics, and therefore what data should be collected?
- What measures and measurement processes are appropriate for the measurement of electronic service access, digital collections, access to remote collections, costs, support requirements and access, and web usage?
- How can publishers of electronic journals and books and libraries work together in the generation and usage of performance statistics?
- What is the relationship between usage statistics and performance indicators?
- How can digital library performance indicators be used alongside traditional library usage and customer satisfaction data in blended environments?

Impact assessment

There is some concern that performance measurement has focused on efficiency rather than effectiveness. Performance indicators can be too focused on input, such as workstation to user ratio, or opening hours, rather than output. This has recently provoked a renewed interest in *service impact* and impact assessment (Markless and Streatfield, 2004). Impact assessment takes a wider perspective and examines the contribution that the library is making to organizational or societal 'success'. For example, academic libraries need to consider how they might measure their impact on learning, school libraries might seek to understand their role in promoting literacy, health information services would seek to understand their role in evidence-based practice, health education, and patient treatment and recovery, and public libraries would benefit from measures relating to social inclusion, learning and digital citizenship. The recent DCMS initiative *Inspiring Learning for All* (MLA, n.d.) is designed to stimulate practitioners working in museums, archives and libraries to focus on and improve the impact that they have in supporting learning (see Figure 6.4).

PEOPLE – *Providing more effective learning opportunities*	**PLACES – *Creating inspiring and accessible learning environments***
As a museum, archive or library, you:	As a museum, archive or library, you:
1.1 Engage and consult with a broad range of people to develop learning opportunities	2.1 Create environments that are conducive to learning
1.2 Provide opportunities for people to engage in learning	2.2 Develop your staff to provide support for learners
1.3 Broaden the range of learning opportunities to engage with new and diverse users	2.3 Promote the museum, archive or library as a centre for learning, inspiration and enjoyment.
1.4 Stimulate discovery and research	
1.5 Evaluate the outcomes of services, programmes and activities.	
PARTNERSHIPS – *Building creative learning partnerships*	**POLICIES, PLANS, PERFORMANCE – *Placing learning at the heart of the MAL***
As a museum, archive or library, you:	As a museum, archive or library, you:
3.1 Identify potential partners and the benefits of working in partnership to support learning	4.1 Identify and seek to influence local, regional and national initiatives relating to learning
3.2 Work with suitable partners to plan and develop learning opportunities	4.2 Respond to local, regional and national initiatives in your plans and priorities
3.3 Invite contributions from outside the organization to broaden its appeal, bring new perspectives and extend learning opportunities.	4.3 Demonstrate that your museum, archive or library is a learning organization through your staff development and evaluation processes.

Figure 6.4 Thinking about impact: elements of *Inspiring Learning for All* (adapted from MLA, n.d.)
Reproduced with permission of the Museums, Libraries and Archives Council (MLA).

Often, however, it is difficult to measure impact. For example, to measure the impact of a university library in student learning, it is necessary to be able to identify appropriate measures of student library use, and then to measure study outcomes and student achievement and look for correlations between these two.

   The alternative to the pursuit of quantitative measures of impact is to embed evaluation of performance of information services in the quality assurance and management processes of their parent organization. For example, academic libraries in England are currently participants in the UK Quality Assurance

Agency's Institutional Audit processes, and can for example:

- Ensure that university documentation covers the experience of students as learner including access to learning facilities. This may include how the service contributes to shaping the student learning environment, liaison with academic departments, service evaluation and contribution to institutional quality assurance processes.
- Support disciplines selected for an audit trail, by helping the department to articulate their strategy for building up appropriate collections and facilities, services, support and course input.
- Ensure that any recent evaluations/surveys are published and available.
- Ensure that the IS has an established policy for collaboration with other organizations and for the support of the learning and teaching of remotely located students.

Other quality accreditation schemes
Charter Mark

The *Charter Mark* (www.chartermark.gov.uk) is a scheme implemented by the UK Cabinet Office to promote improvement and modernization in service delivery in the public sector. The Charter Mark is a results-based scheme in that its criteria focus on the service that the customer receives. The Charter Mark criteria are used in organizational self-assessment, to help organizations to identify both their strengths and any areas for improvement. Organizations seeking the award of the Charter Mark need to undertake an assessment process, through which they generate evidence that they meet the scheme's criteria. This evidence and the written submission is then triangulated by an assessor who will visit the organization, discuss the application and collect further evidence of the organization's performance against the criteria, in order to complete the assessment as to whether the organization has met the standard.

The Charter Mark criteria, which were revised for 2003, are summarized in Figure 6.5.

Charter Mark also maintains a database of good practice examples as part of the Public Sector Benchmarking Service.

1. *Set standards and perform well* – Organizations must show that they set clear service and performance standards, with customer consultation, meet those standards, monitor and review performance against standards, and publish the results, all with as little paperwork and administration as possible.
2. *Actively engage with our customers, partners and staff* – Organizations must show that they work actively with, and consult and involve customers, partners and staff in pursuit of quality, are open and communicate clearly, providing full information about services, costs and performance.
3. *Be fair and accessible to everyone and promote choice* – Organizations must show that they make services easily available to everyone who needs them, offering choice where possible, and treating everybody fairly in relation to service access.
4. *Continuously develop and improve* – Organizations must show that they are always looking to improve services and facilities, put things right quickly and effectively, and learn from a complaints procedure, compliments and suggestions.
5. *Use resources effectively and imaginatively* – Organizations need to show that their financial management is effective and that resources are used to provide best value for taxpayers and customers.
6. *Continue to improve opportunities and quality of life in the communities served* – Organizations need to show that they have reviewed their impact and potential usefulness in the local and national communities that they serve and have made some contribution to enriching the social or economic life of those communities.

Figure 6.5 The Charter Mark criteria

Investors in People

Investors in People (IiP) (www.iip.co.uk) is a national quality standard which sets a level of good practice for improving an organization's performance through its people. The standard provides a national framework for improving business performance and competitiveness through a planned approach to setting and communicating business objectives and developing people to meet these objectives. First developed in 1991 by the UK Department of Trade and Industry, the IiP is now used in many countries.

IiP is cyclical and is designed to engender a culture of continuous improvement. The IiP standard is based on four key principles:

- *commitment* to invest in people to achieve business goals
- *planning* how skills, individuals and teams are to be developed to achieve these goals
- taking *action* to develop and use necessary skills in a well-defined and continuing programme directly tied to business objectives.
- *evaluating* outcomes of training and development for individual progress towards goals, the value achieved and future needs.

These principles are translated into 12 indicators (Figure 6.6), which, like the indicators in the Charter Mark and the EFQM, can be used for self-assessment, as a basis for planning change, and as an element in the external assessment and

1. The organization is committed to supporting the development of its people.	7. People understand how they contribute to achieving the organization's aims and objectives.
2. People are encouraged to improve their own and other people's performance.	8. Managers are effective in supporting the development of people.
3. People believe their contribution to the organization is recognized.	9. People learn and develop effectively.
4. The organization is committed to ensuring equality of opportunity in the development of its people.	10. The development of people improves the performance of the organization, teams and individuals.
5. The organization has a plan with clear aims and objectives that are understood by everyone.	11. People understand the impact of the development of people on the performance of the organization, teams and individuals.
6. The development of people is in line with the organization's aims and objectives.	12. The organization gets better at developing its people.

Figure 6.6 The IiP criteria

accreditation process that leads to recognition as an Investor in People.

It is suggested that benefits for employees include increased motivation, commitment, loyalty, confidence, job satisfaction and career prospects. Organizational benefits include improved productivity, enhanced quality, reduced absenteeism and staff turnover, flexibility and response to change. Having Investor in People status raises an organization's profile in the eyes of current and potential employees, partner organizations and customers.

Reflection: Compare and contrast the criteria for Charter Mark and IiP. Would it be realistic for an organization to be able to use the same evidence in support of their case for meeting both sets of criteria?

Summary and conclusions

Quality management embraces quality assurance and quality enhancement. Quality management needs to operate at all levels of the organization, involving staff and engendering commitment while at the same time responding to the agendas of other stakeholders, such as public sector funding bodies. Quality is defined in terms of user perceptions of fitness for purpose. The work on service quality and its measurement, through the development of instruments such as SERVQUAL and LibQUAL, offers some important perspectives on and approaches to the issue of customer satisfaction. However, information organizations also need to use other methods to listen to and learn from their customers. Total quality management as a philosophy lays down some important parameters about the nature of quality enhancement processes. The European Foundation for Quality Management award scheme has embedded and developed these principles. Benchmarking is a process whereby organizations learn from each other and thereby develop towards excellence in their practice. The Public Sector Benchmarking Service (UK) defines different types of benchmarking and provides support and advice on benchmarking processes. Performance measurement focuses on the definition and application of appropriate performance measures or indicators; these are a necessary element in the formulation of performance targets, which can challenge teams toward quality enhancement. Other quality accreditation schemes include IiP and Charter Mark.

Quality management is a complex process. Library and information managers and their staff must seek to balance the tension between processes, measures and activities that promote quality enhancement at the same time as responding to expectations, targets and systems defined by external stakeholders, some of whom have the ultimate power of the funding body. In addition developing agendas associated with quality management in digital libraries and information services, and the quest for demonstrating impact, provide a further level of challenge.

REVIEW QUESTIONS

1 What do you understand by the term quality? How do different definitions of quality impact on notions of quality assurance, quality enhancement and quality management?

2 Compare and contrast the dimensions of service quality proposed by the two instruments SERVQUAL and LibQUAL. What does this comparison say about the nature of LIS as services?

3 What are the different approaches that an IS might use to collect data from its customers in relation to their opinions of the quality of the service that they have experienced?

4 What do you understand by total quality management (TQM)? How are the principles of TQM embedded in the characteristics of award winners of the European Foundation for Quality Management?

5 Discuss the concept of benchmarking. How can benchmarking be employed by an IS?

6 Explain the concepts of performance indicators and performance measurement, with specific reference to their role in quality management.

7 Compare and contrast the criteria for Charter Mark and IiP. How do the differences between these criteria demonstrate the differences in the emphases of these two accreditation schemes?

8 Discuss some of the quality assessment processes that apply to a library in a specific sector.

CASE STUDY
Customer satisfaction surveys

1. **Which is your mode of study?**
   Full time/Part time/Distance

2. **Which is your current year of study?**
   1/2/3/4/Other

3. **Did you have an introductory tour of the library?**
   Yes/No

4. **Have you had at least one timetabled session about information searching (e.g. using databases such as Web of Science)?**
   Yes/No

5. **If your answer to question 4 was YES, how satisfied were you with the information searching sessions?**
   • Very satisfied
   • Fairly satisfied
   • Neither satisfied nor dissatisfied
   • Fairly dissatisfied
   • Very dissatisfied
   • Can't remember

6. **On average, how often do you visit the library?**
   • Every day
   • At least 3 times per week
   • At least once per week
   • About once per fortnight
   • About once per month
   • Less than once per month
   • Never

7. **Thinking about your most recent visit to the library, WHAT did you use the library for?**
   • Study or research
   • Return or borrow short loan
   • Return or borrow other items
   • Photocopying
   • E-mail
   • Use online library resource
   • Consult a member of library staff

Figure 6.7 Extract from a library customer satisfaction survey (after University of Wales, Bangor Library Service Survey 2004)

Examine each of the questions in Figure 6.7 in turn, and answer the following:

1 Is this an open or closed question? For closed questions, are these reasonable options to offer?
2 What does the library hope to learn from this question? How might the answers to this question help the library to improve services from the user's perspective?
3 How do you think that the opportunity to complete this questionnaire online might affect the responses collected?

CHALLENGES

1 How can an information service manager prioritize and integrate their responses to different quality accreditation schemes such as IiP, Charter Mark, and sectoral

schemes such as the QAA.

2 How can an information organization minimize the amount of evidence or records that it maintains, but still ensure compliance with the requirements of any external agencies with which it is required, or chooses, to engage?

3 Does evidence gathering and record keeping get in the way of quality enhancement – after all there are only so many hours in the working day?

4 How can organizations cultivate a positive teamworking and sharing culture, when knowledge and information lend individuals power?

5 How can library and information managers deliver a quality service through online channels, when the quality of that service is dependent upon partnerships with database providers, online service suppliers, publishers and others?

6 Does accreditation under, for example, IiP have a sufficient impact on external and internal stakeholders' perceptions to make it worth the work and resources input? How could this be evaluated?

References and additional reading

Bainton, T. (1998) SCONUL and Research Libraries, *Library Review*, **47** (5/6), 267–71.

Brophy, P. (2001) Assessing the Performance of Electronic Library Services: the EQUINOX project, *The New Review of Academic Librarianship*, **7**, 3–18.

Brophy, P. (2002) Performance Measures for 21st Century Libraries. In Stein, J., Kyrillidou, M. and Davis, D. (eds), *Proceedings of the 4th Northumbria International Conference on Performance Measurement in Libraries and Information Services, Pittsburgh, USA, 12–16 August 2001*, Washington, Association of Research Libraries, 1–8.

Brophy, P. (2003) Marketing and Quality: using dimensional analysis to achieve success. In Gupta, D. K. and Jambhektar, A. (eds), *An Integrated Approach to Services Marketing: a book of readings on marketing of library and information services*, , Mumbai, India, Allied Publishers Private, 84–91.

Brophy, P. and Couling, K. (1996) *Quality Management for Information and Library Managers*, London, Aslib/Gower.

Cabinet Office, www.servicefirst.gov.uk.

Cabinet Office, www.goodpractice.org.uk.

Chivers, B. and Thebridge, S. (2000) Best Value in Public Libraries: the role of research, *Library Management*, **21** (9), 454–64.

Choudhury, G. S., Hobbs, B., Lorie, M. and Flores, N. E. (2002) A Framework for Evaluating Digital Library Services, *D-Lib Magazine*, **8** (7/8), www.dlib.org/ dlib/july02/choudhury/07choudhury.html.

Cook, C., Heath, F., Thompson, B. and Webster, D. (2002) LibQual+™: preliminary results from 2002, *Performance Measurement and Metrics*, **4** (1), 38–47.

Cook, C. and Heath, F. (2001) User's Perceptions of Library Service Quality: a LibQUAL+™ qualitative study, *Library Trends*, **49** (4), 548–84.

Creaser, C. (2003) *Statistics in Practice – measuring and managing,* LISU Occasional Paper 32, Loughborough, LISU.

Creaser, C., Maynard, S. and White, S. (2003) *LISU Annual Library Statistics*, Loughborough, Library and Information Statistics Unit (LISU).

Department for Culture, Media and Sport (2001) *Comprehensive, Efficient and Modern Public Libraries – standards and assessment*, London, DCMS.

Gadd, E. (2002) Meeting the Library Needs of Distance Learners without Additional Funding, *Library Management*, **23** (8/9), 359–69.

Hart, L. (2001) Comparing Ourselves: using benchmarking techniques to measure performance among academic libraries: report of the LIRG seminar, the effective academic library held in June 2001, *Library and Information Research News*, **25** (80), 23–34.

Heath, F., Kyrillidou, M., Webster, D., Choudhury, S., Hobbs, B., Lorie, M. and Flores, N. (2003) Emerging Tools for Evaluating Digital Library Services: conceptual adaptations of LibQUAL+ and CAPM, *Journal of Digital Information*, **4** (2), www.libqual.org/publications.

Kaplan, R. S. and Norton, D. P. (1996) *The Balanced Scorecard: translating energy into action*, Boston, MA, Harvard Business School Press.

Laeven, H. and Smit, A. (2003) A Project to Benchmark University Libraries in the Netherlands, *Library Management*, **24** (6/7), 291–305.

LibQUAL+ ™, www.libqual.org.

Lilley, E. and Usherwood, B. (2000) Wanting It All: the relationship between expectations and the public's perceptions of public library services, *Library Management*, **21** (1), 13–25.

McNaught, B. and Fleming, M. (2002) Assuring Quality. In Melling, M. and Little, J. (eds), *Building a Successful Customer-service Culture: a guide for library and information management*, London, Facet Publishing, 116–42.

Majid, S., Anwar, M. A. and Eisenschitz, T. S. (2001) User Perceptions of Library Effectiveness in Malaysian Agricultural Libraries, *Library Review*, **50** (4), 176–87.

Markless, S. and Streatfield, D. (2004) *Evaluating the Impact of Your Library*, London, Facet Publishing.

Morse, E. L. (2002) Evaluation Methodologies for Information Management Systems, *D-Lib Magazine,* **8** (9), www.dlib.org/dlib/september02/morse/09morse.html.

Museums, Libraries and Archives Council (n.d.) *Inspiring Learning for All*, London, MLA, www.inspiringlearningforall.gov.uk.

Parasuraman, A., Zeithaml, V. A. and Berry, L. L. (1988) SERVQUAL: a multiple-item scale for measuring customer perceptions of service quality, *Journal of Retailing*, **64**, 12–40.

Perrow, D. (2001) Supporting Off-campus Learning and Ensuring Service Quality, SCONUL Autumn Conference, 20 November 2001, The British Library Conference Centre, *SCONUL Newsletter*, **24**, 63–70.

Public Sector Benchmarking Service, www.benchmarking.gov.uk.

Rowley, J. E. (1995) A New Lecturer's Simple Guide to Quality Issues in Higher Education, *International Journal of Education Management*, **9** (1), 22–5.

Rowley, J. (1996) Implementing TQM for Library Services, *Aslib Proceedings*, **48** (11), 17–21.

Rowley, J. (1998) Quality Measurement in the Public Sector: some perspectives from the service quality literature, *Total Quality Management*, **9** (2/3), 347–59.

Ruthven, T. and Magnay, S. (2002) Top Performing Interlending Operations: results of the Australian benchmarking study, *Interlending & Document Supply*, **30** (2), 73–80.

Shaughnessy, T. W. (1996) Perspective on Quality in Libraries – special issue, *Library Trends*, **44** (3).

Snoj, B. and Petermanec, Z. (2001) Let Users Judge the Quality of Faculty Library Services, *New Library World*, **102**, 1168, 314–25.

Train, B. and Elkin, J. (2001) 'Measuring the Immeasurable': reader development and its impact on performance measurement in the public library sector, *Library Review*, **50** (6), 295–305.

Wang, R., Wu, J. and Wu, J. (2000) Shanghai Library's Quality Service, *Library Management*, **21** (8), 404–9.

Weeks, J. and Mason, T. (2003) *Standards and Guidelines for Museums, Libraries and Archives in the UK,* MLA, www.mla.gov.uk/documents/sg2003-xdom.pdf.

White, S. (2004) *Public Library Materials Fund and Budget Survey 2002–2004*, Loughborough, LISU.

Young, P. R. (2001) Electronic Services and Library Performance Measurement: a definitional challenge, presented at the *4th Northumbria International Conference on Performance Measurement in Libraries and Information Services; Meaningful Measures for Emerging Realities*, Pittsburgh, PA, August 2001, www.arl.org/stats/north.

Zeithaml, V. A., Parasuraman, A. and Malhotra, A. (2000) *A Conceptual Framework for Understanding E-service Quality: implications for future research and managerial practice*, Cambridge, MA, Marketing Science Institute Report 00–115.

7 Finance and resources

The future success of every information service is directly dependent on managerial ability to plan, direct, organise and control financial resources.

(Corrall, 2000, 165)

LEARNING OBJECTIVES

After reading this chapter you should be able to:

- be aware of the key financial and resourcing challenges facing information service managers
- understand the diversity of resources and approaches to their effective management
- discuss different approaches to budget setting and planning
- understand approaches to staffing, revenue and capital budgets
- explore the impact of the electronic library on resourcing strategies and options
- be able to discuss entrepreneurial approaches to service development
- be aware of developments in finance and resources management, for example charging and bidding
- understand the skills and knowledge information professionals require for effective and efficient financial and resource management.

Introduction

Information service managers must be able to acquire, manage and maximize all the resources at their disposal. These will include human, technical, financial and information resources. Resource management and financial planning are interlinked as the necessary finances must be obtained and effectively deployed to ensure the right resources are available to meet service objectives. It is in this way that finance and resources are both prerequisites to successful strategic management, as without them strategy cannot be realized. This chapter explores the critical importance of financial and resources management at both a strategic and operational level, beginning with the key challenges that information professionals face in the current context and an exploration of why we need to be increasingly financially astute whether in the private or public sectors. Ford observes that 'many librarians do not recognise the need to think in economic terms' (1997, 41); such a view must surely be becoming obsolete as library and information professionals have to provide the best levels of service possible for the (often limited) funds available. Moving from challenges and strategy, this chapter encompasses different budgeting and accounting methods and approaches; costing and pricing; staffing, revenue and capital budgets, including the impact of the electronic library on all three; and entrepreneurialism, including bidding for funds and approaches to income generation. Underpinning the chapter are reflections on the skills and knowledge the information manager needs to operate successfully in this aspect of their role. As with other dimensions of management practice, the concepts and frameworks explored here will be determined by organizational climate – policies, procedures, methods and politics.

Key challenges and trends

The increased complexity of resource management in the digital age is coupled with an increasing need for information professionals to be financially astute. The latter has been recognized as fundamental across library and information service sectors, no more so than in the public sector which some may argue has not, in the past, been overly concerned with efficiency and best value. The shift from 'how shall we spend our money' to 'what will it cost to achieve our goals' (Corrall, 2000) can be explained by several factors:

- *Decreasing unit of resource* in real terms – This is a common feature globally and across all sectors. For example, in UK higher education the unit of funding has dropped considerably during the expansion of student numbers in the 1990s, naturally impacting on library and information service budgets. The American Library Association highlights some general trends on library funding in the USA, including libraries reporting reductions of personnel, salary freezes, reductions in opening hours, decreased books and materials budgets, and increased dependence on volunteers and part-time employees. However, this must be set against increased funding in the UK for public libraries with the People's Network and New Opportunities Fund, and the massive explosion in electronic information availability and use. Evidence does point to a decrease in resources but this does not mean that information services aren't developing, providing new services or exploiting the electronic medium – rather, they are having to find more creative ways of operating. This is also leading to a more prevalent bidding culture and the need for more entrepreneurial activity to supplement core funding.

- *Increasing customer expectations* and the dizzying options for services and information.
- *Devolution* – Budgets are being increasingly devolved with a focus on accountability and transparency.
- *Best value/value for money concepts* – The need for organizations to demonstrate effectiveness, efficiency and value for money to their stakeholders, including their users and funding bodies.
- *Pace of change* – As explored in Chapter 2, Management and Leadership, information services operate in a context of dynamic and unrelenting change. How can this be planned for and implemented within a fixed resource envelope?
- *Increasing costs*, particularly with regard to printed materials such as journals, and because of a dependency on a robust technical infrastructure.
- *Impact of networked information environment* – The development of hybrid and fully virtual services, the unpredictability of electronic resource costs and issues of copyright and digitization all impact on capital equipment spending.

This increasingly complex environment is leading information managers to invest more time on finance and resourcing with the recognition that effective resource strategies and budgeting are fundamental to meet service objectives and goals. Moreover, managers are having to explore increasingly creative solutions to maximize scarce resources and these will be explored throughout this chapter.

The trends explored above imply multiple barriers to effective financial and resource management. Table 7.1 foregrounds such barriers and stresses the connection between them and the human elements of organizations.

Table 7.1   Barriers to effective resource management

Barrier	Question to raise
Organizational culture	How is financial management and accountability viewed? Is it seen as a priority? Is it recognized, developed and rewarded?
Funding position	Are the funds simply not available? Can alternative funds be found, exploited?
Financial policies	Are these easily understood? Do they promote transparency, accountability and efficiency?
Professional attitudes and approaches	Are managers willing to rethink service provision in the light of budget restraints? And to think creatively about resources?
Organizational politics	Are certain services privileged over others? Are budgets and resources allocated transparently and fairly?
Lack of awareness and skills	Can the managers' financial and resource management skills be developed further? Are they using best practice?
Inability to measure and visibly demonstrate impact of services	Is the information service seen as impacting on the core business of the organization and being aligned with corporate goals?

Resources and their effective management

Resource management is at the heart of every information organization, and is the topic of countless books and articles. This chapter can only aim to provide a broad overview of the diversity of resources being managed within information organizations, the changes affecting them and their impact upon the information professional's role. Most information organizations will have developed a resource management strategy. Such a strategy must be aligned to service and organizational strategy; for example, an educational institution aiming to move into distance and e-learning would require a resources strategy that foregrounded the shift from print to electronic collections, while a public library with a mission to provide access to ICT would prioritize technical investment. The information professional must, based on an analysis of the mission and strategic direction of their organization, identify what resources are required, why they are needed, how they meet service needs, and then how to obtain the finances in order to purchase them. As Figure 7.1 illustrates, strategy and resources are interlinked at several levels.

Figure 7.1   Resource management strategy

The types of resources an information professional manages may include the following (with the specific balance dependent on the nature of the library and service):

- *sources of information* – printed books, journals, archives, special collections, multimedia (videos, DVDs, CD-ROMs), electronic information (electronic journals, electronic books, datasets, databases, web-based resources, digital collections)
- *buildings/spaces and facilities* – the building itself, infrastructure, furniture, shelving, security systems
- *technology* – ICT hardware, software, peripherals (e.g. scanners, printers, digital cameras)
- *equipment* – variable but could include photocopiers, office equipment, specialized preservation equipment
- *human resources* – see Chapter 4
- *others* – depending on the nature of the service, e.g. artefacts and objects, children's toy libraries and collections, slide collections.

Reflection: *Consider a library you use – what type and range of resources are within its remit? What challenges do they pose to the manager?*

Two particular aspects of the management of resources will be explored in further detail as they both represent crucial aspects of the information professional's role and are also extremely challenging. These are collection development and management and space management.

Collection development and management

Collection development and collection management are two distinct yet interrelated concepts. Collection development refers to the building of collections through the selection and acquisition of materials. Collection development, according to Jenkins and Morley (1999), is more demanding and wider in scope, encompassing policies on housing, preservation, weeding and discarding. Collection management is therefore focused on ensuring a collection is 'alive' and relevant to users. Both concepts are key management functions within the information organization, made far more complex in the networked environment. Most library and information services will develop their own, bespoke Collection Development and Management Policy, which forms a subset of an overall Resources Management Policy and Strategy. The content of such a policy will vary but would generally include:

- the strategic context and broad intent
- the criteria for selection
- the process of acquisition
- retention and deselection criteria
- preservation policy
- roles and responsibilities (including input of users and stakeholders).

Interestingly, a collection development policy will be closely interlinked with space planning, challenges and strategies – i.e. if space is at a premium, new methods may be needed (a shift to digital collections, more rigorous selection and deselection) – and with technological innovations, for example the rise of the e-book which is now beginning to infiltrate further and higher education libraries, if not yet other sectors. Approaches to collection development are predicated upon the perceived functions of the organization and service, with many still maintaining a traditional archival function, as the preservation of knowledge or cultural heritage is seen as the libraries' raison d'être. Such an emphasis can be very expensive, even a 'burden', as resources (including space) are prioritized to this end.

As briefly highlighted in Chapter 2, Information Organizations, there has been considerable debate on the shift in the role of academic libraries, from *archive* to *access*. This shift is also mirrored across sectors, with most information organizations now seeing their role as the organization and management of access to resources, rather than simply the collection of resources themselves. The increase in document creation and, for example, the numbers of books and journals published, never could be matched by acquisition budgets. In addition, many digital resources, such as electronic journals and web resources, are not made available for 'ownership'; they are available under licences for specified periods of time, or for specific payment. Accordingly, information services have sought other routes to ensure that their users have maximum access to the information resources that they might need. This involves negotiating appropriate access arrangements for both print and digital resources, including licensing arrangements for electronic journals and other databases, and interlibrary loans for print documents. In addition, many libraries are members of schemes which provide users with access, and often borrowing, across a range of partners (for example SCONUL Research Extra – see www.sconul.ac.uk). Given the diversity of resources and the complexity of access routes, each with their associated financial and copyright implications, the information service increasingly takes on the role of information intermediary, guiding users towards the resources that can best assist in their enterprise.

Nevertheless, it is important to emphasize that university and other libraries also continue to have an archival function, and some manage major special collections of rare books, original manuscripts from significant literary, cultural and political figures, items of original artwork, and a wide variety of other artefacts. All of these need to be preserved and maintained at considerable cost, including staff time and expertise.

The fundamental challenge for managers is the tension between identifying the resources required and obtaining the funds needed to acquire them. This is particularly difficult in the context of escalating costs. Problems face information professionals in relation to inflation as journals prices alone continue to rise by between 10 and 30% annually (it can be more with scientific titles), with the resulting necessary budget increases being unsustainable year on year. In such a demanding environment the selection of suppliers and the development of effective relationships with them is crucial. When selecting suppliers information managers must consider what they can offer with regard to speed of delivery, coverage, discounts and added value. Most information organizations will work with several suppliers, particularly to meet specialist needs. Purchasing consortia for books and journals (both printed and electronic) offer considerable benefits in relation to discounts and are common across sectors; many organizations are also members of wider consortia which provide discounts across a range of resources such as ICT equipment.

Impact of the electronic or hybrid library on resource management

An underpinning theme of this book is the impact of the networked environment, or the electronic library, on information organizations and the information professional. This is evidently demonstrated in relation to resources management and many collection development and management policies reflect the increasing change of balance between different media. The information service manager must attempt to establish a framework for the resourcing of libraries in this new environment. As Ashcroft (2002) highlights, libraries are 'no longer simply storehouses of information' but are rather transmitters of information in a competitive marketplace (see Chapter 5, Marketing and User Relationships, for more on this). Authors and practitioners also agree that approaches still have to reflect the hybrid reality, with collections a balance between the physical and the virtual. Graham (1998) suggests that the impact of electronic resources on the resources strategy and budget is felt not only in terms of the materials themselves but also in terms of equipment, staffing and space. The advent of the electronic journal, new publishing models (pay-per-use in contrast with free-at-the-point-of-use collections), licensing deals and closer integration of resources and services is leading to more choice and more opportunities to tailor services and resources to user needs (e.g. by alerting services, cross-database searching).

Such resource development does bring its issues, most notably the increasingly complex licence agreements and the software and hardware requirements. The digital revolution is not necessarily a money saver but does provide added value and there has been considerable debate with regard to the budgetary merits of paper vs electronic (for example Connaway and Lawrence, 2003). While Montgomery and Sparks (2000) argue that e-journal collections are cheaper than the print equivalent, e-publishing should not be seen as a panacea for financial problems; but it certainly is a route to increasing accessibility and user satisfaction. Such added value is, however, viewed by many users as a part of the standard service, with the internet raising their expectations with regard to access to information, free at the point of use and available 24 hours a day.

This 'added value' is reflected in the introduction of the e-book by companies such as netLibrary (www.netlibrary.com/Gateway.aspx) and ebrary (www.ebrary.com/). Interestingly, despite debates on the threat posed by internet-based services to libraries, netLibrary's home page stresses the continuing importance of libraries and librarians in the digital environment, as 'Technology may bring more options, but, in our view, libraries and librarians will remain a primary link between those bringing knowledge to the world and those seeking it. It is with their participation that our vision for eBooks has become a successful reality.'

With e-book collections there are multiple pricing models – for example, cost per item as if buying a 'real' book, or licensing agreements to 'rent' collections – that do not appear to offer cheaper alternatives to the printed equivalents. However, they do offer flexible access to any user who has an internet connection, ensuring savings on space and processing costs, and enabling effective management with no fines. Consortia deals, such as that described in the case cameo below, demonstrate the potential that both e-books and partnership approaches can have.

Despite reservations that e-books and e-journals will never fully replace printed material (given people's apparent lack of desire to read large amounts of text from a screen) the e-journal has transformed the journals market and the e-book is beginning to have an impact. In addition, electronic resources are leading to new partnerships as consortial deals can provide more cost effective options – 'The electronic revolution ... has clear elements which are tending to compel collection managers to look more beyond the confines of their own institution' (Ford, 1997, 282). Such purchasing consortia are in strong positions to negotiate with publishers and subscription agents.

CASE CAMEO

Example of e-books consortial purchasing

The NoWAL (North West Academic Libraries – www.nowal.ac.uk) consortium of 15 higher education libraries in the north-west of England, together with Keele University, purchased 12,000 netLibrary e-book titles in 2003. At the time, this made it the largest collection of e-books in Europe, serving more than 160,000 students. Operating alone, individual libraries would not have been able to afford access to such an extensive collection. Following complex negotiations, members of NoWAL who subscribed to the deal have access to an evolving collection of netLibrary e-book titles through a programme that extends to June 2006.

The agreement with netLibrary will allow NoWAL members to have access to a comprehensive collection of e-book material ranging from classic works of fiction, academic monographs, reference works and training guides to recommended background reading and high-demand short-loan items. Users can quickly view the e-books from any internet-enabled PC, both on and off campus. A cross-consortium implementation group worked to establish the framework to operationalize the deal, including approaches to monitoring and evaluation, staff development and the selection of material.

Reflection: What do you think are the positive and negative aspects of using e-books?

Within such a rapidly developing marketplace and with such diversification of products and materials, information managers need to develop holistic resource management strategies that consider electronic resources alongside print and other formats. Only then can managers develop resourcing models to meet user needs and understand the synergies between different media.

Space management

The issue of the development and management of collections, still within a hybrid context for the majority of information organizations, is closely inter-related with that of space – either physical or virtual. As McDonald (1997) cautions, space planning and management is an often overlooked aspect of library and information services development, yet is key to the quality of service and is an expensive resource. Despite the shift to increasingly hybrid collections, libraries *do* still have walls and are important as places to house resources (as information repositories), as learning environments, as social spaces and as centres providing help and guidance. The type of building and spaces will communicate powerful messages to users and staff related to the culture and ethos of the organization. In many library and information service buildings there are numerous and diverse activities occurring, including the introduction of internet cafés, skills centres, children's play areas. Despite concern and warnings that the 'self-service virtual library with scaled-down stock, skeleton staff and a minimal physical presence is a model which is very attractive to paymasters' (Corrall and Brewerton, 1999, 215) such a model is still not a prevalent reality.

A library and information service manager may be involved in a new build project or in refurbishments and extensions. In fact, despite the advent of virtual collections and learning environments, there is still evidence of numerous new build and extension projects. Good practice in relation to the principles of building design exhorts managers to consider the following checklist:

1 How adaptable is the building or space?
2 Is it inviting and accessible (particularly to users and staff with disabilities, e.g. people in wheelchairs or with visual impairments)? Is it welcoming and user-friendly?
3 Is it varied, interactive and well organized?
4 Is it conducive to the functions you wish to take place there, e.g. quiet study, group discussion?
5 Are there suitable environmental conditions (i.e. heat, light, ventilation)?
6 Is it safe and secure?
7 Is it efficient (i.e. economical to operate)?
8 Is it suitable for information technology? (after McDonald, 1997)

Reflection: *Consider a library building you frequent and assess it against the principles listed above. Where could improvements be made?*

Whether involved in new-build projects or not, every service manager must continuously review the spaces and facilities at their disposal, anticipating in a proactive way future needs (e.g. growth in customer numbers, need for different environments, impact of electronic collections) with a focus on their users. Service observations can be helpful in this context as a means of ensuring both a high-quality environment and a way of taking a fresh look at spaces. The three fundamental questions to constantly consider are – *Does the building or space match the functions of the service? How easy is it to use? How economical is it?*

The rapid developments in electronic information has led some authors and managers to question the continuing need for the library as space. However, there is evidence to demonstrate that increasing access to electronic resources can have a positive impact on user visits to the physical buildings. In addition, as highlighted above, building and spaces are taking on other roles as well as the more traditional one of being information repositories. Such trends will need to be carefully monitored to ensure fitness for purpose and adaptation as necessary.

Funding models and principles

Sources of funding for different sectors have been explored in Chapter 1. Funding models will depend on the organizational context but generally can take the form of one of the following:

- *Formula funding* – This is where the library and information service gets a percentage of the income of the organization as a whole. Unfortunately this is not always related to the resources that the service actually needs to fulfil its strategy and mission.
- *Lump sum funding* – In this scenario the service is provided with one lump sum, which can be extremely variable depending on the organization's priorities.
- *Incremental funding* – This takes into account factors such as inflation, plans for growth and financial constraints. It is usually based on the previous year's budget with some increase.

Funding will predominantly be from the parent organization and be allocated on an annual basis. This can cause problems for change management processes and developments given the rapid pace of change and managers' occasional inability to predict what might happen, even in the foreseeable future. Internal markets are also common in many organizations with different sections recharging for services or products, for example cleaning, catering or maintenance. This is also common within academic libraries where academic departments are recharged for the services and resources provided. An increasingly common feature of funding models and principles is *multiple sourcing* with diverse income streams, partly to supplement the standard funding and to protect a service from cuts, but also to fund special initiatives (see 'Entrepreneurialism' below). Fundraising is also increasingly common, particularly in the USA, with donations, sponsorship and the selling of services to external customers raising additional income.

Strategic budget management

The purpose of any budget is to ensure that strategy is realized, as the budget is 'the means by which resources and activities are funded to achieve the library's or information centre's goals' (Bryson, 1990, 345). The budget is often viewed as the central planning document of any service and there are integral links between the budget, strategic plan and the management of risks. Budget setting cycles will be present in every organization and related to the corporate planning process. As Corrall (2000) highlights, managers must view the budget as a strategic document as it plays a 'crucial integrative role in translating strategic plans into current action' (173). Figure 7.2 illustrates the close relationship between strategy and budget.

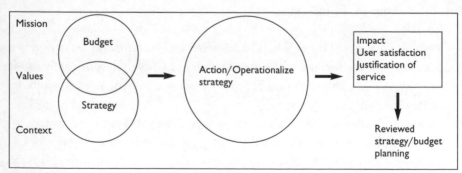

Figure 7.2 The relationship between budget and strategy

The challenges for the information manager in preparing their budget within a strategic context can be summarized as:

- The need to allocate (often scarce) resources among *competing activities* or services. Therefore, how to prioritize and justify the budget.
- The *management information* required to support the budget proposal and to estimate future trends. This will be both qualitative and quantitative, external

and internal (see Table 7.2). Clearly the analysis of the management information forms part of a service's quality strategy and this is closely aligned with budget decision making and arguments for funding.

Table 7.2   Management information for budget setting

	Internal	External
Qualitative	User satisfaction survey	Benchmarking with competitors to establish service shortfalls or gaps
Quantitative	Usage statistics of electronic resources	Data on average cost of books, journals (e.g. LISU – Library and Information Statistical Unit – at Loughborough University in the UK) and average expenditure across sectors (e.g. *Bowker Annual Library and Book Trade Almanac* in the USA)

Reflection: *What information would you need to estimate your journals budget for the coming year?*

- The importance of *involving staff*, communicating key issues and keeping them informed, particularly if there are difficulties ahead as they will have to work with these on the ground, e.g. cuts to opening hours, collections or staffing.
- The *budget cycle* itself which is predominantly annual (although the financial year will vary, e.g. calendar year, April–March, August–July) and therefore does not lend itself to longer-term strategic planning.
- The *political nature* of the budget process must also not be underestimated – how can information service managers influence the budget they are allocated? (See Chapter 3, People in Organizations, for more on politics.) Justification for resources shouldn't be simply a one-off activity, but rather embedded into activity and discussion throughout the year so that those responsible for allocating funding are aware of the service's strengths and needs, and how the budget proposal can add value to the organization. In this context credibility is crucial and the budget holder and service must consistently ensure their credibility through the quality and accuracy of information provided, ongoing critical reflection on services and their efficiency and effectiveness, and by demonstrating where changes have been made to save money or improve services. In many ways, the skills for budgeting are interpersonal as much as technical, with the requirement to influence and motivate. Consultation with stakeholders and their feedback can also act as powerful influencers during the budget process.

Approaches to budget setting

Approaches to budget setting will once again vary depending on the parent organization but the possible methods can be categorized and assessed for positive and negative features as follows:

- *Line-by-line* (incremental budgeting) – This focuses on inputs rather than outputs and doesn't relate the spend to service objectives. It is incremental, i.e. based on last year's budget with some additions, and is therefore based on existing known need with little room for major developments.
- *Programme* (functional budgeting) – The budget is designed around service areas, reflecting organizational structures, e.g. enquiry services. Staff and other costs will be calculated for each area of activity, therefore providing a 'real' cost for each element of the service. Can be extremely time consuming. This is linked with costing and pricing trends (see below).
- *Performance* (effectiveness budgeting) - This moves on from programme budgeting by evaluating the effectiveness of the budget allocation to each service area by identifying measures of performance. It begins by identifying goals, considering different approaches to achieving them and the output indicators to measure success. It's very complex!
- *Zero base* (bottom-up budgeting) – This requires full justification of the budget at all levels and is not dependent on budget allocation in previous years. It is the least-used method as it is the most complex and time consuming.
- *Option or contingency budgets* – This method involves applying different percentage increases or decreases to the budget and exploring implications and actions. For example, if your staffing budget fell by 10% how would this impact upon the service's opening hours? This isn't a holistic or strategic approach but is a useful exercise in exploring different situations and how the service could respond.

Most budget processes will probably encompass several of the variants listed above. What is noticeable across most organizations is the shift from techniques that simply focus on how to spend the resources available to those that begin with service goals and then look at what resources are needed to reach them. This philosophy reflects the move from *input-driven* management to *output-oriented* management discussed in Chapter 2, with an emphasis on answering such questions as 'What is the impact of our services?' and 'How can they become more efficient and effective?' Given the networked environment, there are a greater range of options for service delivery and consequently different costing models to be explored, some of which are included later in this chapter.

A budget manager must above all constantly ask why they do certain things, what would happen if they stopped doing them and could they do them differently. Technology has aided such thinking, for example with electronic document supply, self-issue and digitization, although clearly where some costs are saved (staff time, binding and preservation of printed materials) others take their place (hardware, technical upskilling). An additional challenge for information organizations is the inclusion of some degree of flexibility within the budget once set as there is often very little margin with the majority of the budget committed to set costs.

Costing and pricing

Costing and pricing has become popular in some sectors and is related to the accountability agenda. *Costing* principles are based on the assumption that everything has an associated cost which can be calculated. As highlighted in budget setting approaches, the establishment of costs for different elements of services can be extremely useful when making budget decisions; for example, a manager must know how much it costs to operate an enquiry service if they are considering extending the hours of operation. Costs must also be calculated if recharges are to be made either internally to other parts of the organization or externally.

Three categories of costs have been identified by Hutchins (1997):

* *materials* – costs associated with the acquisition and maintenance of information resources
* *operations* – costs associated with the library services, e.g. lending, shelving, enquiry services
* *overheads* – costs of administering the building, purchasing and maintaining equipment and furniture, general administration, etc.

However, costing is not an easy task. One problem is the allocation of staff costs when individuals contribute to several, if not many, activities during their working day. Staff costs can be calculated through time logs or diaries where the different contributions to multiple parts of the service can be isolated, for example an assistant who spends a proportion of their time on the circulation desk, shelving materials and receiving new items. Managers do need to know how much different elements of the service are costing in broad terms in order to cost out new activities and to justify additional budget requirements; attempts to break down costs in detail should, however, be approached with caution!

Reflection: *What are the challenges associated with estimating the costs related to the opening hours of a library?*

Pricing relates to the charges, subscriptions and fees generated by a service and is a way of generating income and recovering costs. Corrall (2000) highlights several factors influencing pricing, including service objectives, income targets and external markets (level of demand, competition). Whether library services should be 'free or fee' has been well discussed in the public sector, with authors and practitioners often agreeing that 'additional' services could be charged for but not the core business.

Budgets in operation

To operationalize strategy, and to aid transparent management and accountability, budgets are broken down into *functions* (overall library service), *cost centres* (sub-division of service, e.g. sites or services) and *budget categories* (staffing, staff training, equipment, catering, bookfund, journals). The exact breakdowns will vary but should be manageable and transparent.

Staffing budgets are usually the largest part of any budget (between 50 and 80% of costs) as library and information services are very people intensive, 'high contact customer services' (Hart, 1997, 176). There are also numerous hidden costs associated with staffing budgets, including staff turnover and recruitment, absence, and training and development time. Creative approaches to staffing are often required to develop services within limited resources, for example the employment of flexible workers and the reduction of costs associated with cataloguing by buying in downloaded records. Multi-site services are even more staff intensive and rationalization to fewer sites has led to cost efficiencies in a number of organizations.

Capital expenditure represents long-term investment in one-off payments but there are often associated recurring costs, such as equipment maintenance contracts and insurance. Rolling replacement policies are also necessary for ICT as technology rapidly becomes obsolete. Many organizations lease equipment, for example photocopiers and PCs, with the inclusive maintenance and replacement costs saving on internal staff time and drawing on expertise which is often not available within the service. Budgeting for constantly increasing networked services can put a strain on organizations that don't have the capital funds for large-scale projects; they also have an impact on revenue expenditure which needs to include maintenance, telecoms and consumables. Library management systems would also be considered capital and a project to select and implement a new system would have considerable capital and staffing implications.

Revenue budgets encompass all elements that are neither staffing or capital, for example book funds, journals and subscriptions, equipment (on a small scale), travel and subsistence. The ability to 'vire' (i.e. transfer) funds within the revenue budget, and even between revenue and staffing, can provide welcome flexibility if budgets are tightly controlled but this is dependent on the culture and policies of an organization.

Financial control and accountability

Each organization will have policies and procedures in place to ensure financial control and accountability, and these will usually be set out in the *financial regulations*. In a similar way to their need to be familiar with human resources policies and relationships, an information manager must both be fully aware of their organization's financial regulations and also develop effective working relationships and communication with colleagues in the finance department. There can often be inherent tensions in such relationships as the information service manager's role is to optimize the quality of service within resources provided, while the finance manager's role can be to limit spending. Management information will be provided to the information service manager from the finance department, detailing over the year levels of spending that will be compared with the 'profiling' of spend set at the beginning of the year. This information will also usually provide details on amounts committed as well as actually spent so that the information manager can ascertain exactly what remains of their budget. Regular budget reports need to be accurate, timely, clear and auditable, and it is the responsibility of the information professional to understand the reports and be able to both analyse and interrogate them. Underpinning principles provide useful guidance to ensure effective financial procedures and systems (see Figure 7.3).

Reliable staff	Careful selection and training to attempt to ensure trustworthiness and competent staff
Physical safeguards	Intruder alarms, security systems to protect stock and equipment, carefully developed systems to transfer cash
Job segregation	Ordering, authorizing, receipting and paying for goods should ideally be undertaken by different individuals
Formal procedures and staff training	Procedures for authorizing, spending limits and record keeping should be documented and communicated to staff, plus regularly checked
Record keeping	Records should be accurate, current and complete
Independent checks	Via audit – both internal and external – and own checks to ensure compliance with procedures and regulations

Figure 7.3 Principles for rigorous financial procedures

Changes in approaches to finance and resources

Changes in approaches to resourcing and financial management have occurred as a result of several factors and developments, including the need to cut costs, increase income and to exploit new technologies and ideas. The major change across the library and information sector can be characterized by the rise of *entrepreneurialism*. Most information services have always been involved in some aspects of income generation – from fines to selling items, to charging for services, to bidding for funds. The shift from this as a minor aspect of management to a widespread entrepreneurialism across all sectors has been evident since the 1980s, most probably as a result of the need to acquire funds through diverse income streams and not simply from the parent organization. Entrepreneurialism has been defined as a 'freewheeling and dynamic style of business management' (Pantry and Griffiths, 1998, 4) and is often associated with risk taking and the seizing of new opportunities. Entrepreneurialism is used here as a blanket term to encompass activities and approaches to attract, manage and exploit the maximum resources available. Entrepreneurial activity should always be an integral part of the service's role, because if it is seen as detracting from the service's prime purpose this can result in political difficulties and discontent among both staff and stakeholders. There is also a degree of sensitivity in relation to 'charging' users for services, particularly in the public sector, enhanced by the recognition that customers' expectations are increasing and that they can find alternative service providers, especially via the internet. New IT-based services (e.g. video-conferencing and internet access) are viewed by some managers as opportunities for charging, particularly in public libraries where they have only recently become part of the service.

The rise of entrepreneurialism can also be related to the *bidding culture* that is now felt to dominate public sector information organizations – and can be evidenced in public libraries, HE and FE, and the health service. This is the result of a cultural shift with services having to bid for resources and justify their use, rather than libraries being seen simply as a 'good thing' that should be resourced; public libraries in particular have 'been hard hit by the erosion of traditional forms of funding and bidding for additional funds has become a mainstay of many libraries' activities' (Parker, Ray and Harrop, 2001). Special initiative funds can be used to fund one-off projects (e.g. the digitization of a special collection or implementation of new technology), to develop new services (e.g. current awareness services for doctors in the NHS) or to maintain existing services. Sources of project funding are multiple, coming in the UK, for example, from JISC (Joint Information Systems Committee) for HE and FE information technology initiatives and from the National Lottery Heritage Fund for public libraries, particularly in relation to community work and access to culturally significant collections. Working within a bidding culture can provide many opportunities but can also be stressful, frustrating and uncertain, particularly if core services depend on successful bids rather than recurring funding. The management of special initiative funding also requires certain skills, including effective project management and political awareness if partners are involved. Initiatives such as the New Opportunities Fund for UK public libraries provide avenues to develop digitization projects and staff training; yet they also require a 'new approach from managers in drawing up bids, finding the matched funding, implementing and managing time-limited projects' (Gallimore, 1999). It has also been suggested that the bidding culture effectively funds innovation but can't necessarily sustain it, and this represents a challenge for the information manager. Figure 7.4 demonstrates the characteristics of a good bid.

Other changes in resource and financial management include *service level agreements* (SLAs). Service level agreements are used by information organizations to define the level and nature of services to be provided within a given resourcing envelope, and as such they express 'the minimum acceptable standards' (Corrall

---

- Begin by complying with the requirements – what is the funding body asking for?
- Consider eligibility – will bids only be received from certain types of organizations?
- Use their terminology.
- Ensure you can achieve the specified outcomes – don't promise something that can't be delivered.

- Ensure the political environment is conducive – do you have the support within your own organization?
- Ensure the bid links with the organization and service's mission and prime purpose – 'strategy driven'.
- Include: definition of the topic, methodology, timescales, outputs and resource allocation.

Figure 7.4 Characteristics of a good bid

and Brewerton, 1999, 88) agreed by the different parties involved. SLAs are also used as quality mechanisms (see Chapter 6, Quality Management, for more on quality mechanisms and approaches) to ensure, monitor and evaluate agreed performance and targets, and also to manage partnerships. Most likely there will be a financial element, as services are being costed and charged for, but not exclusively. SLAs can be established between different groups and for different reasons, as exemplified in Figure 7.5.

• With users in relation to an aspect of service – SLA for an enquiry service to set out expectations on both sides, type of service provided, hours of available provision, level of service. • With specific groups of users – SLA between an academic library and an academic department to establish level and nature of research support.	• With another part of the organization – SLA with IT Services to establish level of IT support, rolling programme of replacement for PCs, etc. • With an external body or partner – to provide a specific service that is being charged for, e.g. current awareness services for a business, provision of library services for an NHS Trust, outsourcing arrangements.

Figure 7.5 Types of service level agreements

SLAs can be effective communication tools, clarifying expectations and improving user satisfaction, but they can also be restrictive if too detailed and monitoring can be problematic.

Partnerships to enhance resource and financial management

Internal and external partnerships are often the cornerstone of bids, but partnerships can prove extremely beneficial to general resource and financial management, as previously highlighted in relation to consortial purchasing. The importance of partnership has been clearly established in Chapter 1, Information Organizations. External partnerships can be loosely grouped into the categories described below. It is important to note that any one information service is likely to be engaged in several different partnerships, drawn from several categories.

• *Partnerships in the supply chain* – Information services are intermediaries in the information and document supply chain that starts with document creation by an author, illustrator, composer or artist, and finishes with the user. Information services work in a business-to-business, and often longstanding, relationship with publishers, booksellers, journal subscription agents and others to ensure the optimum availability of resources for their services within their budgetary and other constraints. Some information organizations form purchasing consortia that negotiate with publishers and others for attractive rates for volume sales.

- *Outsourcing relationships* – in which parts of the public service activities are outsourced to private sector partners. Public libraries might, for example, outsource the maintenance of the systems infrastructures for their activities under the People's Network, or contract for private sector businesses to manage a café, bookshop or video hire service.
- *Regional networks* – Most regions in the UK, Australia, Canada and the USA operate regional library schemes, which support reciprocal access for users and interlending, and through which they can organize a regional response to other government agendas, such as lifelong learning or digital library projects. For example, in the north-west of England two different kinds of regional consortia exist. *Liverpool Libraries Together* has members from further education colleges, higher education bodies, and public libraries. *NorthWest Academic Libraries* (NOWAL) is a consortium of the higher education libraries in the north-west of England. The USA has strong regional consortia including *Metro* (www.metro.org) in New York which aims to 'promote and facilitate utilization of existing resources and to develop additional library services in the New York Metropolitan Area' and comprises academic, special, public and school libraries as well as archives.
- *Partnerships in service delivery* – between for example, public libraries, schools, authors, and voluntary organizations.
- *National networks of research libraries* – which focus on access, reciprocal borrowing, and often project-based initiatives. In the USA the *Association of Research Libraries* (ARL; www.arl.org) is a powerful network while in the UK the *Consortium of University Research Libraries* (CURL; www.curl.ac.uk) fulfils a similar purpose.
- *Project-based consortia* – which come together for a short period of time to execute specific projects, possibly funded through regional, national or European government initiatives.

Reflection: *Exploring one of the partnerships detailed above via their website, consider the benefits offered to members.*

Future resource and financial management

Current trends in resource and financial management indicate that there will no longer be guaranteed levels of support for libraries and information services, primarily because of an increasingly competitive environment and the prevailing view that they are no longer inherently a 'good thing'. Libraries must prove their worth, effectiveness and efficiency, with information managers constantly adopting new approaches to save resources, maximize resources and use them in new ways and for new services. Increasing entrepreneurialism will become the norm, as will partnerships to achieve goals, provide value for money and cut costs. Resources are becoming more complex, there is more choice, more change – users therefore need clearer information, direction, guidance and personalization. Success will be increasingly dependent on networking, influencing and leadership skills as managers need to seek out opportunities and be 'far more adventurous' (Parker, Ray and Harrop, 2001).

Summary and conclusions

The information manager must recognize and ensure the crucial link between resources, finances and strategy in order for the organization to achieve its objectives. In many circumstances, a decreasing unit of resource and increasing expectations are leading to more creative ways of managing, especially with the opportunities provided by electronic resources and services, and collaborative and entrepreneurial approaches. This chapter has illustrated how library and information services are now responsible for diverse resources and must take a holistic approach, particularly in considering collection development and space management in the context of a shift from archives to access and new products such as e-books, as 'Libraries must attempt to serve both as owners of information in traditional formats and as gatekeepers' to the huge volume of information available (Baker, 1997, 142). Approaches to budget setting and financial policies and procedures have seen a noticeable change from input-driven to output-focused budgeting, with high value placed on control and accountability. Particular models will very much depend on the organizational context and financial policies. Entrepreneurialism – encompassing income generation, bidding for funds, project working and partnerships – can bring additional resources and opportunities, if aligned to organizational goals, and demands new skills and approaches which the information professional must consider. Above all, the purpose of the information service manager is to obtain and maximize the necessary resources for the end-user, within an environment that promotes access and flexibility, and to think creatively about maximizing resources.

REVIEW QUESTIONS

1   Discuss the barriers to effective resource management.

2 Consider the differences between collection management and collection development.

3 What are the benefits and drawbacks of e-publishing for the information manager?

4 What questions should the information service manager consider in judging the effectiveness of space utilization?

5 Explain the main types of approaches to budget setting.

6 How might the demands of capital resourcing be met by the information manager?

7 Consider the positive features of a bidding culture for library services.

8 When might different partnerships prove advantageous to the development of services and their users?

9 What skills should the information manager develop in order to effectively manage resources and finances?

CASE STUDY

The information service budget and its interpretation

Consider the extract from a library and information service budget in Figure 7.6. Note that it is half way through the financial year. After analysing the budget, address the questions below.

- How healthy is the staffing budget? If savings need to be made what are the options for the service manager?
- Which areas of the budget (i.e. which account codes) would you be most concerned about? Why? How might the manager address these concerns?
- Which areas of the budget could you potentially make savings in?

CHALLENGES

1 In considering the fitness for purpose of library spaces, what might the future bring and how can we strategically plan for possibilities?

2 Why is costing and pricing becoming increasingly important and what might be the inherent difficulties?

3 Could it be argued that new entrepreneurialism detracts from core services and from users?

4 How can managers predict the balance between e-resources and traditional collections? Will we see a shift to digital libraries rather than hybrids?

5 Partnership brings many advantages to a service and its users but how can we reconcile partnership demands and the priorities of the parent organization?

Library Services' Budget 2003–2004 (financial year runs from 1 August–31 July)

Budget update as of May 2004

Account code	Description	Committed, £	Actual, £	Balance remaining, £	Budget allocation, £
21000	Staffing		540,000.00	25,000.00	565,000.00
Revenue Budget					
21050	Travel & Subsistence		5,898.54	(1,898.54)	4,000.00
21051	Inter-Site Travel		2,398.74	1,601.26	4,000.00
21065	Fees Staff Training/Development	457.50	8,421.50	3,121.00	12,000.00
21190	Library Books		160,584.63	64,026.37	224,611.00
21200	CD-ROM & Subscriptions		58,944.44	18,420.56	77,365.00
21201	Annual Subs		8,221.65	(421.65)	7,800.00
21202	Inter-library Loans		10,377.70	4,622.30	15,000.00
21203	Book & Journal Binding	822.50	2,274.05	2,903.45	6,000.00
21220	Periodicals, Magazines & Papers		135,632.77	12,069.23	147,702.00
21310	Computing Consumables	66.50	3,958.06	(24.56)	4,000.00
21330	Software, non capital		1,271.93	(271.93)	1,000.00
21313	Licences & Patents		47,075.31	(9,437.31)	37,638.00
21403	Printing Costs	205.15	1,656.32	138.53	2,000.00
21900	Stationery		5,891.42	2,333.58	8,225.00
22415	Equipment – noncapitalized	7,261.38	19,176.43	(12,914.81)	13,523.00
22200	Telephone/Fax	0.00	105.95	44.05	150.00
Totals		8,813.03	471,889.44	84,311.53	565,014.00

Note: figures in brackets indicate deficit amounts

Figure 7.6 Extract from library and information services budget

References and additional reading

Ashcroft, L. (2002) Issues in Developing, Managing and Marketing Electronic Journals Collections, *Collection Building*, **21** (4),147–54.

Baker, D. (ed.) (1997) *Resource Management in Academic Libraries,* London, Library Association Publishing.

Ball, D. (2003) Public Libraries and the Consortium Purchase of Electronic Resources, *The Electronic Library*, **21** (4), 301–9.

Brown, S., Downey, B. and Race, P. (1997) *500 Tips for Academic Librarians*, London, Library Association Publishing.

Bryson, J. (1990) *Effective Library and Information Centre Management*, Aldershot, Gower.

Bryson, J. (1999) *Effective Library and Information Centre Management*, 2nd edn, Aldershot, Gower.

Connaway, L. S., and Lawrence, S. R. (2003) Comparing Library Resource Allocations for the Paper and the Digital Library: an exploratory study, *D-Lib*

Magazine, **9** (12), (December), www.dlib.org/dlib/december03/connaway/12connaway.html.

Corrall, S. (2000) *Strategic Management of Information Services: a planning handbook*, London, ASLIB/ Information Management International.

Corrall, S. and Brewerton, A. (1999) *The New Professional's Handbook: your guide to information services management*, London, Library Association Publishing.

Ford, G. (1997) Finance and Budgeting. In Jenkins, C. and Morley, M. (eds), *Collection Management in Academic Libraries*, 2nd edn, Aldershot, Gower, 39–70.

Gallimore, A. (1999) Managing the Networked Public Library, *Library Management*, **20** (7), 384–92.

Graham, T. (1998) Overview: resourcing and budgeting issues. In Hanson, T. and Day, J. (eds), *Managing the Electronic Library: a practical guide for information professionals*, London, Bowker-Saur, 185–212.

Hanson, T. and Day, J. (eds) (1998) *Managing the Electronic Library: a practical guide for information professionals,* London, Bowker-Saur.

Hart, E. (1997) Operating Costs. In Baker, D. (ed.), *Resource Management in Academic Libraries*, London, Library Association Publishing, 175–88.

Hutchins, J. (1997) Costing of Materials, Operations and Services. In Baker, D. (ed.) *Resource Management in Academic Libraries*, London, Library Association Publishing, 98–109.

Hyams, E. (2001) Seizing the Opportunity in Cambridgeshire, *Library Association Record*, **103** (7), (July), 420–1.

Jenkins, C. and Morley, M. (eds) (1999) *Collection Management in Academic Libraries,* 2nd edn, Aldershot, Gower.

Lawes, A. (ed.) (1993) *Management Skills for the Information Manager*, Aldershot, Ashgate.

McDonald, A. (1997) Space Planning and Management. In Baker, D. (ed.), *Resource Management in Academic Libraries,* London, Library Association Publishing, 189–206.

Montgomery, C. and Sparks, J. (2000) The Transition to an Electronic Journals Collection: managing the organisational changes, *Serials Review*, **26** (3), 4–18.

Pantry, S. and Griffiths, P. (1998) *Becoming a Successful Intrapreneur: a practical guide to creating an innovative information service,* The Successful LIS Professional series, edited by Sheila Pantry, London, Library Association Publishing.

Pantry, S. and Griffiths, P. (2003) *The Complete Guide to Preparing and Implementing Service Level Agreements*, 2nd edn, London, Facet Publishing.

Parker, S., Ray, K. and Harrop, K. (2001) The Bidding Culture in the UK Public Library – a case study approach, *Library Management*, **22** (8/9), 404–10.

8 Strategy and planning

The strategic planning process recognises that organisations cannot achieve everything they would like to do. Instead it allows for the allocation of resources and planning of strategies on a priority basis to best achieve the organisation's mission within the resource constraints and dynamics of the external environment.

(Bryson, 1999, 41).

LEARNING OBJECTIVES

After reading this chapter you should be able to:

- discuss the concept of strategy, and its relationship to planning
- identify the stages in a strategic planning process
- understand the role of missions, visions and objectives in defining strategic focus
- understand the value of some key strategic planning tools
- discuss operational and project planning.

Introduction

From a practice perspective, strategy should precede and inform virtually all of the activities discussed earlier in this book, such as management, leadership, marketing and quality management. This chapter is placed last because strategy is integrative and it is not possible to engage in discussions of strategy without some appreciation of the elements of the organization, as have been explored in the earlier chapters of this book. Strategy is concerned with matching resources to the environment, and through that process, iteratively, enhancing resources to strengthen the organization for the future. Strategy is closely coupled with marketing but takes a wider perspective, reviewing all of the organizational resources, including people, buildings, stock and finance. In addition strategy is contextualized by factors in its environment, many of which were briefly identified in Chapter 1.

Strategy is concerned with establishing and sharing long-term direction. This means not only developing plans, but making them happen. Strategic management is essentially about planning and leading change, while ensuring that the organization has the capacity and capability to move confidently forward in the right direction. In today's dynamic environment, strategy making is an ongoing process that engages not only top management, but all managers and team leaders and other staff. Managers need the ability to think, plan and act strategically on a continuing basis. Chapter 1, Information Organizations, outlined the contribution that information services are increasingly being expected to make within their organizations and within society generally. The wider and ambitious policy agendas to which information organizations are being expected to respond demand visionary leadership, informed decision making and dynamic strategy-making processes.

This chapter commences with a consideration of the nature of strategy and its link to planning. This leads into an exploration of the strategic planning process, including consideration of the context for the information services strategy, and the stages in the strategic planning process. A particularly important issue is the development of strategic focus and direction, and the articulation of direction in mission, vision, goals, values and objectives. Finally, the chapter introduces a number of strategic planning tools and models that can be used in environmental and situation analysis to assist in the identification of the most appropriate strategic option and to explore the concept of impact.

Defining strategy

> There are three kinds of organisations: those that make things happen; those that watch things happen; those that wonder what happened.
>
> (De Saez, 2002, 15)

Strategy is concerned with the long-term direction of an organization. The 'rational' individual might take this simple definition and leap to the immediate conclusion that understanding and managing long-term direction requires planning, and that therefore strategy and planning are inexorably linked. However, Johnson and Scholes (2002) provide a more extended definition that starts to illustrate why strategy is more than planning:

> Strategy is the direction and scope of an organisation over the long term which achieves advantage for the organisation through its configuration of resources within a changing environment and to fulfil stakeholder expectations. (10)

This definition derives from a number of aspects of the characteristics of strategic decisions:

- Strategic decisions and strategy are usually concerned with the *long-term direction* of an organization.
- Strategy is usually concerned with *strategic advantage*, or being able to offer a better value proposition to customers than competitors can offer.
- Strategy concerns *strategic fit*, or the matching of the resources and activities of an organization to the environment in which it operates in order to achieve maximum strategic advantage.

In turn this means that strategic decisions typically:

- are *complex* in nature
- are made in situations of *uncertainty and risk*, since predicting the long-term future cannot be achieved with certainty
- require an *integrated approach* across the organization
- have major resource implications
- affect a range of operational activities in the organization and provide the context for operational decisions
- drive change within the organization, and the relationship between the organization and other organizations.

To summarize, strategic management is concerned with establishing fundamental parameters, has long-term implications and is organization-wide. This means that strategic planning and management is typically ambiguous, uncertain and complex.

Strategy as *design* is probably the dominant lens that people use to examine strategy. The design lens views strategy development as the deliberate positioning of the organization through a rational, analytic, structured and directive process. The situation is analysed through collecting data, plans are made concerning direction, the allocation of resources is clearly articulated, the organization moves in the planned direction, and mechanisms can be put in place to monitor progress in the planned direction. This lens sees organizations as mechanistic, hierarchical and logical. While this lens is important and drives the strategic planning process as described later in this chapter, it is obvious that this is only part of the real picture.

The strategy as *experience* lens views strategic development as the outcome of individual and collective experience. It argues that strategy formulation and evolution is an incremental development from the status quo, and is therefore constrained by organizational culture, or the basic assumption and beliefs that are shared within an organization, and often across a sector. These constraints limit innovation. This lens sees organizations as culture bound, with strategy constrained by history and past success.

The strategy as *ideas* lens seeks to understand strategy from the perspective of new ideas and innovation. It argues that strategy is the emergence of order and innovation through variety and diversity in and around the organization, which act as drivers for change and direction. This lens sees organizations as complex systems responding to internal and external variety and diversity.

Strategy formulation and development may, then, be seen to be an amalgam of rational planning, cultural and experiential influences, and the complexity and diversity that provide a fertile ground for innovation and creativity.

The complex and culturally and politically charged environment of strategic planning and formulation, coupled with the uncertainty of internal and external factors, means that there is often a difference between what managers plan to happen and what actually happens. *Intended* strategy is an expression of desired strategic direction deliberately formulated or planned by managers. *Realized* strategy, on the other hand, is the strategy actually being followed by an organization in practice. It may be that the realized strategy better meets the organization's objective, or defines a better place for the organization in the marketplace. Big differences between intended strategy and realized strategy can occur with significant changes in leadership and management, organizational structure or marketplace. There is nothing wrong with a mismatch between intended and realized strategy providing that managers are aware of the difference and are taking appropriate actions to manage the situation. Much more serious is strategic drift. *Strategic drift* occurs when the organization's strategy (intended or realized) gradually ceases to be an appropriate response to the organization's context and environment.

The strategic planning process

Strategic planning is an activity or process that provides a systematic structure and framework for considering the future, appraising opportunities and options, and then selecting and implementing the necessary activities for achieving the stated objectives efficiently and effectively. Strategic planning is a cyclical process with typically annual cycles.

The process that is described in this section tends towards the rational, design view of strategy. This approach has a number of advantages:

- It provides a structured context for a manager to analyse and think, question and challenge.
- It encourages forward thinking, possibly over a three- to five-year time window.
- It generates a context for communication and co-ordination.
- Involvement and representation can be structured and controlled.
- The planning document can be used for control and performance monitoring.
- The planning system creates a benchmark for the organization which gives it a shared sense of security and logic.

Orna (1999) argues that the existence of an information policy and strategy within an organization can lead to:

- integrated information activities and resources
- information policy and strategy integrated within corporate policies and priorities
- criteria for assessing how information contributes to organizational objectives
- freer information flow, with better access and sharing
- an evaluation of options for investment in systems, resources and IT that takes into account key organizational goals and what people need to do to achieve them
- systematic intelligence gathering and constant monitoring of internal and external environment.

Each of these outcomes has benefits for the organization.

The structure and nature of the planning process is pivotal to success. As discussed earlier, strategy formulation is a political and cultural process, and the direction at the heart of any strategy is influenced by the experiences, resources, capabilities and value sets of those involved in the planning process.

Successful planning features staff involvement. This can be achieved through a range of different strategies. Quality management processes should surface some opinions, ideas and dialogues. These are often bottom-up processes that generate suggestions that inform the incremental development of strategy. Major changes in direction are more likely to be initiated and led by managers, in a top-down manner, and on the basis of their interpretation of the most appropriate response to the environment. Even with such top-down initiatives it is unlikely that managers will understand all of the consequences at an operational level of changes in strategic direction. Consultation and two-way communication during planning processes is central to drawing on staff expertise, while also keeping them informed and involved. Staff benefit from the opportunity to contribute to the planning process, need to understand that their performance will be evaluated in terms of their contribution to fulfilling objectives identified in the planning process, and need to be empowered to fulfil their job functions in such a way that they are able to make an appropriate contribution. In addition, planning must be based on good market information, interpreted using appropriate forecasting techniques. Finally, there needs to be recognition that most annual plans will not be executed in their entirety. Management involves making appropriate judgements about modifications to plans as the year progresses, without sinking into unsystematic chaos.

There are two different models of the strategic planning process:

• the strategic planning hierarchy, and
• the elements of the strategic planning process (that can be applied at each level in the hierarchy).

Any specific strategy or step in the strategic planning process does not occur in isolation, and it is this factor that can lead to complexity in surfacing and finalizing a strategic plan.

The strategic planning hierarchy

Most organizations have a series of interlinked strategic planning documents and processes. The links between these plans typically reflect the organizational structure, as different organizational structures suggest different approaches to communication within the organization. Many organizations have hierarchical organizational structures, as discussed in Chapter 1, Information Organizations. This leads to the development of a hierarchy of strategies, with strategies matching the business units, departments and divisions within the organization. Corporate-level strategy is concerned with the overall purpose and scope of an organization. Below corporate strategy there may be strategies for each of the business units in an organization, as well as some overarching strategies for functions like marketing or finance. The information service strategic plan will usually be one element in the strategic plan for the local authority, university, school or business organization of which it is part. Each of these strategies will be the subject of a written document, and is likely to be considered and approved by various key stakeholders. For example, a corporate strategy for a university in the UK will be considered and approved by the university's Senate (representing the leaders and managers in the university), and the governing body (with externally appointed governors, whose responsibility it is to ensure the appropriateness of the management and governance of the university). In addition, universities are required to submit their strategic plans to their funding body, HEFCE, on an annual basis.

The corporate strategy document for a university will have some reference to the contribution that information services will make to the continuing development of the learning and research environment for the university. It may have a separate section on information service strategy. Often information service strategies are tightly coupled with, or integrated into, an overarching information systems strategy, that embraces networks, hardware, software, systems, media resources, digital and print resources, and user support and other services.

Finally, as discussed in Chapter 1, organizations often do not work alone, and links need to exist between the strategy and strategic plans of partners in alliances. There are challenges around the long-term commercial position of the outcomes from such initiatives, and related challenges associated with the clear articulation of strategy in relation to them.

Reflection: *Visit a library website. Make a list of the organizations with which the library is engaged in joint projects. How do these projects contribute to the fulfilment of the library's mission?*

The stages in the strategic planning process

Strategic management is more than strategy formulation and decision making. Strategic management is about making things happen. As such, strategic management is concerned with the stages in Figure 8.1. While each of these stages is easy to describe, they are much more difficult to undertake thoroughly. They all involve the collection and analysis of a considerable quantity of data, information and knowledge relating to the organization's environment, competitors, activities, operation and resources. The resource base that informs decision making is informed by experience and history. Some resources will exist in explicit form in databases and from summaries of operational processes; other inputs will be implicit knowledge integral to the experiences and competencies of managers and others.

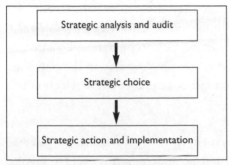

Figure 8.1 The stages in the strategic planning process

Strategic analysis and audit is concerned with the answer to the question 'Where are we now?' It is concerned with understanding the external environment, internal resources and the match between these two, and conducting an environmental situation audit. The PESTEL model (see below) is useful for making sense of the factors in the external environment, and SWOT analysis (also described below) can be used to create a broad picture of the match between internal and external factors. Other tools that might be used at this stage include competitive benchmarking, customer surveys and stakeholder mapping (a process whereby the various stakeholders and their needs, expectations and perspectives are articulated). The environment needs to be analysed in terms of the opportunities and threats posed for the organization. The internal resources should be analysed in terms of their strengths and weaknesses, to yield a profile of the strategic capability of the organization. More detailed analysis can focus on product or service portfolio, and competitors and competitive position, with the aid of portfolio analysis tools (see below) and positioning maps (used to analyse the marketplace position of a business or its products relative to its competitors).

Strategic choice has two components:

- *Deciding direction*, sometimes described as strategic profiling, which is concerned with setting the overarching direction. The key question is: 'Where do we want to be?' This involves the discussion of fundamental issues such as scope, purpose, objectives, future aspirations and goals.
- *Method*, which is concerned with the identification of the most appropriate route to the destination, through the formulation and evaluation of options and choices. The key question is 'How will we arrive at where we want to be?' In order to answer this question the process must identify the possible routes

towards the destination, including, for example, low investment and relatively slow development, and injections of targeted resources into specific key action areas to provoke faster change. Once the possible routes have been identified some criteria for their evaluation need to be developed, and the different options evaluated using these criteria. Scenario development may assist in the evaluation and comparison of different options. In addition, uncertainty in projections and forecasts may be accommodated through assessing events that might happen and their likelihood with the aid of sensitivity analysis (which uses scenarios to identify the impact of specific variants on outcomes) and contingency analysis (which explores different possible events and the outcomes of those events). Ultimately, this stage must conclude with the selection of a specific option.

Strategic action and implementation is concerned with putting things in place to ensure that the organization achieves its strategic direction. It is likely to involve planning at the operational level, including the allocation of resources, budget setting and the specification of departmental or individual responsibility and targets. The link between strategic planning and financial planning should be transparent. Strategic objectives should inform budget allocations. However strategic and financial planning are often not as closely intertwined as they should be, leading to resources constraints hindering strategic progress. Strategic action is concerned with the management of the dynamic between strategy and the key resource areas of an organization: people, information, money and technology.

The final element of implementation is monitoring and control, which measures success in contributing to strategic direction in terms of fulfilment of objectives, and generates data, information and knowledge that feed into the strategic analysis and audit stage of the next (annual) strategic planning cycle. Although an annual review offers an opportunity to take an overview, progress towards objectives should also be monitored over shorter intervals, of say, one month or three months. Failure to achieve interim targets should provoke a review of elements of the plan. The knowledge-based organization will use this evaluation process and the reports that emanate from it to drive organizational learning and development.

In conclusion, different models of the planning process will be appropriate for different information organizations, depending on the size of the organization, the nature of its activities and services, and the customer profile. However, all information organizations need to:

- understand the relationship between corporate or organizational objectives and their resources
- understand the context, resources and constraints which impact on the achievement of objectives
- formulate a plan which includes a range of actions
- monitor progress with implementation of the plan, and the effectiveness of the plan and the planning process.

Strategic focus and direction

Strategy formulation and development is concerned with developing direction. Statements of mission, vision, values, objectives, goals and performance measures are pivotal in the process of setting direction and will continue to be relevant through uncertain times and over periods of years. These can all be set at both organizational level and at, for example, information service level, and the usage of each of these varies. Table 8.1 provides a summary of some of the key vocabulary in this area, and presents a useful starting point. This section explores and illustrates the way in which mission and vision statements, goals and objectives can be used to articulate direction. Figures 8.3 and 8.4 illustrate how linkages can be achieved in practice. Figure 8.3 shows linkages between a goal and its objec-

Table 8.1 Strategy vocabulary (developed from Johnson and Scholes, 2002)

Term	Definition	Example for a university library
Mission	Overriding purpose in line with the values or expectations of stakeholders	To offer a leading edge information service in support of teaching and learning
Vision or strategic intent	Desired future state: the aspiration of the organization	To be recognized as an innovative information service
Goal	General statement of aim or purpose	To enhance service availability for remote users
Objective	Quantification (if possible) or more precise statement of the goal	To implement a website that integrates services for remote users, by 31.12.2004
Value	Statements of beliefs or principles that underpin organizational or professional philosophies	Diversity, integrity, literacy, privacy, preservation of cultural heritage
Policy	Statements of principles intended to provide a framework for decisions on a continuing basis	Borrowing entitlement, scope of collections.

tives, performance measures and strategies. Figure 8.4 demonstrates links between mission, values and corporate objectives.

Mission and vision statements should be clear declarations of an organization's beliefs about its own nature and distinctive competencies. They should answer the following questions:

- What are we doing?
- Who are we doing it for?
- Why are we doing it?
- What should we be doing?

Figure 8.2 includes some information service mission statements. These vary in length and explicitness. Some would argue that every member of staff and even every customer should be able to recite a mission statement; this suggests a brief statement is appropriate, but writing truly representative brief statements that

1. 'To achieve excellence in the provision and promotion of information services to meet the research, teaching and learning needs of the University.'

2. 'To inspire and enable every individual in Bristol to participate actively in the cultural, economic and democratic life of the city through the exploitation of information, learning opportunities, and the enjoyment of books and other media.'

3. 'To underpin and secure our democratic society by
   a. Providing and promoting access to information, books and other materials and knowledge
   b. Supporting everyone to play active roles as citizens
   c. Facilitating the use of information, the reading experience and literature through mediation and assistance
   d. Actively encouraging use, especially by members of ethnic minority groups.'

4. 'To be the best public library service in the country.'

5. 'The New York Public Library is one of the cornerstones of the American tradition of equal opportunity. It provides free and open access to the accumulated wisdom of the world, without distinction as to income, religion, nationality, or other human condition. It is everyone's university; the scholar's and author's haven; the statesman's, scientist's, and businessman's essential resource; the nation's memory. It guarantees freedom of information and independence of thought. It enables each individual to pursue learning at his/her own personal level of interest, preparation, ability, and desire. It helps ensure the free trade in ideas and the right of dissent.
   The mission of The New York Public Library is to use its available resources in a balanced program of collecting, cataloging, and conserving books and other materials, and providing ready access directly to individual library users and to users elsewhere through cooperating libraries and library networks. The New York Public Library's responsibility is to serve as a great storehouse of knowledge at the heart of one of the world's information centers, and to function as an integral part of a fabric of information and learning that stretches across the nation and the world.'

6. 'To enable the University to achieve excellence in teaching, research and scholarship by the provision and promotion of recorded knowledge.'

Figure 8.2 Some information service mission statements

uniquely reflect the information services mission and differentiate it from that of other organizations can be a challenge. Mission and vision statements provide a context for the development of goals, objectives, performance measures and strategies.

Reflection: *Which of the mission statements in Figure 8.2 on page 220 do you think is the most appropriate? Why?*

Goal 4. *To maintain the provision of services by best management practices, demonstrating leadership in the innovative use of resources and technology*

The new information environment requires that the Library management infrastructure must be able to accommodate change readily while maintaining efficiency in its operations. It must also gain adequate financial support to achieve its mission of excellence.

Objectives to achieve this goal are to:
- Maintain a high and credible profile within the University, the tertiary sector and the community which will create support for and enhance the reputation of the institution.
- Allocate the Library's budget according to priorities.
- Work in co-operation with other areas of the University to develop, introduce and advise on new techniques for the transmission of scholarly information.
- Foster entrepreneurial activity.
- Make effective use of the Library's buildings, space, collections and equipment to satisfy user, staff and safety needs.

Performance measures will be:
- Extent to which unit costs of operations are reduced or maintained
- Reputation of the Library both within the University and on the national and international scene
- Optimal allocation of overall resources between stock, staff and equipment
- Benefits accrued to the Library and the University through both internal and external cooperation.

Strategies include:
- Being actively involved in the planning of new University initiatives which require additional Library resources.
- Maximising the efficiency of Library operations.
- Monitoring information technology developments relating to the network.
- Working with academic staff on campus to develop electronic publishing skills required for teaching or research.
- Providing services for the local community on a commercial basis.
- Providing advice and consultancy services on a local, national and international basis.

Figure 8.3 Linking goals, objectives, performance measures and strategies: Australian National University Library (anulib.anu.edu.au)

Reflection: *Examine the statements of roles, values and objectives in Figure 8.4 on page 222.*

- *How do they link together?*
- *To what extent do they define the future direction not only for MLA, but also for library and information services in the UK?*

MLA's roles
Our mission is to enable the collections and services of the museums, archives and libraries sector to touch the lives of everyone.

We deliver our mission through our core roles, which encompass all aspects of our work:

* providing strategic leadership
* acting as a powerful advocate
* developing capacity within the sector
* promoting innovation and change.

In fulfilling these roles we work in partnership and through collaboration with a wide range of institutions, umbrella bodies, government departments and national and international organisations, both within and beyond our sector.

Our core values
All of MLA's work is informed and underpinned by our core values. We believe that:

* museums, archives and libraries have a central role to play in sustaining and developing cultural, social, educational and economic well-being.
* the care, maintenance and enrichment of collections provides an essential starting point for the development of the sector.
* the services provided by museums, archives

and libraries should be focused on the needs of actual and potential users.
* these services should recognise and promote access and social inclusion and cultural diversity.
* the development of the sector should be based upon vigorous and informed debate and rigorous research.
* partnership and cooperation are essential components of success.

Our corporate objectives
Our key corporate objectives for the period 2002–03 to 2004–05 are:

* to develop the organisational and funding infrastructure that will support the sector's development, meeting the needs of the English regions, aligned with the priorities of Northern Ireland, Scotland and Wales, and in dialogue with the wider international community
* to encourage the development of accessible and inclusive collections and services that provide learning, inspiration and enjoyment for everyone
* to demonstrate the impact of our sector on society and the economy
* to determine the strategic needs and priorities of our sector
* to ensure MLA's increasing operational effectiveness.

Figure 8.4 MLA's (The Museums, Libraries and Archives Council) mission, values and corporate objectives (www.mla.gov.uk)
Reproduced with permission of the Museums, Libraries and Archives Council (MLA)

Goals and objectives

Goals are general statements of aims of purpose. Typically they can be further articulated through a series of objectives, and achievement towards goals can be measured in terms of performance measures or indicators, as illustrated in Figure 8.3.

The Balanced Scorecard of Organizational Goals (see page 173) suggests that organizations need to articulate goals and evaluate performance in all four quarters of the scorecard, viz: financial, process, customer and internal. Balanced scorecards acknowledge the need to incorporate both short- and long-term goals, objectives and measures, and to combine qualitative and quantitative measures. Information services need to remain financially healthy, to continue to enhance processes that support service delivery (such as cataloguing and licensing arrangements), to work on enhancing service delivery and to cultivate the commitment, motivation and development of their staff.

Objectives are a more precise statement of the goal, which make it easier to identify action towards the goal and to measure progress and performance. Objectives are statements of specific outcomes that are to be achieved (Johnson and Scholes, 2002).

Objectives should be SMART:

• Specific, or focused, giving details of services and target groups
• Measurable, or quantifiable
• Achievable, within the contexts and resources available
• Relevant, in that they contribute to organizational success, and are aligned with corporate objectives, and
• Timely so that actions are taken at the right time to achieve market success; this involves judging market readiness.

Some strategic planning tools

There are many strategic planning tools; in order to illustrate their use this section introduces some that are widely used. These tools can be used to inform organizational strategic planning or to examine the specific contributions of individual departments. Many of them can be used at different stages in the strategic planning process. For example, they may be used in situation audit in the strategic analysis stage of the planning process, or they may be used in strategy definition to evaluate specific strategic options. Such tools can assist individual managers to assess and evaluate, but they are also frequently used in group situations such as strategic planning workshops or away days to provide a structure to group discussion and idea generation.

PESTEL analysis and the organizational environment

All organizations need to gather as much intelligence as possible about the environment in which they are operating. The environment comprises a macroenvironment and a microenvironment. The microenvironment comprises the actors close to the organization that affect its ability to serve its customers, and includes suppliers, marketing intermediaries, customer markets, competitors and publics. The macroenvironment embraces the wider societal forces that affect the microenvironment; these include demographic, economic, natural, technological, political and cultural forces.

Library and information managers need to undertake *environmental scanning*, to remain informed as to the profile of, and potential changes within, both micro and macroenvironments. Gathering marketplace intelligence, spotting opportunities and long-term trends is a key management competence. Knowledge, information and data can be collected from a wide range of person-to-person (sometimes grapevine) sources, as well as through scanning electronic and print documents such as announcements, newsletters, newspapers, magazines and professional journals. In addition, analysis of use statistics, budget allocations and expenditure, staff deployment and other details on internal operations provides insights into the competencies and opportunities relating to specific elements of services.

PESTEL analysis is a useful tool for analysing the factors that exist in an organization's macroenvironment. The model suggests that there are six categories of factors that may affect any organization (or part of an organization): Political, Economic, Social, Technological, Environmental and Legal. Organizations need to identify individual factors in each of these categories, to be aware of any constraints that these factors pose and to monitor any changes or developments. Figure 8.5 suggests some typical factors in the macroenvironment for information services.

Political factors
- Central and local funding decisions for public and national libraries
- Funding decisions for higher education
- Increases in student numbers in further and higher education
- Governmental and institutional controls that suggest that library services should be provided 'free' to the customer

Economic forces
- Changes in income and consumer spending patterns
- Subscription rates for journals
- Prices of books
- Licence fees for bibliographic databases and electronic journals

Social factors
- Age distribution of target market
- Changes in educational levels
- Changes in family structures
- Increases in diversity in relation to ethnicity, race, sexuality and disabilities

- Changes in beliefs about the relationship between individuals and society
- Diversity of culture, as exhibited through preferences for music, art, drama and literature

Technological factors
- Telecommunications standards and protocols
- New software products, such as improved search engine technology
- Innovations in telecommunications, including digital television and mobile technologies.

Environmental factors
- Sustainability agenda
- Availability and depletion of natural resources

Legal factors
- Health and safety legislation
- Legislation defining the roles of libraries
- Legislation relating to employment
- Copyright legislation
- Licensing agreements in respect of the use of data downloaded from databases

Figure 8.5 Factors in the macroenvironment for information services

SWOT analysis and situation audit

SWOT analysis, otherwise described as opportunity/issue analysis, is a widely used tool for situation audit. It encourages managers to summarize the position in terms of:

- Strengths
- Weaknesses
- Opportunities, and
- Threats.

Strengths and weaknesses focus on the present and past, and summarize 'where we are now'. An assessment of strengths and weaknesses provides a capability audit of the present internal situation. Strengths should be developed as the basis for future success. Weaknesses need to be acknowledged and overcome, or minimized.

Opportunities and threats encourage consideration of the present and the future, taking a more forward- and outward-looking view of future strategic directions. They focus on the external factors. Opportunities can be taken. Threats need to be overcome. They may summarize 'where we want to be', 'where we do not want to be, but might end up' or 'where we could be if we pursued certain courses of action'.

The gap between strengths and weaknesses and opportunities and threats represents: 'what we have to do to get there' and needs to be filled by managerial imagination, inspiration and leadership. An organization that is high in threats and low in opportunities faces an uncertain future, whereas an organization that has numerous opportunities but few threats has much potential. Most information services have their fair share of both opportunities and threats with the balance shifting in one direction or another over time.

The 7-S framework and situation analysis

The '7-S' framework developed by the McKinsey consulting firm identifies seven interrelated factors that determine the effectiveness of an organization and its ability to change. The factors identified are:

- Strategy
- Structure
- Systems

- Staff
- Style
- Shared values
- Skills.

The first three of these are sometimes described as the hard Ss, whereas the later four, which have to do with people, are described as the soft Ss. The primary message of this model is that these factors are inter-related, and it is difficult to make progress on one dimension without progress on all of the others. The 7-S framework can be used as a checklist to structure situation analysis, and to assess the link between strategic direction and implementation. Corrall (2000) proposes a modified framework for information services, which has the following elements: seeker (information seeker), sources (information sources), space (physical environment), service, systems, security (of physical asset and intellectual property) and skills.

Reflection: Do you think that any of the 7-Ss are more important than the others?

Analysing and developing the portfolio – the Boston Consulting Group Growth Share Matrix and Ansoff's Growth Matrix

A number of tools have been developed to support the analysis and development of product portfolios (see Chapter 5). This section introduces the two best known of these, the Boston Consulting Group's (BCG) Growth Share Matrix and Ansoff's Growth Matrix. Information services can use such tools to profile and analyse their portfolio of services to identify the relative contributions of different services and to consider portfolio development.

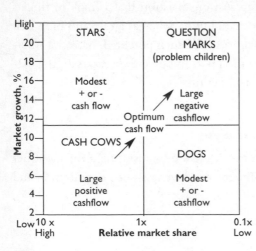

Figure 8.6 Boston Consulting Group Growth Share Matrix

The BCG Growth Share Matrix (see Figure 8.6) can be used for portfolio analysis at the organization, business unit, department, product or service level. Using the Matrix an organization can map each of their business units or products/services in a way that supports an analysis of their current and potential future contribution to the organization in terms of their market strength. Each business unit (department or service activity) is plotted on the Matrix in such as way as to reflect:

- *market growth rate* – the annual growth rate of the market in which the business unit operates; this is a measure of the potential for growth of the business, on the assumption that it is generally easier to grow a business in an expanding market than it is in a steady state or declining market
- *relative market share* – the specific business unit's market share relative to its largest competitor in the segment; this is a measure of strength in that segment.

The matrix has four cells, labelled respectively:

- *Cash cows* – business units that are in a market with little growth, but in which the business unit has a large relative market share. Such products are typically associated with a large positive cash flow or, in more general terms, a large value investment into the organization. Cash cows need to be monitored and supported to ensure that they do not decline into dogs.
- *Stars* are in markets with high market growth, and have a relatively high market share. Because stars are often newer business units their value contribution to the organization is relatively small, since they still require investment for promotion and innovation. Management of the cash flow associated with stars can convert them into the cash cows of the future.
- *Question marks* or problem children are in markets with high growth, but have not achieved a significant relative market share. Supporting question marks may be expensive, and they are typically associated with a large negative cash flow. The optimal solution is to seek to grow market share and to convert question marks into stars, but this typically requires even more resource commitment.
- *Dogs* are in markets with limited growth, and do not have a significant market share in that market. They deliver a modest positive or negative cash flow and need to be monitored carefully to ensure that they do not drain resources from other businesses or products.

This model can be used by an information service to review the different services that it offers, although the concepts of relative market share, market growth and cash flow might need translation. Cash flow might be measured in terms of resources committed to the delivery of a specific service element, relative market share might be measured in terms of how important or significant the service is to the user community, and market growth might be replaced with some measure of the likely future importance of the specific service. Using the model would support an analysis of a service portfolio. It may help to identify services for deletion from the portfolio and services that might justify further commitment of resources. It may also contribute to the assessment of the overall health of the service portfolio of the organization. A portfolio that has only dogs and question marks is draining value and resources from the organization and the organization will eventually fail. A healthy portfolio has a mixture of cows, stars, dogs and possibly question marks.

Products / Markets	Existing	New
Existing	Market penetration	Product development
New	Market development	Diversification

Figure 8.7 Ansoff's Growth Matrix

Ansoff's Growth Matrix (see Figure 8.7) categorizes the opportunities for developing an organization's position in the marketplace. It identifies four development strategies on the basis of whether the innovation is in relation to the product or the target market:

- *Market penetration* involves seeking to sell more existing products into existing markets, or for a public service, seeking to extend the user group within an existing market, for existing services. This is always the least risky option towards the strengthening of market position, but it may not always be possible.
- *Market development* involves seeking to sell more products by selling existing products into new markets. This require investment in promotion and reputation building with new market groups, and the risks associated with achieving success in unknown markets.
- *Product development* involves seeking to develop new products for existing markets. This incurs new development and promotion costs, but does have the advantage that the organization has knowledge of the market.
- *Diversification* involves the launch of new products into new markets. This is by far the riskiest option, because resources need to be invested into both product and market development and the organization has limited prior knowledge on which to base its predictions of the level of success that the diversification will achieve.

Ansoff's model is useful for information services thinking about new services. It encourages an assessment of the level of novelty of a new service proposal and the associated level of predictability of success, and offers a basis for risk assessment. It may, for example, suggest a step-wise innovation strategy in which a new service is first implemented with an existing user group before being rolled out to new communities, even if it is recognized that the needs of the two groups might not be identical. For example, a new database or online catalogue interface may be made available to on-site staff and users, before being launched to remote business users, where any problems with service delivery may be less easy to detect and to eliminate.

Reflection: *Explain why Ansoff's Growth Matrix might be useful in analysing the strategic options open to an information service. Explain how it encapsulates the concept of risk.*

Models for impact and importance analysis

The information systems strategy literature exhibits a preoccupation with the strategic significance of information technology applications and information systems (IS). A key question in establishing the status and role of information systems in an organization is the extent to which they provide competitive advantage or have a strategic impact on the long-term success of an organization. These models can often be applied to assess both the overall importance of IS within an organization and also the significance of specific applications. There are clear parallels with information services, and indeed in many organizations the two are the responsibility of a merged service. This section introduces two models that illustrate approaches to the consideration of strategic impact. The topic of impact was discussed from the quality management perspective in Chapter 6.

The Information Intensity Matrix, shown in Figure 8.8, identifies different industrial sectors and category sectors on the basis of the information intensity of the value chain and the information intensity of the product. Information services and systems are likely to have a greater strategic impact in sectors with high information intensity in both the value chain and the product.

Information intensity of the value chain	High	Oil refining Legal services	Newspapers Banking Education Airlines
	Low	Cement Bricks	Fashion Perishables
		Low	High
	Information intensity of the product		

Figure 8.8 The Information Intensity Matrix (based on Robson, 1997)

The Strategic Importance Matrix (Figure 8.9) is derived from the BCG Matrix. It can be used to separate business units on the basis of the extent to which the organization is functionally dependent upon IS today or the degree to which IS developments will create competitive edge, or to examine the contribution of specific IS applications to the organization:

- *Strategic systems* are the systems upon which the organization depends now and will do in the future.
- *Turnaround systems* are those with low critical importance, but which are expected to become more significant in the future.
- *Factory systems* are those of high current value but low predicted value for the future.
- *Support systems* are those of low importance now, and are likely to continue to be of low importance in the future.

Strategic importance of planned	High	Turnaround	Strategic
	Low	Support	Factory
LIS			
		Low	High
	Strategic importance of current IS		

Figure 8.9 The Strategic Importance Matrix (based on Robson, 1997)

This matrix can be used in a similar way to the BCG Matrix to make investment decisions for the future. In terms of cash flow, organizations should be investing in strategic systems or services, examining the potential of investment in turnaround systems, tightly controlling expenditure on support systems, and milking income from factory systems, to support future developments.

Reflection: Discuss why the Strategic Importance Matrix and the BCG Matrix might be useful in strategic planning for information organizations.

Operational and project planning

Strategic plans require a range of operational and project plans in order to ensure that things get done. Typically such plans focus on:

- what actions need to be taken
- what budgets and resources are required/available
- who (individual or teams) will be responsible for undertaking actions
- who is responsible for ensuring that actions and tasks have been completed
- when will action be taken, and when will it be completed.

For example, each of the strategies in Figure 8.4 involves a number of actions by teams or individuals over the period of the plan. Many activities are ongoing, and it may not be necessary to specify the resources and mechanisms for their completion on an annual basis. Action plans often focus on new initiatives. Where an action involves a specific change, such as the introduction of a new service, the construction of a new building, or the replacement of an information system, this is likely to be identified as a project, and a specific project plan will need to be developed and implemented.

An identified project will typically have a project team and a project leader. In most instances members of the team, including the leader, will undertake their team role as part of their wider job role. The project team is responsible for ensuring that the actions necessary to complete the project are undertaken. This means that they will work together and with others to progress and complete the project. For a larger project some of the team, including the leader, may be temporarily and/or partially seconded from their main role. The project team may be led and primarily comprise members from the staff of the information service, or information service staff may contribute to a project team with a wider organizational remit. If additional expertise or staff resources are required to complete the project, short-term contract staff or consultants may be used, depending on the nature of the task to be completed and the expertise required. Significant projects can also benefit from a project management team and a project champion. A project champion is a senior manager who is committed to the project, and can support the project team in negotiating resources and lend senior management expertise and power when it is needed. A project management team might also perform these functions, but can also aid in communication between the project team and the wider organization, and contribute to ensuring the match between project outcomes and strategic direction.

Each project is different; they require different actions and run over different timescales. Nevertheless it is possible to identify five generic stages in a project, and two intertwinned processes. The intertwined processes are:

- Managing the activities that lead to the successful delivery of the project outcomes, as discussed below
- Managing the communication, approval, consultation, and political processes. At each stage of the project key stakeholders need to be consulted, to ensure that the delivered project will meet their requirements and, most importantly, to ensure that the necessary resource allocation for the project is approved and available.

Reflection: *Suggest some projects that might be conducted in an information organiza-*
tion.

Typical stages in a project are:

1 *Definition of objectives*, based on the initial awareness of the need for the project and a full situation audit. This stage is likely to involve discussion with a range of interested parties with a view to articulating shared views on desirable outcomes, and developing an appreciation of the political and change environment within which the project will take place.
2 *Development of a requirements specification*, which gives a clear and explicit view of what is required. For a new building project, this requirements specification will indicate room sizes, space layouts, design features, telecommunications networking, etc. For a new service, the specification of requirements might identify the databases, staff and staff training, and IT facilities needed to deliver the service. If the project merits external contractors (as, for example, with a new building or with some new information systems), the requirements specification is an important document in any tender process.
3 *Design.* This stage is concerned with working through the details of the design of the new service, building, training series or information system. Prototypes and models may be used to aid communication with interested parties. The outcome of this process is a detailed specification of the outcome from the project.
4 *Implementation.* Two things happen during implementation. First 'things get built'. Buildings are constructed, courseware for new training programmes is created and information systems are installed. Secondly, 'people start using things'. This may involve moving staff and library stock to a new building, marketing and running a new training course, or going operational with a new information system.
5 *Evaluation.* Evaluation of projects should take place while the project is ongoing, at the end of the project, during the early weeks of use and after the innovation from the project has been in operation for some time. Evaluation leads to the identification of minor and, hopefully only occasionally, more major problems, and offers an opportunity to put things right.

While in general projects progress in a linear manner through these stages, there is likely to be re-working of some aspects of earlier stages as projects progress and it becomes apparent that earlier decisions need to be reviewed. Figure 8.10 summarizes some of the activities in a typical information systems project.

Definition of objectives	Terms of reference developed, initial needs analysis in the form of a study proposal leads to feasibility study, including initial evaluation of options and analysis of existing systems
Development of a requirements specification	Specification of systems requirements, in terms of systems functionality, and technical hardware and software requirements
Design	Selection of a systems supplier and subsequent working with them, to define the design parameters to meet the systems specification. Contracting and ordering of hardware and software
Implementation	Planning and preparation of environment. Installation of hardware and software, database creation, education and training, systems switch-over
Evaluation	Ongoing evaluation during project, initial evaluation after project, and finally ongoing monitoring, maintenance and evolution

Figure 8.10 Summary of stages in an information systems project

Summary and conclusions

Strategic planning and management are concerned with the long-term direction of an organization. As such they are often complex, risky, uncertain and ambiguous. The 'rational' model of strategy is encapsulated by the 'strategy as design' lens, which privileges the relationship between planning and strategy, but the reality is much more complex and it is important to acknowledge that strategic planning and management are influenced by experience, environment and political and cultural processes. The strategic planning and management process is negotiated through the organizational structure and involves a series of inter-linked documents and processes. Each of these processes has three main components: strategic analysis and audit, strategic choice and strategic analysis and implementation. Organizational direction is encapsulated and shared through mission and vision statements. For action and implementation these need to be translated into goals and objectives, which in their turn have matching performance measures or indicators. There are a range of strategic planning tools or models that can be applied to assist managers in their analysis of the strategic situation and options. PESTEL analysis aids in profiling the macroenvironment. SWOT analysis provides an approach to situation audit. The 7-S framework identifies seven inter-related factors that determine the effectiveness of an organization and its ability to change. The BCG Matrix and Ansoff's Matrix can be useful in analysing business, product or service portfolios, and in identifying potential developments. Other models support impact and importance analysis. Operational and project planning focuses on specific elements of strategic plans, and identifies actions and how they will be completed. A typical project involves the following stages: definition of objectives, requirements specification, design, implementation and evaluation.

REVIEW QUESTIONS

1 In what sense is strategy different from planning?
2 Why is the planned or design approach to strategy valuable to organizations?
3 Explain how organizational structure impacts on strategic planning and management.
4 What are the stages in the strategic planning process?
5 Give some examples of information service mission statements. What do they communicate about service priorities and values?
6 Explain and illustrate the difference between mission, value, goal, objective and performance measure. Why do all of these need to be embedded in strategic planning and management?
7 Compare and contrast analyses conducted using the PESTEL, SWOT and '7-S' models.
8 Explain the contribution that the BCG Matrix can make to strategic analysis of the portfolio of an information service.
9 Discuss how the Information Intensity Matrix and the Strategic Importance Matrix can be used to explore the contribution of information systems and services to an organization.
10 What are the stages in project planning? Discuss how these might be applied in a project to renovate part of a library building, which is normally accessible to the public.

CASE STUDY

Strategic plans

As a management consultant your brief is to develop a strategic plan for the development of a school library in a school that has received special status and funding to allow its development as a specialist technology school. You want to conduct a strategic audit in order to be able to assess the situation and to use this assessment for the development of scenarios for future development. In order to assist with this analysis you want to be able to use SWOT, PESTEL, the 7Ss and the BCG Matrix. Taking each of these tools in turn, describe the data that you would need to collect in order to support the application of these models/tools.

CHALLENGES

1 How can information service managers ensure that staff are making an appropriate contribution to the achievement of the service's mission, in a rapidly changing

environment in which written plans are only partly realized?

2   Is strategic analysis and audit always distinct from strategic action and implementation?

3   What do words like 'excellence', 'best' and 'enable' mean in an information service mission statement (see Figure 8.2)?

4   What is the difference between a service portfolio, as for example in the range of
services that an information service offers to different groups, and a product portfolio?

5   What impact would commitment to knowledge management within an organization have on the strategic planning and management for the information service in
that organization?

References and additional reading

Bryson, J. (1999) *Effective Library and Information Centre Management*, 2nd edn,
Aldershot, Gower.

Cohn, J. M., Kelsey, A. L. and Fiels, K. M. (2002) *Planning for Integrated Systems and
Technologies: a how-to-do-it manual for librarians*, 2nd edn, edited by D. Salter,
London, Facet Publishing.

Corrall, S. (1998) Scenario Planning: a strategic management tool for the future,
Managing Information, **5** (9), 34–7.

Corrall, S. (2000) *Strategic Management of Information Services: a planning handbook*,
London, ASLIB/Information Management International.

De Saez, E. E. (2002) *Marketing Concepts for Libraries and Information Services*, 2nd edn,
London, Facet Publishing.

Evans, G. E., Layzell Ward, P. and Rugaas, B. (2000) *Management Basics for Information
Professionals*, New York, Neal-Schuman.

Galliers, R. D., Baker, B. S.H. and Leidner, D. E. (2002) *Strategic Information
Management: challenges and strategies in managing information systems*, Oxford,
Butterworth-Heinemann.

Hannagan, T. (2002) *Mastering Strategic Management*, Basingstoke: Palgrave.

Himmel, E. and Wilson, W. J. (1999) *Planning for Results: a public library transformation
process*, Chicago, American Library Association.

Johnson, G. and Scholes, K. (2002) *Exploring Corporate Strategy*, 6th edn, Harlow, FT
Prentice Hall.

Mason, M. G. (2000) *Strategic Management for Today's Libraries*, Chicago, American
Library Association.

Nelson, S. (2002) *The New Planning for Results: a streamlined approach*, Chicago,

American Library Association.

Orna, E. (1999) *Practical Information Policies*, Aldershot, Gower.

Pantry, S. and Griffiths, P. (2000) *Developing a Successful Service Plan*, London, Library Association Publishing.

Robson, W. (1997) *Strategic Management & Information Systems*, 2nd edn, FT Prentice Hall.

Ward, J. and Peppard, J. (2002) *Strategic Planning for Information Systems*, Chichester, Wiley.

Ward, P. L. (2003) Management and the Management of Information, Knowledge-based and Library Services 2002, *Library Management*, **24** (3), 126–50.

Index